# Tales of Fashionable Life by Maria Edgeworth

*Tutta la gente in lieta fronte udiva*
*Le graziose e finte istorielle,*
*Ed ì difetti altrui tosto scopriva*
*Ciascuno, e non i proprj espressi in quelle;*
*O se de' proprj sospettava, ignoti*
*Credeali a ciascun altro, e a se sol noti.*

Maria Edgeworth was born at Black Bourton, Oxfordshire on January 1st 1768. Her early years were with her mother's family in England. Sadly, her mother died when Maria was five.

Maria was educated at Mrs Lattafière's school in Derby in 1775. There she studied dancing, French and other subjects. Maria transferred to Mrs Devis's school in Upper Wimpole Street, London. Her father began to focus more attention on Maria in 1781 when she nearly lost her sight to an eye infection.

She returned home to Ireland at 14 and took charge of her younger siblings. She herself was home-tutored by her father in Irish economics and politics, science, literature and law. Despite her youth literature was in her blood. Maria also became her father's assistant in managing the family's large Edgeworthstown estate.

Maria first published 1795 with 'Letters for Literary Ladies'. That same year 'An Essay on the Noble Science of Self-Justification', written for a female audience, advised women on how to obtain better rights in general and specifically from their husbands.

'Practical Education' (1798) is a progressive work on education. Maria's ambition was to create an independent thinker who understands the consequences of his or her actions.

Her first novel, 'Castle Rackrent' was published anonymously in 1800 without her father's knowledge. It was an immediate success and firmly established Maria's appeal to the public.

Her father married four times and the last of these to Frances, a year younger and a confidante of Maria, who pushed them to travel more widely: London, Britain and Europe were all now visited.

The second series of 'Tales of Fashionable Life' (1812) did so well that she was now the most commercially successful novelist of her age.

She particularly worked hard to improve the living standards of the poor in Edgeworthstown and to provide schools for the local children of all and any denomination.

After a visit to see her relations Maria had severe chest pains and died suddenly of a heart attack in Edgeworthstown on 22nd May 1849. She was 81.

## Index of Contents

## PREFACE

My daughter asks me for a Preface to the following volumes; from a pardonable weakness she calls upon me for parental protection: but, in fact, the public judges of every work, not from the sex, but from the merit of the author.

What we feel, and see, and hear, and read, affects our conduct from the moment when we begin, till the moment when we cease to think. It has therefore been my daughter's aim to promote, by all her writings, the progress of education from the cradle to the grave.

Miss Edgeworth's former works consist of tales for children—of stories for young men and women—and of tales suited to that great mass which does not move in the circles of fashion. The present volumes are intended to point out some of those errors to which the higher classes of society are disposed.

All the parts of this series of moral fictions bear upon the faults and excellencies of different ages and classes; and they have all arisen from that view of society which we have laid before the public in more didactic works on education. In the PARENT'S ASSISTANT, in MORAL and in POPULAR TALES, it was my daughter's aim to exemplify the principles contained in PRACTICAL EDUCATION. In these volumes, and in others which are to follow, she endeavours to disseminate, in a familiar form, some of the ideas that are unfolded in ESSAYS ON PROFESSIONAL EDUCATION.

The first of these stories is called

ENNUI.—The causes, curses, and cure of this disease are exemplified, I hope, in such a manner, as not to make the remedy worse than the disease. Thiebauld tells us, that a prize-essay on Ennui was read to the Academy of Berlin, which put all the judges to sleep.

THE DUN—is intended as a lesson against the common folly of believing that a debtor is able, by a few cant phrases, to alter the nature of right and wrong. We had once thoughts of giving to these books the title of FASHIONABLE TALES: alas! the Dun could never have found favour with fashionable readers.

Difference of rank is a continual excitement to laudable emulation; but those who consider the being admitted into circles of fashion as the summit of human bliss and elevation, will here find how grievously such frivolous ambition may be disappointed and chastised.

I may be permitted to add a word on the respect with which Miss Edgeworth treats the public—their former indulgence has not made her careless or presuming. The dates subjoined to these stories show that they have not been hastily intruded upon the reader.

*RICHARD LOVELL EDGEWORTH.*
*Edgeworthstown,*
*March, 1809.*


ENNUI; OR, MEMOIRS OF THE EARL OF GLENTHORN.

*"'Que faites-vous à Potzdam?' demandois-je un jour an prince Guillaume. 'Monsieur,' me répondit-il, 'nous passons notre vie à conjuguer tous le même verbe; Je m'ennuie, tu t'ennuies, il s'ennuie, nous nous ennuyons, vous vous ennuyez, ils s'ennuient; je m'ennuyois, je m'ennuierai,'" &c.*
THIEBAULD, *Mém. de Frédéric le Grand.*


## CHAPTER I

Bred up in luxurious indolence, I was surrounded by friends who seemed to have no business in this world but to save me the trouble of thinking or acting for myself; and I was confirmed in the pride of helplessness by being continually reminded that I was the only son and heir of the Earl of Glenthorn. My mother died a few weeks after I was born; and I lost my father when I was very young. I was left to the care of a guardian, who, in hopes of winning my affection, never controlled my wishes or even my whims: I changed schools and masters as often as I pleased, and consequently learned nothing. At last I found a private tutor who suited me exactly, for he was completely of my own opinion, "that every thing which the young Earl of Glenthorn did not know by the instinct of genius was not worth his learning." Money could purchase a reputation for talents, and with money I was immoderately supplied; for my guardian expected to bribe me with a part of my own fortune, to forbear inquiring what had become of a certain deficiency in the remainder. This tacit compact I perfectly understood: we were consequently on the most amicable terms imaginable, and the most confidential; for I thought it better to deal with my guardian than with Jews. Thus at an age when other young men are subject to some restraint, either from the necessity of their circumstances, or the discretion of their friends, I became completely master of myself and of my fortune. My companions envied me; but even their envy was not sufficient to make me happy. Whilst yet a boy, I began to feel the dreadful symptoms of that mental malady which baffles the skill of medicine, and for which wealth can purchase only temporary alleviation. For this complaint there is no precise English name; but, alas! the foreign term is now naturalized in England. Among the higher classes, whether in the wealthy or the fashionable world, who is unacquainted with ennui? At first I was unconscious of being subject to this disease; I felt that something was the matter with me, but I did not know what: yet the symptoms were sufficiently marked. I was afflicted with frequent fits of fidgeting, yawning, and stretching, with a constant restlessness of mind and body; an aversion to the place I was in, or the thing I was doing, or rather to that which was passing before my eyes, for I was never doing any thing; I had an utter abhorrence and an incapacity of voluntary exertion. Unless roused by external stimulus, I sank into that kind of apathy, and vacancy of ideas, vulgarly known by the name of a brown study. If confined in a room for more than half an hour by bad weather or other contrarieties, I would pace backwards and forwards, like the restless cavia in his den, with a fretful, unmeaning pertinacity. I felt an insatiable longing for something new, and a childish love of locomotion.

My physician and my guardian, not knowing what else to do with me, sent me abroad. I set out upon my travels in my eighteenth year, attended by my favourite tutor as my companion. We perfectly agreed in our ideas of travelling; we hurried from place to place as fast as horses and wheels, and curses and guineas, could carry us. Milord Anglois rattled over half the globe without getting one inch farther from his ennui. Three years were to be consumed before I should be of age. What sums did I spend during this interval in expedition-money to Time! but the more I tried to hasten him, the slower the rogue went. I lost my money and my temper.

At last the day for which I had so long panted arrived—I was twenty-one! and I took possession of my estate. The bells rang, the bonfires blazed, the tables were spread, the wine flowed, huzzas resounded, friends and tenants crowded about me, and nothing but the voice of joy and congratulation was to be heard. The bustle of my situation kept me awake for some weeks; the pleasure of property was new, and, as long as the novelty lasted, delightful. I cannot say that I was satisfied; but my mind was distended by the sense of the magnitude of my possessions. I had large estates in England; and in one of the remote maritime counties of Ireland, I was lord over an immense territory, annexed to the ancient castle of Glenthorn;—a noble pile of antiquity! worth ten degenerate castles of modern days. It was placed in a bold romantic situation: at least as far as I could judge of it by a picture, said to be a striking likeness, which hung in my hall at Sherwood Park in England. I was born in Ireland, and nursed, as I was told, in an Irish cabin: for my father had an idea that this would make me hardy; he left me with my Irish nurse till I was two years old, and from that time forward neither he nor I ever revisited Ireland. He had a dislike to that country, and I grew up in his prejudices. I declared that I would always reside in England. Sherwood Park, my English country-seat, had but one fault, it was completely finished. The house was magnificent, and in the modern taste; the furniture fashionably elegant, and in all the gloss of novelty. Not a single luxury omitted; not a fault could be found by the most fastidious critic. My park, my grounds, displayed all the beauties of nature and of art, judiciously combined. Majestic woods, waving their dark foliage, overhung—But I will spare my readers the description, for I remember falling asleep myself whilst a poet was reading to me an ode on the beauties of Sherwood Park. These beauties too soon became familiar to my eye; and even the idea of being the proprietor of this enchanting place soon palled upon my vanity. Every casual visitor, all the strangers, even the common people, who were allowed once a week to walk in my pleasure-grounds, enjoyed them a thousand times more than I could. I remember, that, about six weeks after I came to Sherwood Park, I one evening escaped from the crowds of friends who filled my house, to indulge myself in a solitary, melancholy walk. I saw at some distance a party of people, who were coming to admire the place; and to avoid meeting them I took shelter under a fine tree, the branches of which, hanging to the ground, concealed me from the view of passengers. Thus seated, I was checked in the middle of a desperate yawn, by hearing one among the party of strangers exclaiming—

"How happy the owner of this place must be!"

Yes, had I known how to enjoy the goods of life, I might have been happy; but want of occupation, and antipathy to exertion, rendered me one of the most miserable men upon earth. Still I imagined that the cause of my discontent proceeded from some external circumstance. Soon after my coming of age, business of various sorts required my attention; papers were to be signed, and lands were to be let: these things appeared to me terrible difficulties. Not even that minister of state, who so feelingly describes his horror at the first appearance of the secretary with the great portfolio, ever experienced sensations so oppressive as mine were, when my steward began to talk to me of my own affairs. In the peevishness of my indolence, I declared that I thought the pains overbalanced the pleasures of property. Captain Crawley, a friend—a sort of a friend—a humble companion of mine, a gross, unblushing, thorough-going flatterer, happened to be present when I made this declaration: he kindly undertook to stand between me and the shadow of trouble. I accepted this offer.

"Ay, Crawley," said I, "do see and settle with these people."

I had not the slightest confidence in the person into whose hands, to save myself from the labour of thinking, I thus threw all my affairs; but I satisfied my understanding, by resolving that, when I should have leisure, I would look out for an agent upon whom I could depend.

I had now been nearly two months at Sherwood Park; too long a time, I thought, to remain in any place, and I was impatient to get away. My steward, who disliked the idea of my spending my summers at home, found it easy to persuade me that the water on my estate had a brackish unwholesome taste. The man who told me this stood before me in perfect health, though he had drunk this insalubrious water all his life: but it was too laborious a task for my intellects to compare the evidence of my different senses, and I found it most easy to believe what I heard, though it was in direct opposition to what I saw. Away I hurried to a watering-place, after the example of many of my noble contemporaries, who leave their delightful country-seats, to pay, by the inch, for being squeezed up in lodging-houses, with all imaginable inconvenience, during the hottest months in summer. I whiled away my time at Brighton, cursing the heat of the weather, till the winter came, and then cursing the cold, and longing for the London winter.

The London winter commenced; and the young Earl of Glenthorn, and his entertainments, and his equipages, and extravagance, were the conversation of all the world, and the joy of the newspapers. The immense cost of the fruit at my desserts was recorded; the annual expense of the vast nosegays of hot-house flowers worn daily by the footmen who clung behind my coach was calculated; the hundreds of wax lights, which burned nightly in my house, were numbered by the idle admirers of folly; and it was known by every body that Lord Glenthorn suffered nothing but wax to be burned in his stables; that his servants drank nothing but claret and champagne; that his liveries, surpassing the imagination of ambassadors, vied with regal magnificence, whilst their golden trappings could have stood even the test of Chinese curiosity. My coachmaker's bill for this year, if laid before the public, would amuse and astonish sober-minded people, as much as some charges which have lately appeared in our courts of justice for extraordinary coaches, and very extraordinary landaus. I will not enter into the detail of my extravagance in minor articles of expense; these, I thought, could never be felt by such a fortune as that of the Earl of Glenthorn; but, for the information of those who have the same course to run or to avoid, I should observe, that my diurnal visits to jewellers' shops amounted, in time, to sums worth mentioning. Of the multitude of baubles that I bought, the rings, the seals, the chains, I will give no account; it would pass the belief of man, and the imagination of woman. Those who have the least value for their time have usually the greatest number of watches, and are the most anxious about the exactness of their going. I and my repeaters were my own plagues, and the profit of all the fashionable watchmakers, whose shops I regularly visited for a lounge. My history, at this period, would be a complete lounger's journal; but I will spare my readers this diary. I wish, however, as I have had ample experience, to impress it on the minds of all whom it may concern, that a lounger of fortune must be extravagant. I went into shops merely to pass an idle hour, but I could not help buying something; and I was ever at the mercy of tradesmen, who took advantage of my indolence, and who thought my fortune inexhaustible. I really had not any taste for expense; but I let all who dealt with me, especially my servants, do as they pleased, rather than be at the trouble of making them do as they ought. They assured me, that Lord Glenthorn must have such and such things, and must do so and so; and I quietly submitted to this imaginary necessity.

All this time I was the envy of my acquaintance; but I was more deserving of their compassion. Without anxiety or exertion, I possessed every thing they wanted; but then I had no motive—I had nothing to desire. I had an immense fortune, and I was the Earl of Glenthorn: my title and wealth were sufficient distinctions; how could I be anxious about my boots, or the cape of my coat, or any of those trifles which so happily interest and occupy the lives of fashionable young men, who have not the misfortune to possess large estates? Most of my companions had some real or imaginary grievance, some old uncle or father, some cursed profession to complain of; but I had none. They had hopes and fears; but I had none. I was on the pinnacle of glory, which they were endeavouring to reach; and I had nothing to do but to sit still, and enjoy the barrenness of the prospect.

In this recital I have communicated, I hope, to my readers some portion of that ennui which I endured; otherwise they cannot form an adequate idea of my temptation to become a gambler. I really had no vice, nor any of those propensities which lead to vice; but ennui produced most of the effects that are usually attributed to strong passions or a vicious disposition.

CHAPTER II

"O! ressource assurée,
Viens ranimer leur langueur desoeuvrée:
Leur âme vide est du moins amusée
Par l'avarice en plaisir deguisée."

Gaming relieved me from that insuperable listlessness by which I was oppressed. I became interested—I became agitated; in short, I found a new kind of stimulus, and I indulged in it most intemperately. I grew immoderately fond of that which supplied me with sensations. My days and nights were passed at the gaming-table. I remember once spending three days and three nights in the hazard-room of a well-known house in St. James's-street: the shutters were closed, the curtains down, and we had candles the whole time; even in the adjoining rooms we had candles, that when our doors were opened to bring in refreshments, no obtrusive gleam of daylight might remind us how the hours had passed. How human nature supported the fatigue, I know not. We scarcely allowed ourselves a moment's pause to take the sustenance our bodies required. At last, one of the markers, who had been in the room with us the whole time, declared that he could hold out no longer, and that sleep he must. With difficulty he obtained an hour's truce: the moment he got out of the room he fell asleep, absolutely at the very threshold of our door. By the rules of the house he was entitled to a bonus on every transfer of property at the hazard-table; and he had made, in the course of these three days, upwards of three hundred pounds. Sleep and avarice had struggled to the utmost, but, with his vulgar habits, sleep prevailed. We were wide awake. I shall never forget the figure of one of my noble associates, who sat holding his watch, his eager eyes fixed upon the minute-hand, whilst he exclaimed continually, "This hour will never be over!" Then he listened to discover whether his watch had stopped; then cursed the lazy fellow for falling asleep, protesting that, for his part, he never would again consent to such waste of time. The very instant the hour was ended, he ordered "that dog" to be awakened, and to work we went. At this sitting 35,000l. were lost and won. I was very fortunate, for I lost a mere trifle—ten thousand pounds; but I could not expect to be always so lucky.—Now we come to the old story of being ruined by play. My English John o'-the-Scales warned me that he could advance no more money; my Irish agent, upon whom my drafts had indeed been unmerciful, could not oblige me any longer, and he threw up his agency, after having made his fortune at my expense. I railed, but railing would not pay my debts of honour. I inveighed against my grandfather for having tied me up so tight; I could neither mortgage nor sell: my Irish estate would have been sold instantly, had it not been settled upon a Mr. Delamere. The pleasure of abusing him, whom I had never seen, and of whom I knew nothing but that he was to be my heir, relieved me wonderfully. He died, and left only a daughter, a mere child. My chance of possessing the estate in fee-simple increased: I sold this increased value to the Jews, and gamed on. Miss Delamere, some time afterwards, had the smallpox. Upon the event of her illness I laid bets to an amazing amount.

She recovered. No more money could be raised, and my debts were to be paid. In this dilemma I recollected that I once had a guardian, and that I had never settled accounts with him. Crawley, who continued to be my factotum and flatterer in ordinary and extraordinary, informed me, upon looking over these accounts, that there was a mine of money due to me, if I could but obtain it by law or equity. To law I went: and the anxiety of a lawsuit might have, in some degree, supplied the place of gambling, but that all my business was managed for me by Crawley, and I charged him never to mention the subject to me till a verdict should be obtained.

A verdict was obtained against me. It was proved in open court, by my own witnesses, that I was a fool; but as no judge, jury, or chancellor, could believe that I was so great a fool as my carelessness indicated, my guardian stood acquitted in equity of being so great a rogue as he really was. What was now to be done? I saw my doom. As a highwayman knows that he must come to the gallows at last, and acts accordingly, so a fashionably extravagant youth knows that, sooner or later, he must come to matrimony. No one could have more horror of this catastrophe than I felt; but it was in vain to oppose my destiny. My opinion of women had been formed from the commonplace jests of my companions, and from my own acquaintance with the worst part of the sex. I had never felt the passion of love, and, of course, believed it to be something that might have existed in former ages, but that it was in our days quite obsolete, at least, among the knowing part of the world. In my imagination young women were divided into two classes; those who were to be purchased, and those who were to purchase. Between these two classes, though the division was to be marked externally by a certain degree of ceremony, yet I was internally persuaded that there was no essential difference. In my feelings towards them there was some distinction; of the first class I was tired, and of the second I was afraid. Afraid! Yes—afraid of being taken in. With these fears, and these sentiments, I was now to choose a wife. I chose her by the numeration table: Units, tens, hundreds, thousands, tens of thousands, hundreds of thousands. I was content, in the language of the newspapers, to lead to the Hymeneal altar any fashionable fair one whose fortune came under the sixth place of figures. No sooner were my dispositions known than the friends of a young heiress, who wanted to purchase a coronet, settled a match between us. My bride had one hundred wedding-dresses, elegant as a select committee of dress-makers and milliners, French and English, could devise. The least expensive of these robes, as well as I remember, cost fifty guineas: the most admired came to about five hundred pounds, and was thought, by the best judges in these matters, to be wonderfully cheap, as it was of lace such as had never before been trailed in English dust, even by the lady of a nabob. These things were shown in London as a spectacle for some days, by the dress-maker, who declared that she had lost many a night's rest in contriving how to make such a variety of dresses sufficiently magnificent and distinguished. The jewellers also requested and obtained permission to exhibit the different sets of jewels: these were so numerous that Lady Glenthorn scarcely knew them all. One day, soon after her marriage, somebody at court, observing that her diamonds were prodigiously fine, asked where she bought them. "Really," said she, "I cannot tell. I have so many sets, I declare I don't know whether it's my Paris, or my Hamburgh, or my London set."

Poor young creature! I believe her chief idea of happiness in marriage was the possession of the jewels and paraphernalia of a countess—I am sure it was the only hope she could have, that was likely to be realized, in marrying me. I thought it manly and fashionable to be indifferent, if not contemptuous to my wife: I considered her only as an incumbrance, that I was obliged to take along with my fortune. Besides the disagreeable ideas generally connected with the word wife, I had some peculiar reasons for my aversion to my Lady Glenthorn. Before her friends would suffer me to take possession of her fortune, they required from me a solemn oath against gambling: so I was compelled to abjure the hazard-table and the turf, the only two objects in life that could keep me awake. This extorted vow I set down entirely to my bride's account; and I therefore became even more averse to her than men usually are who marry for money. Yet this dislike subsided. Lady Glenthorn was only childish—I, of an easy temper. I thought her ridiculous, but it was too much trouble to tell her so continually. I let the occasions pass, and even forgot her ladyship, when she was not absolutely in my way. She was too frivolous to be hated, and the passion of hatred was not to be easily sustained in my mind. The habit of ennui was stronger than all my passions put together.

## CHAPTER III

*"Or realize what we think fabulous,*
*I' th' bill of fare of Eliogabalus."*

After my marriage, my old malady rose to an insupportable height. The pleasures of the table were all that seemed left to me in life. Most of the young men of any ton, either were, or pretended to be, connoisseurs in the science of good eating. Their talk was of sauces and of cooks, what dishes each cook was famous for; whether his forte lay in white sauces or brown, in soups, lentilles, fricandeaus, bechemele, matelotes, daubes, &c. Then the history and genealogy of the cooks came after the discussion of the merit of the works; whom my Lord C—'s cook lived with formerly—what my Lord D— gave his cook—where they met with these great geniuses, &c. I cannot boast that our conversation at these select dinners, from which the ladies were excluded, was very entertaining; but true good eaters detest wit at dinner-time, and sentiment at all times. I think I observed that amongst these cognoscenti there was scarcely one to whom the delicacy of taste did not daily prove a source of more pain than pleasure. There was always a cruel something that spoiled the rest; or if the dinner were excellent, beyond the power of the most fastidious palate to condemn, yet there was the hazard of being placed far from the favourite dish, or the still greater danger of being deputed to carve at the head or foot of the table. How I have seen a heavy nobleman of this set dexterously manoeuvre to avoid the dangerous honour of carving a haunch of venison! "But, good Heavens!" said I, when a confidential whisper first pointed out this to my notice, "why does he not like to carve?—he would have it in his power to help himself to his mind, which nobody else can do so well."—"No! if he carve, he must give the nice bits to others; every body here understands them as well as he—each knows what is upon his neighbour's plate, and what ought to be there, and what must be in the dish." I found that it was an affair of calculation—a game at which nobody can cheat without being discovered and disgraced. I emulated, and soon equalled my experienced friends. I became a perfect epicure, and gloried in the character, for it could be supported without any intellectual exertion, and it was fashionable. I cannot say that I could ever eat as much as some of my companions. One of them I once heard exclaim, after a monstrous dinner, "I wish my digestion were equal to my appetite." I would not be thought to exaggerate, therefore I shall not recount the wonders I have seen performed by these capacious heroes of the table. After what I have beheld, to say nothing of what I have achieved, I can believe any thing that is related of the capacity of the human stomach. I can credit even the account of the dinner which Madame de Bavière affirms she saw eaten by Lewis the Fourteenth; viz. "quatre assiettes de différentes soupes; un faisan tout entier; un perdrix; une grande assiette pleine de salade; du mouton coupé dans son jus avec de l'ail; deux bons morceaux de jambon; une assiette pleine de patisserie! du fruit et des confitures!" Nor can I doubt the accuracy of the historian, who assures us that a Roman emperor, one of the most moderate of those imperial gluttons, took for his breakfast, 500 figs, 100 peaches, 10 melons, 100 beccaficoes, and 400 oysters.

Epicurism was scarcely more prevalent during the decline of the Roman empire than it is at this day amongst some of the wealthy and noble youths of Britain. Not one of my select dinner-party but would have been worthy of a place at the turbot consultation immortalized by the Roman satirist. A friend of mine, a bishop, one day went into his kitchen, to look at a large turbot, which the cook was dressing. The cook had found it so large that he had cut off the fins: "What a shame!" cried the bishop; and immediately calling for the cook's apron, he spread it before his cassock, and actually sewed the fins again to the turbot with his own episcopal hands.

If I might judge from my own experience, I should attribute fashionable epicurism in a great measure to ennui. Many affect it, because they have nothing else to do; and sensual indulgences are all that exist for those who have not sufficient energy to enjoy intellectual pleasures. I dare say, that if Heliogabalus could be brought in evidence in his own case, and could be made to understand the meaning of the word ennui, he would agree with me in opinion, that it was the cause of half his vices. His offered reward for the discovery of a new pleasure is stronger evidence than any confession he could make. I thank God that I was not born an emperor, or I might have become a monster. Though not in the least inclined to cruelty, I might have acquired the taste for it, merely for desire of the emotion which real tragedies excite. Fortunately, I was only an earl and an epicure.

My indulgence in the excesses of the table injured my health; violent bodily exercise was necessary to counteract the effects of intemperance. It was my maxim, that a man could never eat or drink too much, if he would but take exercise enough. I killed fourteen horses, and survived; but I grew tired of killing horses, and I continued to eat immoderately. I was seized with a nervous complaint, attended with extreme melancholy. Frequently the thoughts of putting an end to my existence occurred; and I had many times determined upon the means; but very small and apparently inadequate and ridiculous motives, prevented the execution of my design. Once I was kept alive by a piggery, which I wanted to see finished. Another time, I delayed destroying myself, till a statue, which I had just purchased at a vast expense, should be put up in my Egyptian salon. By the awkwardness of the unpacker, the statue's thumb was broken. This broken thumb saved my life; it converted ennui into anger. Like Montaigne and his sausage, I had now something to complain of, and I was happy. But at last my anger subsided, the thumb would serve me no longer as a subject of conversation, and I relapsed into silence and black melancholy. I was "a'weary of the sun;" my old thoughts recurred. At this time I was just entering my twenty-fifth year. Rejoicings were preparing for my birthday. My Lady Glenthorn had prevailed upon me to spend the summer at Sherwood Park, because it was new to her. She filled the house with company and noise; but this only increased my discontent. My birthday arrived—I wished myself dead—and I resolved to shoot myself at the close of the day. I put a pistol into my pocket, and stole out towards the evening, unobserved by my jovial companions. Lady Glenthorn and her set were dancing, and I was tired of these sounds of gaiety. I took the private way to the forest, which was near the house; but one of my grooms met me with a fine horse, which an old tenant had just sent as a present on my birthday. The horse was saddled and bridled; the groom held the stirrup, and up I got. The fellow told me the private gate was locked, and I turned as he pointed to go through the grand entrance. At the outside of the gate sat upon the ground, huddled in a great red cloak, an old woman, who started up and sprang forwards the moment she saw me, stretching out her arms and her cloak with one and the same motion.

"Ogh! is it you I see?" cried she, in a strong Irish tone.

At this sound and this sight, my horse, that was shy, backed a little. I called to the woman to stand out of my way.

"Heaven bless your sweet face! I'm the nurse that suckled yees when ye was a baby in Ireland. Many's the day I've been longing to see you," continued she, clasping her hands, and standing her ground in the middle of the gateway, regardless of my horse, which I was pressing forward.

"Stand out of the way, for God's sake, my good woman, or I shall certainly ride over you. So! so! so!" said I, patting my restless horse.

"Oh! he's only shy, God bless him! he's as quite now as a lamb; and kiss one or other of yees, I must," cried she, throwing her arms about the horse's neck.

The horse, unaccustomed to this mode of salutation, suddenly plunged, and threw me. My head fell against the pier of the gate. The last sound I heard was the report of a pistol; but I can give no account of what happened afterwards. I was stunned by my fall, and senseless. When I opened my eyes, I found myself stretched on one of the cushions of my landau, and surrounded by a crowd of people, who seemed to be all talking at once: in the buzz of voices I could not distinguish any thing that was said, till I heard Captain Crawley's voice above the rest, saying,

"Send for a surgeon instantly: but it's all over! it's all over! Take the body the back way to the banqueting-house; I must run to Lady Glenthorn."

I perceived that they thought me dead. I did not at this moment feel that I was hurt. I was curious to know what they would all do; so I closed my eyes again before any one perceived that I had opened them. I lay motionless, and they proceeded with me, according to Captain Crawley's orders, to the banqueting-house. When we arrived there, my servants laid me on one of the Turkish sofas; and the crowd, after having satisfied their' curiosity, dropped off one by one, till I was left with a single footman and my steward.

"I don't believe he's quite dead," said the footman, "for his heart beats."

"Oh, he's the same as dead, for he does not stir hand or foot, and his skull, they say, is fractured for certain; but it will all be seen when the surgeon comes. I am sure he will never do. Crawley will have every thing his own way now, and I may as well decamp."

"Ay; and among them," said the footman, "I only hope I may get my wages."

"What a fool that Crawley made of my lord!" said the steward.

"What a fool my lord made of himself," said the footman, "to be ruled, and let all his people be ruled, by such an upstart! With your leave, Mr. Turner, I'll just run to the house to say one word to James, and be back immediately."

"No, no, you must stay, Robert, whilst I step home to lock my places, before Crawley begins to rummage."

The footman was now left alone with me. Scarcely had the steward been gone two minutes, when I heard a low voice near me saying, in a tone of great anxiety, "Is he dead?"

I half opened my eyes to see who it was that spoke. The voice came from the door which was opposite to me; and whilst the footman turned his back, I raised my head, and beheld the figure of the old woman, who had been the cause of my accident. She was upon her knees on the threshold—her arms crossed over her breast. I never shall forget her face, it was so expressive of despair.

"Is he dead?" she repeated.

"I tell you yes," replied the footman.

"For the love of God, let me come in, if he is here," cried she.

"Come in, then, and stay here whilst I run to the house."

The footman ran off; and my old nurse, on seeing me, burst into an agony of grief. I did not understand one word she uttered, as she spoke in her native language; but her lamentations went to my heart, for they came from hers. She hung over me, and I felt her tears dropping upon my forehead. I could not refrain from whispering, "Don't cry—I am alive."

"Blessings on him!" exclaimed she, starting back: she then dropped down on her knees to thank God. Then calling me by every fondling name that nurses use to their children, she begged my forgiveness, and alternately cursed herself and prayed for me.

The strong affections of this poor woman touched me more than any thing I had ever yet felt in my life; she seemed to be the only person upon earth who really cared for me; and in spite of her vulgarity, and my prejudice against the tone in which she spoke, she excited in my mind emotions of tenderness and gratitude. "My good woman, if I live, I will do something for you: tell me what I can do," said I. "Live! live! God bless you, live; that's all in the wide world I want of you, my jewel; and, till you are well, let me watch over you at nights, as I used to do when you were a child, and I had you in my arms all to myself, dear."

Three or four people now ran into the room, to get before Captain Crawley, whose voice was heard at this instant at a distance. I had only time to make the poor woman understand that I wished to appear to be dead; she took the hint with surprising quickness. Captain Crawley came up the steps, talking in the tone of a master to the steward and people who followed.

"What is this old hag doing here? Where is Robert? Where is Thomas? I ordered them to stay till I came. Mr. Turner, why did not you stay? What! has not the coroner been here yet? The coroner must see the body, I tell you. Good God! What a parcel of blockheads you all are! How many times must I tell you the same thing? Nothing can be done till the coroner has seen him; then we'll talk about the funeral, Mr. Turner—one thing at a time. Every thing shall be done properly, Mr. Turner. Lady Glenthorn trusts every thing to me—Lady Glenthorn wishes that I should order every thing."

"To be sure—no doubt—very proper—I don't say against that."

"But," continued Crawley, turning towards the sofa upon which I lay, and seeing Ellinor kneeling beside me, "what keeps this old Irish witch here still? What business have you here, pray; and who are you, or what are you?"

"Plase your honour, I was his nurse formerly, and so had a nat'ral longing to see him once again before I would die."

"And did you come all the way from Ireland on this wise errand?"

"Troth I did—every inch of the way from his own sweet place."

"Why, you are little better than a fool, I think," said Crawley.

"Little better, plase your honour; but I was always so about them childer that I nursed."

"Childer! Well, get along about your business now; you see your nursing is not wanted here."

"I'll not stir out of this, while he is here," said my nurse, catching hold of the leg of the sofa, and clinging to it.

"You'll not stir, you say," cried Captain Crawley: "Turn her out!"

"Oh, sure you would not have the cru'lty to turn his old nurse out before he's even cowld. And won't you let me see him buried?"

"Out with her! out with her! the old Irish hag! We'll have no howling here. Out with her, John!" said Crawley to my groom.

The groom hesitated, I fancy; for Crawley repeated the order more imperiously: "Out with her! or go yourself."

"May be it's you that will go first yourself," said she.

"Go first myself!" cried Captain Crawley, furiously: "Are you insolent to me?"

"And are not you cru'l to me, and to my child I nursed, that lies all as one as dead before you, and was a good friend to you in his day, no doubt?"

Crawley seized hold of her: but she resisted with so much energy, that she dragged along with her the sofa to which she clung, and on which I lay.

"Stop!" cried I, starting up. There was sudden silence. I looked round, but could not utter another syllable. Now, for the first time, I was sensible that I had been really hurt by the fall. My head grew giddy, and my stomach sick. I just saw Crawley's fallen countenance, and him and the steward looking at one another; they were like hideous faces in a dream. I sunk back.

"Ay, lie down, my darling; don't be disturbing yourself for such as them," said my nurse. "Let them do what they will with me; it's little I'd care for them, if you were but once in safe hands."

I beckoned to the groom, who had hesitated to turn out Ellinor, and bid him go to the housekeeper, and have me put to bed. "She," added I, pointing to my old nurse, "is to sit up with me at night." It was all I could say. What they did with me afterwards, I do not know; but I was in my bed, and a bandage was round my temples, and my poor nurse was kneeling on one side of the bed, with a string of beads in her hand; and a surgeon and physician, and Crawley and my Lady Glenthorn were on the other side, whispering together. The curtain was drawn between me and them; but the motion I made on wakening was instantly observed by Crawley, who immediately left the room. Lady Glenthorn drew back my curtain, and began to ask me how I did: but when I fixed my eyes upon her, she sunk upon the bed, trembling violently, and could not finish her sentence. I begged her to go to rest, and she retired. The physician ordered that I should be kept quiet, and seemed to think I was in danger. I asked what was the matter with me? and the surgeon, with a very grave face, informed me that I had an ugly contusion on my head. I had heard of a concussion of the brain; but I did not know distinctly what it was, and my fears were increased by my ignorance. The life which, but a few hours before, I had been on the point of voluntarily destroying, because it was insupportably burdensome, I was now, the moment it was in danger, most anxious to preserve; and the interest which I perceived others had in getting rid of me, increased my desire to recover. My recovery was, however, for some time doubtful. I was seized with a fever, which left me in a state of alarming debility. My old nurse, whom I shall henceforward call by her name of Ellinor, attended me with the most affectionate solicitude during my illness; she scarcely stirred from my bedside, night or day; and, indeed, when I came to the use of my senses, she was the only person whom I really liked to have near me. I knew that she was sincere; and, however unpolished her manners, and however awkward her assistance, the good-will with which it was given, made me prefer it to the most delicate and dexterous attentions which I believed to be interested. The very want of a sense of propriety, and the freedom with which she talked to me, regardless of what was suited to her station, or due to my rank, instead of offending or disgusting me, became agreeable; besides, the novelty of her dialect, and of her turn of thought, entertained me as much as a sick man could be entertained. I remember once her telling me, that, "if it plased God, she would like to die on a Christmas-day, of all days; because the gates of Heaven, they say, will be open all that day; and who knows but a body might slip in unknownst?" When she sat up with me at nights she talked on eternally; for she assured me there was nothing like talking, as she had found, to put one asy asleep. I listened or not, just as I liked; any way she was contint. She was inexhaustible in her anecdotes of my ancestors, all tending to the honour and glory of the family; she had also an excellent memory for all the insults, or traditions of insults, which the Glenthorns had received for many ages back, even to the times of the old kings of Ireland; long and long before they stooped to be lorded; when their "names, which it was a pity and a murder, and moreover a burning shame, to change, was, O'Shaughnessy." She was well-stored with histories of Irish and Scotish chiefs. The story of O'Neill, the Irish blackbeard, I am sure I ought to remember, for Ellinor told it to me at least six times. Then she had a large assortment of fairies and shadowless witches, and banshees; and besides, she had legions of spirits and ghosts, and haunted castles without end, my own castle of Glenthorn not excepted, in the description of which she was extremely eloquent; she absolutely excited in my mind some desire to see it. For many a long year, she said, it had been her nightly prayer, that she might live to see me in my own castle; and often and often she was coming over to England to tell me so, only her husband, as long as he lived, would not let her set out on what he called a fool's errand: but it pleased God to take him to himself last fair day, and then she resolved that nothing should hinder her to be with her own child against his birthday: and now, could she see me in my own Castle Glenthorn, she would die contint—and what a pity but I should be in it! I was only a lord, as she said, in England; but I could be all as one as a king in Ireland.

Ellinor impressed me with the idea of the sort of feudal power I should possess in my vast territory, over tenants who were almost vassals, and amongst a numerous train of dependents. We resist the efforts made by those who, we think, exert authority or employ artifice to change our determinations; whilst the perverse mind insensibly yields to those who appear not to have power, or reason, or address, sufficient to obtain a victory. I should not have heard any human being with patience try to persuade me to go to Ireland, except this ignorant poor nurse, who spoke, as I thought, merely from the instinct of affection to me and to her native country. I promised her that I would, some time or other, visit Glenthorn Castle: but this was only a vague promise, and it was but little likely that it should be accomplished. As I regained my strength, my mind turned, or rather was turned, to other thoughts.


## CHAPTER IV

One morning—it was the day after my physicians had pronounced me out of all danger—Crawley sent me a note by Ellinor, congratulating me upon my recovery, and begging to speak to me for half an hour. I refused to see him; and said, that I was not yet well enough to do business. The same morning Ellinor came with a message from Turner, my steward, who, with his humble duty, requested to see me for five minutes, to communicate to me something of importance. I consented to see Turner. He entered with a face of suppressed joy and affected melancholy.

"Sad news I am bound in duty to be the bearer of, my lord. I was determined, whatever came to pass, however, not to speak till your honour was out of danger, which, I thank Heaven, is now the case, and I am happy to be able to congratulate your lordship upon looking as well as—"

"Never mind my looks. I will excuse your congratulations, Mr. Turner," said I, impatiently; for the recollection of the banqueting-house, and the undertaker whom Turner was so eager to introduce, came full into my mind. "Go on, if you please; five minutes is all I am at present able to give to any business, and you sent me word you had something of importance to communicate."

"True, my lord; but in case your lordship is not at present well enough, or not so disposed, I will wait your lordship's leisure."

"Now or never, Mr. Turner. Speak, but speak at once."

"My lord, I would have done so long ago, but was loth to make mischief; and besides, could not believe what I heard whispered, and would scarce believe what I verily saw; though now, as I cannot reasonably have a doubt, I think it would be a sin, and a burden upon my conscience, not to speak; only that I am unwilling to shock your lordship too much, when but just recovering, for that is not the time one would wish to tell or to hear disagreeable things."

"Mr. Turner, either come to the point at once, or leave me; for I am not strong enough to bear this suspense."

"I beg pardon, my lord: why then, my lord, the point is Captain Crawley."

"What of him? I never desire to hear his name again."

"Nor I, I am sure, my lord; but there are some in the house might not be of our opinion."

"Who? you sneaking fellow; speak out, can't you?"

"My lady—my lord—Now it is out. She'll go off with him this night, if not prevented."

My surprise and indignation were as great as if I had always been the fondest and the most attentive of husbands. I was at length roused from that indifference and apathy into which I had sunk; and though I had never loved my wife, the moment I knew she was lost to me for ever was exquisitely painful. Astonishment, the sense of disgrace, the feeling of rage against that treacherous parasite by whom she had been seduced, all combined to overwhelm me. I could command my voice only enough to bid Turner leave the room, and tell no one that he had spoken to me on this subject. "Not a soul," he said, "should be told, or could guess it."

Left to my own reflections, as soon as the first emotions of anger subsided, I blamed myself for my conduct to Lady Glenthorn. I considered that she had been married to me by her friends, when she was too young and too childish to judge for herself; that from the first day of our marriage I had never made the slightest effort to win her affections, or to guide her conduct; that, on the contrary, I had shown her marked indifference, if not aversion. With fashionable airs, I had professed, that provided she left me at liberty to spend the large fortune which she brought me, and in consideration of which she enjoyed the title of Countess of Glenthorn, I cared for nothing farther. With the consequences of my neglect I now reproached myself in vain. Lady Glenthorn's immense fortune had paid my debts, and had for two years supplied my extravagance, or rather my indolence: little remained, and she was now, in her twenty-third year, to be consigned to public disgrace, and to a man whom I knew to be destitute of honour and feeling. I pitied her, and resolved to go instantly and make an effort to save her from destruction.

Ellinor, who watched all Crawley's motions, informed me, that he was gone to a neighbouring town, and had left word that he should not be home till after dinner. Lady Glenthorn was in her dressing-room, which was at a part of the house farthest from that which I now inhabited. I had never left my room since my illness, and had scarcely walked farther than from my bed to my arm-chair; but I was so much roused by my feelings at this instant, that, to Ellinor's great astonishment, I started from my chair, and, forbidding her to follow me, walked without any assistance along the corridor, which led to the back-stairs, and to Lady Glenthorn's apartment. I opened the private door of her dressing-room suddenly—the room was in great disorder—her woman was upon her knees packing a trunk: Lady Glenthorn was standing at a table, with a parcel of open letters before her, and a diamond necklace in her hand. She started at the sight of me as if she had beheld a ghost: the maid screamed, and ran to a door at the farther end of the room, to make her escape, but that was bolted. Lady Glenthorn was pale and motionless, till I approached; and then, recollecting herself, she reddened all over, and thrust the letters into her table-drawer. Her woman, at the same instant, snatched a casket of jewels, swept up in her arms a heap of clothes, and huddled them all together into the half-packed trunk.

"Leave the room," said I to her sternly. She locked the trunk, pocketed the key, and obeyed.

I placed a chair for Lady Glenthorn, and sat down myself. We were almost equally unable to stand. We were silent for some moments. Her eyes were fixed upon the ground, and she leaned her head upon her hand in an attitude of despair. I could scarcely articulate; but making an effort to command my voice, I at last said—

"Lady Glenthorn, I blame myself more than you for all that has happened."

"For what?" said she, making a feeble attempt at evasion, yet at the same time casting a guilty look towards the drawer of letters.

"You have nothing to conceal from me," said I.

"Nothing!" said she, in a feeble voice.

"Nothing," said I; "for I know every thing"—she started—"and am willing to pardon every thing."

She looked up in my face astonished. "I am conscious," continued I, "that you have not been well treated by me. You have had much reason to complain of my neglect. To this I attribute your error. Forget the past—I will set you the example. Promise me never to see the man more, and what has happened shall never be known to the world."

She made me no answer, but burst into a flood of tears. She seemed incapable of decision, or even of thought. I felt suddenly inspired with energy.

"Write this moment," continued I, placing a pen and ink before her, "write to forbid him ever to return to this house, or ever more to appear in your presence. If he should appear in mine, I know how to chastise him, and to vindicate my own honour. To preserve your reputation, I refrain, upon these conditions, from making my contempt of him public."

I put a pen into Lady Glenthorn's hand; but she trembled so that she could not write. She made several ineffectual attempts, then tore the paper; and again giving way to tears, exclaimed, "I cannot write—I cannot think—I do not know what to say. Write what you will, and I will sign it."

"I write to Captain Crawley! Write what I will! Lady Glenthorn, it must be your will to write, not mine. If it be not your will, say so."

"Oh! I do not say so—I do not say that. Give me a moment's time. I do not know what I say. I have been very foolish—very wicked. You are very good—but it is too late: it will all be known. Crawley will betray me; he will tell it to Mrs. Mattocks: so whichever way I turn, I am undone. Oh! what will become of me?"

She wrung her hands and wept, and was for an hour in this state, in all the indecision and imbecility of a child. At last, she wrote a few scarcely legible lines to Crawley, forbidding him to see or think of her more. I despatched the note, and she was full of penitence, and gratitude, and tears. The next morning, when I wakened, I in my turn received a note from her ladyship.

"Since I saw you, Captain Crawley has convinced me that I am his wife, in the eye of Heaven, and I therefore desire a divorce, as much as your whole conduct, since my marriage, convinces me you must in your heart, whatever may be your motives to pretend otherwise. Before you receive this I shall be out of your way and beyond your reach; so do not think of pursuing one who is no longer,

"Yours,

"A. CRAWLEY."

After reading this note, I thought not of pursuing or saving Lady Glenthorn. I was as anxious for a divorce as she could be. Some months afterwards the affair was brought to a public trial. When the cause came on, so many circumstances were brought in mitigation of damages, to prove my utter carelessness respecting my wife's conduct, that a suspicion of collusion arose. From this imputation I was clear in the opinion of all who really knew me; and I repelled the charge publicly, with a degree of indignation that surprised all who knew the usual apathy of my temper. I must observe, that during the whole time my divorce-bill was pending, and whilst I was in the greatest possible anxiety, my health was perfectly good. But no sooner was the affair settled, and a decision made in my favour, than I relapsed into my old nervous complaints.


CHAPTER V

*"'Twas doing nothing was his curse;—*
*Is there a vice can plague us worse?*
*The wretch who digs the mine for bread,*
*Or ploughs, that others may be fed,*
*Feels less fatigue than that decreed*
*To him who cannot think or read."*

Illness was a sort of occupation to me, and I was always sorry to get well. When the interest of being in danger ceased, I had no other to supply its place. I fancied that I should enjoy my liberty after my divorce; but "even freedom grew tasteless." I do not recollect any thing that wakened me from my torpor, during two months after my divorce, except a violent quarrel between all my English servants and my Irish nurse. Whether she assumed too much, upon the idea that she was a favourite, or whether national prejudice was alone the cause of the hatred, that prevailed against her, I know not; but they one and all declared that they could not, and would not, live with her. She expressed the same dislike to consorting with them; "but would put up with worse, ay, with the devils themselves, to oblige my honour, and to lie under the same roof wid my honour."

The rest of the servants laughed at her blunders. This she could bear with good-humour; but when they seriously affected to reproach her with having, by her uncouth appearance, at her first presenting herself at Sherwood Park, endangered my life, she retorted, "And who cared for him in the wide world but I, amongst you all, when he lay for dead? I ask you that," said she.

To this there was no reply; and they hated her the more for their having been silenced by her shrewdness. I protected her as long as I could; but, for the sake of peace, I at last yielded to the combined forces of the steward's room and the servants' hall, and despatched Ellinor to Ireland, with a renewal of the promise that I would visit Glenthorn Castle this year or the next. To comfort her at parting, I would have made her a considerable present; but she would take only a few guineas, to bear her expenses back to her native place. The sacrifice I made did not procure me a peace of any continuance in my own house:—ruined by indulgence, and by my indolent, reckless temper, my servants were now my masters. In a large, ill-regulated establishment, domestics become, like spoiled children, discontented, capricious, and the tyrants over those who have not the sense or steadiness to command. I remember one delicate puppy parted with me, because, as he informed me, the curtains of his bed did not close at the foot; he had never been used to such a thing, and had told the housekeeper so three times, but could obtain no redress, which necessitated him to beg my permission to retire from the service.

In his stead another coxcomb came to offer himself, who, with an incomparably easy air, begged to know whether I wanted a man of figure or a man of parts? For the benefit of those to whom this fashionable classification of domestics may not be familiar, I should observe, that the department of a man of figure is specially and solely to announce company on gala days; the business of the man of parts is multifarious: to write cards of invitation, to speak to impertinent tradesmen, to carry confidential messages, et cetera. Now, where there is an et cetera in an agreement, there is always an opening for dispute. The functions of the man of parts not being accurately defined, I unluckily required from him some service which was not in his bond; I believe it was to go for my pocket handkerchief: "He could not possibly do it, because it was not his business;" and I, the laziest of mortals, after waiting a full quarter of an hour, whilst they were settling whose business it was to obey me, was forced to get up and go for what I wanted. I comforted myself by the recollection of the poor king of Spain and le brasier. With a regal precedent I could not but be satisfied. All great people, said I to myself, are obliged to submit to these inconveniences. I submitted with so good a grace, that my submission was scarcely felt to be a condescension. My bachelor's house soon exhibited in perfection "High Life below Stairs."

It is said that a foreign nobleman permitted his servants to take their own way so completely, that one night he and his guests being kept waiting an unconscionable time for supper, he at last went down stairs to inquire into the cause of the delay: he found the servant, whose business it was to take up supper, quietly at cards with a large party of his friends. The man coolly remonstrated, that it was impossible to leave his game unfinished. The master candidly acknowledged the force of his plea; but insisted upon the man's going up stairs to lay the cloth for supper, whilst he took his cards, sat down, and finished the game for him.

The suavity of my temper never absolutely reached this degree of complaisance. My home was disagreeable to me: I had not the resolution to remove the causes of the discontents. Every day I swore I would part with all these rascals the next morning; but still they stayed. Abroad I was not happier than at home. I was disgusted with my former companions: they had convinced me, the night of my accident at Sherwood Park, that they cared not whether I was alive or dead; and ever since that time I had been more and more struck with their selfishness as well as folly. It was inexpressibly fatiguing and irksome to me to keep up a show of good fellowship and joviality with these people, though I had not sufficient energy to make the attempt to quit them. When these dashers and loungers found that I was not always at their disposal, they discovered that Glenthorn had always something odd about him; that Glenthorn had always a melancholy turn; that it ran in the family, &c. Satisfied with these phrases, they let me take my own way, and forgot my existence. Public amusements had lost their charm; I had sufficient steadiness to resist the temptation to game: but, for want of stimulus, I could hardly endure the tedium of my days. At this period of my life, ennui was very near turning into misanthropy. I balanced between becoming a misanthrope and a democrat.

Whilst I was in this critical state of ineptitude, my attention was accidentally roused by the sight of a boxing-match. My feelings were so much excited, and the excitation was so delightful, that I was now in danger of becoming an amateur of the pugilistic art. It did not occur to me, that it was beneath the dignity of a British nobleman to learn the vulgar terms of the boxing trade. I soon began to talk very knowingly of first-rate bruisers, game men, and pleasing fighters; making play—beating a man under the ropes—sparring—rallying—sawing—and chopping. What farther proficiency I might have made in this language, or how long my interest in these feats of prize-fighters might have continued, had I been left to myself, I cannot determine; but I was unexpectedly seized with a fit of national shame, on hearing a foreigner of rank and reputation express astonishment at our taste for these savage spectacles. It was in vain that I repeated the arguments of some of the parliamentary panegyrists of boxing and bull-baiting; and asserted, that these diversions render a people hardy and courageous. My opponent replied, that he did not perceive the necessary connexion between cruelty and courage; that he did not comprehend how the standing by in safety to see two men bruise each other almost to death could evince or inspire heroic sentiments or warlike dispositions. He observed, that the Romans were most eager for the fights of gladiators during the reigns of the most effeminate and cruel emperors, and in the decline of all public spirit and virtue. These arguments would have probably made but a feeble impression on an understanding like mine, unaccustomed to general reasoning, and on a temper habituated to pursue, without thought of consequences, my immediate individual gratification; but it happened that my feelings were touched at this time by the dreadful sufferings of one of the pugilistic combatants. He died a few hours after the battle. He was an Irishman: most of the spectators being English, and triumphing in the victory of their countryman, the poor fellow's fate was scarcely noticed. I spoke to him a little while before he died, and found that he came from my own county. His name was Michael Noonan. He made it his dying request, that I would carry half-a-guinea, the only money he possessed, to his aged father, and a silk handkerchief he had worn round his neck, to his sister. Pity for this unfortunate Irishman recalled Ireland to my thoughts. Many small reasons concurred to make me now desirous of going to that country. I should get rid at once of a tormenting establishment, and of servants, without the odium of turning them away; for most of them declined going into banishment, as they called it. Besides this, I should leave my companions, with whom I was disgusted. I was tired of England, and wanted to see something new, even if it were to be worse than what I had seen before. These were not my ostensible reasons: I professed to have more exalted motives for my journey. It was my duty, I said, to visit my Irish estate, and to encourage my tenantry, by residing some time among them. Duties often spring up to our view at a convenient opportunity. Then my promise to poor Ellinor; it was impossible for a man of honour to break a promise, even to an old woman: in short, when people are determined upon any action, they seldom fail to find arguments capable of convincing them that their resolution is reasonable. Mixed motives govern the conduct of half mankind; so I set out upon my journey to Ireland.

## CHAPTER VI

*"Es tu contente à la fleur de tes ans?*
*As tu des goûts et des amusemens?*
*Tu dois mener une assez douce vie.*
*L'autre en deux mots répondait 'Je m'ennuie.'*
*C'est un grand mal, dit la fée, et je crois*
*Qu'un beau secret est de rester chez soi."—*

I was detained six days by contrary winds at Holyhead. Sick of that miserable place, in my ill-humour I cursed Ireland, and twice resolved to return to London: but the wind changed, my carriage was on board the packet; so I sailed and landly safely in Dublin. I was surprised by the excellence of the hotel at which I was lodged. I had not conceived that such accommodation could have been found in Dublin. The house had, as I was told, belonged to a nobleman: it was fitted up and appointed with a degree of elegance, and even magnificence, beyond what I had been used to in the most fashionable hotels in London.

"Ah! sir," said an Irish gentleman, who found me in admiration upon the staircase, "this is all very good, very fine, but it is too good and too fine to last; come here again in two years, and I am afraid you will see all this going to rack and ruin. This is too often the case with us in Ireland: we can project, but we can't calculate; we must have every thing upon too large a scale. We mistake a grand beginning for a good beginning. We begin like princes, and we end like beggars."

I rested only a few days in a capital in which, I took it for granted, there could be nothing worth seeing by a person who was just come from London. In driving through the streets, I was, however, surprised to see buildings, which my prejudices could scarcely believe to be Irish. I also saw some things, which recalled to my mind the observations I had heard at my hotel. I was struck with instances of grand beginnings and lamentable want of finish, with mixture of the magnificent and the paltry; of admirable and execrable taste. Though my understanding was wholly uncultivated, these things struck my eye. Of all the faculties of my mind, my taste had been most exercised, because its exercise had given me least trouble.

Impatient to see my own castle, I left Dublin. I was again astonished by the beauty of the prospects, and the excellence of the roads. I had in my ignorance believed that I was never to see a tree in Ireland, and that the roads were almost impassable. With the promptitude of credulity, I now went from one extreme to the other: I concluded that we should travel with the same celerity as upon the Bath road; and I expected, that a journey for which four days had been allotted might be performed in two. Like all those who have nothing to do any where, I was always in a prodigious hurry to get from place to place; and I ever had a noble ambition to go over as much ground as possible in a given space of time. I travelled in a light barouche, and with my own horses. My own man (an Englishman), and my cook (a Frenchman), followed in a hackney chaise; I cared not how, so that they kept up with me; the rest was their affair. At night, my gentleman complained bitterly of the Irish post carriages, and besought me to let him follow at an easier rate the next day; but to this I could by no means consent: for how could I exist without my own man and my French cook? In the morning, just as I was ready to set off, and had thrown myself back in my carriage, my Englishman and Frenchman came to the door, both in so great a rage, that the one was inarticulate and the other unintelligible. At length the object of their indignation spoke for itself. From the inn yard came a hackney chaise, in a most deplorable crazy state; the body mounted up to a prodigious height, on unbending springs, nodding forwards, one door swinging open, three blinds up, because they could not be let down, the perch tied in two places, the iron of the wheels half off, half loose, wooden pegs for linch-pins, and ropes for harness. The horses were worthy of the harness; wretched little dog-tired creatures, that looked as if they had been driven to the last gasp, and as if they had never been rubbed down in their lives; their bones starting through their skin; one lame, the other blind; one with a raw back, the other with a galled breast; one with his neck poking down over his collar, and the other with his head dragged forward by a bit of a broken bridle, held at arm's length by a man dressed like a mad beggar, in half a hat and half a wig, both awry in opposite directions; a long tattered great-coat, tied round his waist by a hay-rope; the jagged rents in the skirts of his coat showing his bare legs marbled of many colours; while something like stockings hung loose about his ankles. The noises he made by way of threatening or encouraging his steeds, I pretend not to describe.

In an indignant voice I called to the landlord, "I hope these are not the horses—I hope this is not the chaise, intended for my servants."

The innkeeper, and the pauper who was preparing to officiate as postilion, both in the same instant exclaimed, "Sorrow better chaise in the county!"

"Sorrow" said I; "what do you mean by sorrow?"

"That there's no better, plase your honour, can be seen. We have two more, to be sure; but one has no top, and the other no bottom. Any way there's no better can be seen than this same."

"And these horses!" cried I; "why, this horse is so lame he can hardly stand."

"Oh, plase your honour, tho' he can't stand, he'll go fast enough. He has a great deal of the rogue in him, plase your honour. He's always that way at first setting out."

"And that wretched animal with the galled breast!"

"He's all the better for it, when once he warms; it's he that will go with the speed of light, plase your honour. Sure, is not he Knockecroghery? and didn't I give fifteen guineas for him, barring the luck penny, at the fair of Knockecroghery, and he rising four year old at the same time?"

I could not avoid smiling at this speech: but my gentleman, maintaining his angry gravity, declared, in a sullen tone, that he would be cursed if he went with such horses; and the Frenchman, with abundance of gesticulation, made a prodigious chattering, which no mortal understood.

"Then I'll tell you what you'll do," said Paddy; "you'll take four, as becomes gentlemen of your quality, and you'll see how we'll powder along."

And straight he put the knuckle of his fore-finger in his mouth, and whistled shrill and strong; and, in a moment, a whistle somewhere out in the fields answered him.

I protested against these proceedings, but in vain; before the first pair of horses were fastened to the chaise, up came a little boy with the others fresh from the plough. They were quick enough in putting these to; yet how they managed it with their tackle, I know not. "Now we're fixed handsomely," said Paddy.

"But this chaise will break down the first mile."

"Is it this chaise, plase your honour? I'll engage it will go the world's end. The universe wouldn't break it down now; sure it was mended but last night."

Then seizing his whip and reins in one hand, he clawed up his stockings with the other: so with one easy step he got into his place, and seated himself, coachman-like, upon a well-worn bar of wood, that served as a coach-box. "Throw me the loan of a trusty Bartly, for a cushion," said he. A frieze coat was thrown up over the horses' heads—Paddy caught it. "Where are you, Hosey?" cried he. "Sure I'm only rowling a wisp of straw on my leg," replied Hosey. "Throw me up," added this paragon of postilions, turning to one of the crowd of idle bystanders. "Arrah, push me up, can't ye?"

A man took hold of his knee, and threw him upon the horse: he was in his seat in a trice; then clinging by the mane of his horse, he scrambled for the bridle, which was under the other horse's feet—reached it, and, well satisfied with himself, looked round at Paddy, who looked back to the chaise-door at my angry servants, "secure in the last event of things." In vain the Englishman in monotonous anger, and the Frenchman in every note of the gamut, abused Paddy: necessity and wit were on Paddy's side; he parried all that was said against his chaise, his horses, himself, and his country, with invincible comic dexterity, till at last, both his adversaries, dumb-foundered, clambered into the vehicle, where they were instantly shut up in straw and darkness. Paddy, in a triumphant tone, called to my postilions, bidding them "get on, and not be stopping the way any longer."

Without uttering a syllable, they drove on; but they could not, nor could I, refrain from looking back to see how those fellows would manage. We saw the fore-horses make towards the right, then to the left, and every way but straight forwards; whilst Paddy bawled to Hosey—"Keep the middle of the road, can't ye? I don't want ye to draw a pound at-all-at-all."

At last, by dint of whipping, the four horses were compelled to set off in a lame gallop; but they stopped short at a hill near the end of the town, whilst a shouting troop of ragged boys followed, and pushed them fairly to the top. Half an hour afterwards, as we were putting on our drag-chain to go down another steep hill,—to my utter astonishment, Paddy, with his horses in full gallop, came rattling and chehupping past us. My people called to warn him that he had no drag: but still he cried "Never fear!" and shaking the long reins, and stamping with his foot, on he went thundering down the hill. My Englishmen were aghast.

"The turn yonder below, at the bottom of the hill, is as sharp and ugly as ever I see," said my postilion, after a moment's stupified silence. "He will break their necks, as sure as my name is John."

Quite the contrary: when we had dragged and undragged, and came up to Paddy, we found him safe on his legs, mending some of his tackle very quietly.

"If that had broken as you were going down the steep hill," said I, "it would have been all over with you, Paddy."

"That's true, plase your honour: but it never happened me going down hill—nor never will, by the blessing of God, if I've any luck."

With this mixed confidence in a special providence, and in his own good luck, Paddy went on, much to my amusement. It was his glory to keep before us; and he rattled on till he came to a narrow part of the road, where they were rebuilding a bridge. Here there was a dead stop. Paddy lashed his horses, and called them all manner of names; but the wheel horse, Knockecroghery, was restive, and at last began to kick most furiously. It seemed inevitable that the first kick which should reach the splinter-bar, at which it was aimed, must demolish it instantly. My English gentleman and my Frenchman both put their heads out of the only window which was pervious, and called most manfully to be let out. "Never fear," said Paddy. To open the door for themselves was beyond their force or skill. One of the hind wheels, which had belonged to another carriage, was too high to suffer the door to be opened, and the blind at the other side prevented their attempts, so they were close prisoners. The men who had been at work on the broken bridge came forward, and rested on their spades to see the battle. As my carriage could not pass, I was also compelled to be a spectator of this contest between man and horse.

"Never fear," reiterated Paddy; "I'll engage I'll be up wid him. Now for it, Knockecroghery! Oh, the rogue, he thinks he has me at a nonplush, but I'll show him the differ."

After this brag of war, Paddy whipped, Knockecroghery kicked; and Paddy, seemingly unconscious of danger, sat within reach of the kicking horse, twitching up first one of his legs, then the other, and shifting as the animal aimed his hoofs, escaping every time as it were by miracle. With a mixture of temerity and presence of mind, which made us alternately look upon him as a madman and a hero, he gloried in the danger, secure of success, and of the sympathy of the spectators.

"Ah! didn't I compass him cleverly then? Oh, the villain, to be browbating me! I'm too cute for him yet. See there, now, he's come to; and I'll be his bail he'll go asy enough wid me. Ogh! he has a fine spirit of his own, but it's I that can match him: 'twould be a poor case if a man like me cou'dn't match a horse any way, let alone a mare, which this is, or it never would be so vicious."

After this hard-fought battle, and suitable rejoicing for the victory, Paddy walked his subdued adversary on a few yards to allow us to pass him; but, to the dismay of my postilions, a hay-rope was at this instant thrown across the road, before our horses, by the road-makers, who, to explain this proceeding, cried out, "Plase your honour, the road is so dry, we'd expect a trifle to wet it."

"What do these fellows mean?" said I.

"It's only a tester or a hog they want, your honour, to give 'em to drink your honour's health," said Paddy.

"A hog to drink my health?"

"Ay, that is a thirteen, plase your honour; all as one as an English shilling."

I threw them a shilling: the hay-rope was withdrawn, and at last we went on. We heard no more of Paddy till evening. He came in two hours after us, and expected to be doubly paid for driving my honour's gentlemen so well.

I must say that on this journey, though I met with many delays and disasters; though one of my horses was lamed in shoeing by a smith, who came home drunk from a funeral; and though the back pannel of my carriage was broken by the pole of a chaise; and though one day I went without my dinner at a large desolate inn, where nothing was to be had but whiskey; and though one night I lay in a little smoky den, in which the meanest of my servants in England would have thought it impossible to sleep; and though I complained bitterly, and swore it was impracticable for a gentleman to travel in Ireland; yet I never remember to have experienced, on any journey, less ennui. I was out of patience twenty times a day, but I certainly felt no ennui; and I am convinced that the benefit some patients receive from a journey is in an inverse proportion to the ease and luxury of their mode of travelling. When they are compelled to exert their faculties, and to use their limbs, they forget their nerves, as I did. Upon this principle I should recommend to wealthy hypochondriacs a journey in Ireland, preferably to any country in the civilized world. I can promise them, that they will not only be moved to anger often enough to make their blood circulate briskly, but they will even, in the acme of their impatience, be thrown into salutary convulsions of laughter, by the comic concomitants of their disasters: besides, if they have hearts, their best feelings cannot fail to be awakened by the warm, generous hospitality they will receive in this country, from the cabin to the castle.

Late in the evening of the fourth day, we came to an inn on the verge of the county where my estate was situate. It was one of the wildest parts of Ireland. We could find no horses, nor accommodations of any sort, and we had several miles farther to go. For our only comfort, the dirty landlady, who had married the hostler, and wore gold drop ear-rings, reminded us, that, "Sure, if we could but wait an hour, and take a fresh egg, we should have a fine moon."

After many fruitless imprecations, my French cook was obliged to mount one of my saddle-horses; my groom was left to follow us the next day; I let my gentleman sit on the barouche box, and proceeded with my own tired horses. The moon, which my landlady had promised me, rose, and I had a full view of the face of the country. As we approached my maritime territories, the cottages were thinly scattered, and the trees had a stunted appearance; they all slanted one way, from the prevalent winds that blew from the ocean. Our road presently stretched along the beach, and I saw nothing to vary the prospect but rocks, and their huge shadows upon the water. The road being sandy, the feet of the horses made no noise, and nothing interrupted the silence of the night but the hissing sound of the carriage-wheels passing through the sand.

"What o'clock is it now, think you, John?" said one of my postilions to the other.

"Past twelve, for sartain," said John; "and this bees a strange Irish place," continued he, in a drawling voice; "with no possible way o' getting at it, as I see." John, after a pause, resumed, "I say, Timothy, to the best of my opinion, this here road is leading on us into the sea." John replied, "that he did suppose there might be such a thing as a boat farther on, but where, he could not say for sartain." Dismayed and helpless, they at last stopped to consult whether they had come the right road to the house. In the midst of their consultation there came up an Irish carman, whistling as he walked beside his horse and car.

"Honest friend, is this the road to Glenthorn Castle?"

"To Glenthorn, sure enough, your honour."

"Whereabouts is the castle?"

"Forenent you, if you go on to the turn."

"Forenent you!" As the postilions pondered upon this word, the carman, leaving his horse, and car, turned back to explain by action what he could not make intelligible by words.

"See, isn't here the castle?" cried he, darting before us to the turn of the road, where he stood pointing at what we could not possibly see, as it was hid by a promontory of rock. When we f reached the spot where he was stationed, we came full upon the view of Glenthorn Castle: it seemed to rise from the sea, abrupt and insulated, in all the gloomy grandeur of ancient times, with turrets and battlements, and a huge gateway, the pointed arch of which receded in perspective between the projecting towers.

"It's my lord himself, I'm fond to believe!" said our guide, taking off his hat; "I had best step on and tell 'em at the castle."

"No, my good friend, there is no occasion to trouble you farther; you had better go back to your horse and car, which you have left on the road."

"Oh! they are used to that, plase your honour; they'll go on very quite, and I'll run like a redshank with the news to the castle."

He ran on before us with surprising velocity, whilst our tired horses dragged us slowly through the sand. As we approached, the gateway of the castle opened, and a number of men, who appeared to be dwarfs when compared with the height of the building, came out with torches in their hands. By their bustle, and the vehemence with which they bawled to one another, one might have thought that the whole castle was in flames; but they were only letting down a drawbridge. As I was going over this bridge, a casement window opened in the castle; and a voice, which I knew to be old Ellinor's, exclaimed, "Mind the big hole in the middle of the bridge, God bless yees!"

I passed over the broken bridge, and through the massive gate, under an arched way, at the farthest end of which a lamp had just been lighted: then I came into a large open area, the court of the castle. The hollow sound of the horses' feet, and of the carriage rumbling over the drawbridge, was immediately succeeded by the strange and eager voices of the people, who filled the court with a variety of noises, contrasting, in the most striking manner, with the silence in which we had travelled over the sands. The great effect that my arrival instantaneously produced upon the multitude of servants and dependants, who issued from the castle, gave me an idea of my own consequence beyond any thing which I had ever felt in England. These people seemed "born for my use:" the officious precipitation with which they ran to and fro; the style in which they addressed me; some crying, "Long life to the Earl of Glenthorn!" some blessing me for coming to reign over them; all together gave more the idea of vassals than of tenants, and carried my imagination centuries back to feudal times.

The first person I saw on entering the hall of my castle was poor Ellinor: she pushed her way up to me—

"'Tis himself!" cried she. Then turning about suddenly, "I've seen him in his own castle—I've seen him; and if it pleases God this minute to take me to himself, I would die with pleasure."

"My good Ellinor," said I, touched to the heart by her affection, "my good Ellinor, I hope you will live many a happy year; and if I can contribute—"

"And himself to speak to me so kind before them all!" interrupted she. "Oh! this is too much—quite too much!" She burst into tears; and, hiding her face with her arm, made her way out of the hall.

The flights of stairs which I had to ascend, and the length of galleries through which I was conducted, before I reached the apartment where supper was served, gave me a vast idea of the extent of my castle; but I was too much fatigued to enjoy fully the gratifications of pride. To the simple pleasures of appetite I was more sensible: I ate heartily of one of the most profusely hospitable suppers that ever was prepared for a noble baron, even in the days when oxen were roasted whole. Then I grew so sleepy, that I was impatient to be shown to my bed. I was ushered through another suite of chambers and galleries; and, as I was traversing one of these, a door of some strange dormitory opened, and a group of female heads were thrust out, in the midst of which I could distinguish old Ellinor's face; but, as I turned my head, the door closed so quickly, that I had no time to speak: I only heard the words, "Blessings on him! that's he!"

I was so sleepy, that I rejoiced having escaped an occasion where I might have been called upon to speak, yet I was really grateful to my poor nurse for her blessing. The state tower, in which, after reiterated entreaties, I was at last left alone to repose, was hung with magnificent, but ancient tapestry. It was so like a room in a haunted castle, that if I had not been too much fatigued to think of any thing, I should certainly have thought of Mrs. Radcliffe. I am sorry to say that I have no mysteries, or even portentous omens, to record of this night; for the moment that I lay down in my antiquated bed, I fell into a profound sleep.

CHAPTER VII

When I awoke, I thought that I was on shipboard; for the first sound I heard was that of the sea booming against the castle walls. I arose, looked out of the window of my bedchamber, and saw that the whole prospect bore an air of savage wildness. As I contemplated the scene, my imagination was seized with the idea of remoteness from civilized society: the melancholy feeling of solitary grandeur took possession of my soul.

From this feeling I was relieved by the affectionate countenance of my old nurse, who at this instant put her head half in at the door.

"I only just made bold to look in at the fire, to see did it burn, because I lighted it myself, and would not be blowing of it for fear of wakening you."

"Come in, Ellinor, come in," said I. "Come quite in."

"I will, since you've nobody with you that I need be afraid of," said she, looking round satisfied, when she saw my own man was not in the room.

"You need never be afraid of any body, Ellinor, whilst I am alive," said I; "for I will always protect you. I do not forget your conduct, when you thought I was dead in the banqueting-room."

"Oh! don't be talking of that; thanks be to God there was nothing in it! I see you well now. Long life to you! Sure you must have been tired to death last night, for this morning early you lay so quite, sleeping like an angel; and I could see a great likeness in yees to what you were when you were a child in my arms."

"But sit down, sit down, my good Ellinor," said I, "and let us talk a little of your own affairs."

"And are not these my own affairs?" said she, rather angrily.

"Certainly; but I mean, that you must tell me how you are going on in the world, and what I can do to make you comfortable and happy."

"There's one thing would make me happy," said she.

"Name it," said I.

"To be let light your fire myself every morning, and open your shutters, dear."

I could not help smiling at the simplicity of the request. I was going to press her to ask something of more consequence, but she heard a servant coming along the gallery, and, starting from her chair, she ran and threw herself upon her knees before the fire, blowing it with her mouth with great vehemence.

The servant came to let me know that Mr. M'Leod, my agent, was waiting for me in the breakfast-room.

"And will I be let light your fire then every morning?" said Ellinor eagerly, turning as she knelt.

"And welcome," said I.

"Then you won't forget to speak about it for me," said she, "else may be I won't be let up by them English. God bless you, and don't forget to speak for me."

"I will remember to speak about it," said I; but I went down stairs and forgot it.

Mr. M'Leod, whom I found reading the newspaper in the breakfast-room, seemed less affected by my presence than any body I had seen since my arrival. He was a hard-featured, strong-built, perpendicular man, with a remarkable quietness of deportment: he spoke with deliberate distinctness, in an accent slightly Scotch; and, in speaking, he made use of no gesticulation, but held himself surprisingly still. No part of him but his eyes moved, and they had an expression of slow, but determined good sense. He was sparing of his words; but the few that he used said much, and went directly to the point. He pressed for the immediate examination and settlement of his accounts: he enumerated several things of importance, which he had done for my service: but he did this without pretending the slightest attachment to me; he mentioned them only as proofs of his having done his duty to his employer, for which he neither expected nor would accept of thanks. He seemed to be cold and upright in his mind as in his body. I was not influenced in his favour even by his striking appearance of plain-dealing, so strong was the general abhorrence of agents which Crawley's treachery had left in my mind. The excess of credulity, when convinced of its error, becomes the extreme of suspicion. Persons not accustomed to reason often argue absurdly, because, from particular instances, they deduce general conclusions, and extend the result of their limited experience of individuals indiscriminately to whole classes. The labour of thinking was so great to me, that, having once come to a conclusion upon any subject, I would rather persist in it, right or wrong, than be at the trouble of going over the process again to revise and rectify my judgment.

Upon this occasion national prejudice heightened the prepossession which circumstances had raised. Mr. M'Leod was not only an agent, but a Scotchman; and I had a notion that all Scotchmen were crafty: therefore I concluded that his blunt manner was assumed, and his plain-dealing but a more refined species of policy.

After breakfast he laid before me a general statement of my affairs; obliged me to name a day for the examination of his accounts; and then, without expressing either mortification or displeasure at the coldness of my behaviour, or at my evident impatience of his presence, he, unmoved of spirit, rang for his horse, wished me a good morning, and departed.

By this time my castle-yard was filled with a crowd of "great-coated suitors," who were all come to see—could they see my lordship? or waiting just to say two words to my honour. In various lounging attitudes, leaning against the walls, or pacing backwards and forwards before the window, to catch my eye, they, with a patience passing the patience of courtiers, waited, hour after hour, the live-long day, for their turn, or their chance, of an audience. I had promised myself the pleasure of viewing my castle this day, and of taking a ride through my grounds; but that was totally out of the question. I was no longer a man with a will of my own, or with time at my own disposal.

"Long may you live to reign over us!" was the signal that I was now to live, like a prince, only for the service of my subjects. How these subjects of mine had contrived to go on for so many years in my absence, I was at a loss to conceive; for, the moment I was present, it seemed evident that they could not exist without me.

One had a wife and six childer, and not a spot in the wide world to live in, if my honour did not let him live under me, in any bit of a skirt of the estate that would feed a cow.

Another had a brother in jail, who could not be got out without me.

Another had three lives dropped in a lase for ever; another wanted a renewal; another a farm; another a house; and one expected my lard would make his son an exciseman; and another that I would make him a policeman; and another was racked, if I did not settle the mearing between him and Corny Corkran; and half a hundred had given in proposals to the agent for lands that would be out next May; and half a hundred more came with legends of traditionary promises from the old lord, my lordship's father that was: and for hours I was forced to listen to long stories out of the face, in which there was such a perplexing and provoking mixture of truth and fiction, involved in language so figurative, and tones so new to my English ears, that, with my utmost patience and strained attention, I could comprehend but a very small portion of what was said to me.

Never were my ears so weary any day of my life as they were this day. I could not have endured the fatigue, if I had not been supported by the agreeable idea of my own power and consequence; a power seemingly next to despotic. This new stimulus sustained me for three days that I was kept a state-prisoner in my own castle, by the crowds who came to do me homage, and to claim my favour and protection. In vain every morning was my horse led about saddled and bridled: I never was permitted to mount. On the fourth morning, when I felt sure of having despatched all my tormentors, I was in astonishment and despair on seeing my levee crowded with a fresh succession of petitioners. I gave orders to my people to say that I was going out, and absolutely could see nobody. I supposed that they did not understand what my English servants said, for they never stirred from their posts. On receiving a second message, they acknowledged that they understood the first; but replied, that they could wait there till my honour came back from my ride. With difficulty I mounted my horse, and escaped from the closing ranks of my persecutors. At night I gave directions to have the gates kept shut, and ordered the porter not to admit any body at his peril. When I got up, I was delighted to see the coast clear; but the moment I went out, lo! at the outside of the gate, the host of besiegers were posted, and in my lawn, and along the road, and through the fields: they pursued me; and when I forbade them to speak to me when I was on horseback, the next day I found parties in ambuscade, who laid wait for me in silence, with their hats off, bowing and bowing, till I could not refrain from saying, "Well, my good friend, what do you stand bowing there for?" Then I was fairly prisoner, and held by the bridle for an hour.

In short, I found that I was now placed in a situation where I could hope neither for privacy nor leisure; but I had the joys of power, my rising passion for which would certainly have been extinguished in a short time by my habitual indolence, if it had not been kept alive by jealousy of Mr. M'Leod.

One day, when I refused to hear an importunate tenant, and declared that I had been persecuted with petitioners ever since my arrival, and that I was absolutely tired to death, the man answered, "True for ye, my lard; and it's a shame to be troubling you this way. Then, may be, it's to Mr. M'Leod I'll go? Sure the agent will do as well, and no more about it. Mr. M'Leod will do every thing the same way as usual."

"Mr. M'Leod will do every thing!" said I, hastily: "no, by no means."

"Who will we speak to, then?" said the man.

"To myself," said I, with as haughty a tone as Louis XIV. could have assumed, when he announced to his court his resolution to be his own minister. After this intrepid declaration to act for myself, I could not yield to my habitual laziness. So much had my pride been hurt, as well as my other feelings, by Captain Crawley's conduct, that I determined to show the world I was not to be duped a second time by an agent.

When, on the day appointed, Mr. M'Leod came to settle accounts with me, I, with an air of self-important capability, as if I had been all my life used to look into my own affairs, sat down to inspect the papers; and, incredible as it may appear, I went through the whole at a sitting, without a single yawn; and, for a man who never before had looked into an account, I understood the nature of debtor and creditor wonderfully well: but, with my utmost desire to evince my arithmetical sagacity, I could not detect the slightest error in the accounts; and it was evident that Mr. M'Leod was not Captain Crawley; yet, rather than believe that he could be both an agent and an honest man, I concluded, that if he did not cheat me out of my money, his aim was to cheat me out of power; and, fancying that he wished to be a man of influence and consequence in the county, I transferred to him instantly the feelings that were passing in my own mind, and took it for granted that he must be actuated by a love of power in every thing that he did apparently for my service.

About this time I remember being much disturbed in my mind, by a letter which Mr. M'Leod received in my presence, and of which he read to me only a part: I never rested till I saw the whole. The epistle proved well worth the trouble of deciphering: it related merely to the paving of my chicken-yard. Like the King of Prussia, who was said to be so jealous of power, that he wanted to regulate all the mousetraps in his dominions, I soon engrossed the management of a perplexing multiplicity of minute insignificant details. Alas! I discovered to my cost, that trouble is the inseparable attendant upon power: and many times, in the course of the first ten days of my reign, I was ready to give up my dignity from excessive fatigue.

## CHAPTER VIII

Early one morning, after having passed a feverish night, tortured in my dreams by the voices and faces of the people who had surrounded me the preceding day, I was awakened by the noise of somebody lighting my fire. I thought it was Ellinor; and the idea of the disinterested affection of this poor woman came full into my mind, contrasted in the strongest manner with the recollection of the selfish encroaching people by whom, of late, I had been worried.

"How do you do, my good Ellinor?" said I; "I have not seen any thing of you this week past."

"It's not Ellinor at all, my lard," said a new voice.

"And why so? Why does not Ellinor light my fire?"

"Myself does not know, my lard."

"Go for her directly."

"She's gone home these three days, my lard."

"Gone! is she sick?"

"Not as I know on, my lard. Myself does not know what ailed her, except she would be jealous of my lighting the fire. But I can't say what ailed her; for she went away without a word good or bad, when she seen me lighting this fire, which I did by the housekeeper's orders."

I now recollected poor Ellinor's request, and reproached myself for having neglected to fulfil my promise, upon an affair which, however trifling in itself, appeared of consequence to her. In the course of my morning's ride I determined to call upon her at her own house, and make my apologies: but first I satisfied my curiosity about a prodigious number of parks and towns which I had heard of upon my estate. Many a ragged man had come to me, with the modest request that I would let him one of the parks near the town. The horse-park, the deer-park, the cow-park, were not quite sufficient to answer the ideas I had attached to the word park: but I was quite astonished and mortified when I beheld the bits and corners of land near the town of Glenthorn, on which these high-sounding titles had been bestowed:—just what would feed a cow is sufficient in Ireland to constitute a park.

When I heard the names of above a hundred towns on the Glenthorn estate, I had an exalted idea of my own territories; and I was impatient to make a progress through my dominions: but, upon visiting a few of these places, my curiosity was satisfied. Two or three cabins gathered together were sufficient to constitute a town, and the land adjoining thereto is called a town-land. The denominations of these town-lands having continued from generation to generation, according to ancient surveys of Ireland, it is sufficient to show the boundaries of a town-land, to prove that there must be a town; and a tradition of a town continues to be satisfactory, even when only a single cabin remains. I turned my horse's head away in disgust from one of these traditionary towns, and desired a boy to show me the way to Ellinor O'Donoghoe's house.

"So I will, plase your honour, my lard; sure I've a right to know, for she's my own granny."

The boy, or, as he was called, the gossoon, ran across some fields where there was abundance of fern and of rabbits. The rabbits, sitting quietly at the entrance of their holes, seemed to consider themselves as proprietors of the soil, and me and my horse as intruders. The boy apologized for the number of rabbit-holes on this part of the estate: "It would not be so, my lard, if I had a gun allowed me by the gamekeeper, which he would give me if he knew it would be plasing to your honour." The ingenuity with which even the young boys can introduce their requests in a favourable moment sometimes provoked me, and sometimes excited my admiration. This boy made his just at the time he was rolling out of my way a car that stopped a gap in the hedge; and he was so hot and out of breath with running in my service, that I could not refuse him a token to the gamekeeper that he might get a gun as soon as I understood what it meant.

We came to Ellinor's house, a wretched-looking, low, and mud-walled cabin; at one end it was propped by a buttress of loose stones, upon which stood a goat reared on his hind legs, to browse on the grass that grew on the house-top. A dung-hill was before the only window, at the other end of the house, and close to the door was a puddle of the dirtiest of dirty water, in which ducks were dabbling. At my approach there came out of the cabin a pig, a calf, a lamb, a kid, and two geese, all with their legs tied; followed by turkeys, cocks, hens, chickens, a dog, a cat, a kitten, a beggar-man, a beggar-woman with a pipe in her mouth, children innumerable, and a stout girl with a pitchfork in her hand; all together more than I, looking down upon the roof as I sat on horseback, and measuring the superficies with my eye, could have possibly supposed the mansion capable of containing. I asked if Ellinor O'Donoghoe was at home; but the dog barked, the geese cackled, the turkeys gobbled, and the beggars begged, with one accord, so loudly, that there was no chance of my being heard. When the girl had at last succeeded in appeasing them all with her pitchfork, she answered, that Ellinor O'Donoghoe was at home, but that she was out with the potatoes; and she ran to fetch her, after calling to the lays, who was within in the room smoking, to come out to his honour. As soon as they had crouched under the door, and were able to stand upright, they welcomed me with a very good grace, and were proud to see me in the kingdom. I asked if they were all Ellinor's sons?

"All entirely," was the first answer.

"Not one but one," was the second answer. The third made the other two intelligible.

"Plase your honour, we are all her sons-in-law, except myself, who am her lawful son."

"Then you are my foster-brother?"

"No, plase your honour, it's not me, but my brother, and he's not in it."

"Not in it?"

"No, plase your honour; becaase he's in the forge, up abow."

"Abow!" said I; "what does he mean?"

"Sure he's the blacksmith, my lard."

"And what are you?"

"I'm Ody, plase your honour; the short for Owen."

"And what is your trade?"

"Trade, plase your honour! I was bred to none, more than another; but expects, only that my mother's not willing to part with me, to go into the militia next month; and I'm sure she'd let me, if your honour's lordship would spake a word to the colonel, to see to get me made a serjeant immadiately."

As Ody made his request, all his companions came forward in sign of sympathy, and closed round my horse's head to make me sinsible of their expectations; but at this instant Ellinor came up, her old face colouring all over with joy when she saw me.

"So, Ellinor," said I, "you were affronted, I hear, and left the castle in anger?"

"In anger! And if I did, more shame for me—but anger does not last long with me any way; and against you, my lord, dear, how could it? Oh, think how good he is, coming to see me in such a poor place!"

"I will make it a better place for you, Ellinor," said I. Far from being eager to obtain promises, she still replied, that "all was good enough for her." I desired that she would come and live with me at the castle, till a better house than her present habitation could be built for her; but she seemed to prefer this hovel. I assured her that she should be permitted to light my fire.

"Oh, it's better for me not," said she; "better keep out of the way. I could not be asy if I got any one ill-will."

I assured her that she should be at liberty to do just as she liked: and whilst I rode home I was planning a pretty cottage for her near the porter's lodge. I was pleased with myself for my gratitude to this poor woman. Before I slept, I actually wrote a letter, which obtained for Ody the honour of being made a serjeant in the — militia; and Ellinor, dazzled by this military glory, was satisfied that he should leave home, though he was her favourite.

"Well, let him leave me then," said she; "I won't stand in his light. I never thought of my living to see Ody a serjeant. Now, Ody, have done being wild, honey-dear, and be a credit to your family, and to his honour's commendation—God bless him for ever for it! From the very first I knew it was he that had the kind heart."

I am not sure that it was a very good action to get a man made a serjeant, of whom I knew nothing but that he was son to my nurse. Self-complacency, however, cherished my first indistinct feelings of benevolence. Though not much accustomed to reflect upon my own sensations, I think I remember, at this period, suspecting that the feeling of benevolence is a greater pleasure than the possession of barouches, and horses, and castles, and parks—greater even than the possession of power. Of this last truth, however, I had not as yet a perfectly clear conception. Even in my benevolence I was as impatient and unreasonable as a child. Money, I thought, had the power of Aladdin's lamp, to procure with magical celerity the gratification of my wishes. I expected that a cottage for Ellinor should rise out of the earth at my command. But the slaves of Aladdin's lamp were not Irishmen. The delays, and difficulties, and blunders, in the execution of my orders, provoked me beyond measure; and it would have been difficult for a cool spectator to decide whether I or my workmen were most in fault; they for their dilatory habits, or I for my impatient temper.

"Well, plase your honour, when the pratees are set, and the turf cut, we'll fall-to at Ellinor's house."

"Confound the potatoes and the turf! you must fall-to, as you call it, directly."

"Is it without the lime, and plase your honour? Sure that same is not drawn yet, nor the stones quarried, since it is of stone it will be—nor the foundations itself dug, and the horses were all putting out dung."

Then after the bog and the potatoes, came funerals and holidays innumerable. The masons were idle one week waiting for the mortar, and the mortar another week waiting for the stones, and then they were at a stand for the carpenter when they came to the door-case, and the carpenter was looking for the sawyer, and the sawyer was gone to have the saw mended. Then there was a stop again at the window-sills for the stone-cutter, and he was at the quarter-sessions, processing his brother for tin and tinpence, hay-money. And when, in spite of all delays and obstacles, the walls reached their destined height, the roof was a new plague; the carpenter, the slater, and the nailer, were all at variance, and I cannot tell which was the most provoking rogue of the three. At last, however, the house was roofed and slated: then I would not wait till the walls were dry before I plastered, and papered, and furnished it. I fitted it up in the most elegant style of English cottages; for I was determined that Ellinor's habitation should be such as had never been seen in this part of the world. The day when it was finished, and when I gave possession of it to Ellinor, paid me for all my trouble; I tasted a species of pleasure that was new to me, and which was the sweeter from having been earned with some difficulty. And now, when I saw a vast number of my tenants assembled at a rural feast which I gave on Ellinor's installation, my benevolence enlarged, even beyond the possibility of its gratification, and I wished to make all my dependants happy, provided I could accomplish it without much trouble. The method of doing good, which seemed to require the least exertion, and which I, therefore, most willingly practised, was giving away money. I did not wait to inquire, much less to examine into the merits of the claimants; but, without selecting proper objects, I relieved myself from the uneasy feeling of pity, by indiscriminate donations to objects apparently the most miserable.

I was quite angry with Mr. M'Leod, my agent, and considered him as a selfish, hard-hearted miser, because he did not seem to sympathize with me, or to applaud my generosity. I was so much irritated by his cold silence, that I could not forbear pressing him to say something.

"I doubt, then," said he, "since you desire me to speak my mind, my lord, I doubt whether the best way of encouraging the industrious is to give premiums to the idle."

"But, idle or not, these poor wretches are so miserable, that I cannot refuse to give them something; and, surely, when one can do it so easily, it is right to relieve misery. Is it not?"

"Undoubtedly, my lord; but the difficulty is, to relieve present misery, without creating more in future. Pity for one class of beings sometimes makes us cruel to others. I am told that there are some Indian Brahmins so very compassionate, that they hire beggars to let fleas feed upon them: I doubt whether it might not be better to let the fleas starve."

I did not in the least understand what Mr. M'Leod meant: but I was soon made to comprehend it, by crowds of eloquent beggars, who soon surrounded me: many who had been resolutely struggling with their difficulties, slackened their exertions, and left their labour for the easier trade of imposing upon my credulity. The money I had bestowed was wasted at the dram-shop, or it became the subject of family-quarrels; and those whom I had relieved returned to my honour, with fresh and insatiable expectations. All this time my industrious tenants grumbled, because no encouragement was given to them; and, looking upon me as a weak good-natured fool, they combined in a resolution to ask me for long leases, or reduction of rent.

The rhetoric of my tenants succeeded in some instances; and again I was mortified by Mr. M'Leod's silence. I was too proud to ask his opinion. I ordered, and was obeyed. A few leases for long terms were signed and sealed; and when I had thus my own way completely, I could not refrain from recurring to Mr. M'Leod's opinion.

"I doubt, my lord," said he, "whether this measure may be as advantageous as you hope. These fellows, these middle-men, will underset the land, and live in idleness, whilst they rack a parcel of wretched under-tenants."

"But they said they would keep the land in their own hands, and improve it; and that the reason why they could not afford to improve before was, that they had not long leases."

"It may be doubted whether long leases alone will make improving tenants; for in the next county to us, there are many farms of the dowager Lady Ormsby's land let at ten shillings an acre, and her tenantry are beggars: and the land now, at the end of the leases, is worn out, and worse than at their commencement."

I was weary listening to this cold reasoning, and resolved to apply no more for explanations to Mr. M'Leod; yet in my indolence I wanted the support of his approbation, at the very time I was jealous of his interference.

At one time I had a mind to raise the wages of labour; but Mr. M'Leod said, "It might be doubted whether the people would not work less, when they could with less work have money enough to support them."

I was puzzled: and then I had a mind to lower the wages of labour, to force them to work or starve. Still provoking Mr. M'Leod said, "It might be doubted whether it would not be better to leave them alone."

I gave marriage-portions to the daughters of my tenants, and rewards to those who had children; for I had always heard that legislators should encourage population. Still Mr. M'Leod hesitated to approve; he observed, "that my estate was so populous, that the complaint in each family was, that they had not land for the sons. It might be doubted whether, if a farm could support but ten people, it were wise to encourage the birth of twenty. It might be doubted whether it were not better for ten to live, and be well fed, than for twenty to be born, and to be half-starved."

To encourage manufactures in my town of Glenthorn, I proposed putting a clause in my leases, compelling my tenants to buy stuffs and linens manufactured at Glenthorn, and no where else. Stubborn M'Leod, as usual, began with, "I doubt whether that will not encourage the manufacturers at Glenthorn to make bad stuffs and bad linen, since they are sure of a sale, and without danger of competition."

At all events, I thought my tenants would grow rich and independent, if they made every thing at home that they wanted: yet Mr. M'Leod perplexed me by his "doubt whether it would not be better for a man to buy shoes, if he could buy them cheaper than he could make them." He added something about the division of labour, and Smith's Wealth of Nations; to which I could only answer—"Smith's a Scotchman."

I cannot express how much I dreaded Mr. M'Leod's I doubt—and—It may be doubted.

From the pain of doubt, and the labour of thought, I was soon most agreeably reprieved by the company of a Mr. Hardcastle, whose visits I constantly encouraged by a most gracious reception. Mr. Hardcastle was the agent of the dowager Lady Ormsby, who had a large estate in my neighbourhood: he was the very reverse of my Mr. M'Leod in his deportment and conversation. Talkative, self-sufficient, peremptory, he seemed not to know what it was to doubt; he considered doubt as a proof of ignorance, imbecility, or cowardice. "Can any man doubt?" was his usual beginning. On every subject of human knowledge, taste, morals, politics, economy, legislation; on all affairs, civil, military, or ecclesiastical, he decided at once in the most confident tone. Yet he "never read, not he!" he had nothing to do with books; he consulted only his own eyes and ears, and appealed only to common sense. As to theory, he had no opinion of theory; for his part, he only pretended to understand practice and experience—and his practice was confined steadily to his own practice, and his experience uniformly to what he had tried at New-town-Hardcastle.

At first I thought him a mighty clever man, and I really rejoiced to see my doubter silenced. After dinner, when he had finished speaking in this decisive manner, I used frequently to back him with a—Very true—very fair—very clear—though I understood what he said as little as he did himself; but it was an ease to my mind to have a disputed point settled—and I filled my glass with an air of triumph, whilst M'Leod never contradicted my assertions, nor controverted Mr. Hardcastle's arguments. There was still an air of content and quiet self-satisfaction in M'Leod's very silence, which surprised and vexed me.

One day, when Hardcastle was laying down the law upon several subjects in his usual dictatorial manner, telling us how he managed his people, and what order he kept them in, I was determined that M'Leod should not enjoy the security of his silence, and I urged him to give us his general opinion, as to the means of improving the poor people in Ireland.

"I doubt," said M'Leod, "whether any thing effectual can be done till they have a better education."

"Education!—Pshaw!—There it is now—these book-men," cried Hardcastle: "Why, my dear sir, can any man alive, who knows this country, doubt that the common people have already too much education, as it is called—a vast deal too much? Too many of them know how to read, and write, and cipher, which I presume is all you mean by education."

"Not entirely," said M'Leod; "a good education comprehends something more."

"The more the worse," interrupted Hardcastle. "The more they know, the worse they are, sir, depend on that; I know the people of this country, sir; I have a good right to know them, sir, being born amongst them, and bred amongst them; so I think I may speak with some confidence on these matters. And I give it as my decided humble opinion, founded on irrefragable experience, which is what I always build upon, that the way to ruin the poor of Ireland would be to educate them, sir. Look at the poor scholars, as they call themselves; and what are they? a parcel of young vagabonds in rags, with a book under their arm instead of a spade or a shovel, sir. And what comes of this? that they grow up the worst-disposed, and the most troublesome seditiousrascals in the community. I allow none of them about New-town-Hardcastle—none—banished them all. Useless vagrants—hornets, vipers, sir: and show me a quieter, better-managed set of people than I have made of mine. I go upon experience, sir; and that's the only thing to go upon; and I'll go no farther than New-town-Hardcastle: if that won't bring conviction home to you, nothing will."

"I never was at New-town-Hardcastle," said M'Leod, drily.

"Well, sir, I hope it will not be the case long. But in the mean time, my good sir, do give me leave to put it to your own common sense, what can reading or writing do for a poor man, unless he is to be a bailiff or an exciseman? and you know all men can't expect to be bailiffs or excisemen. Can all the book-learning in the world, sir, dig a poor man's potatoes for him, or plough his land, or cut his turf? Then, sir, in this country, where's the advantage of education, I humbly ask? No, sir, no, trust me—keep the Irish common people ignorant, and you keep 'em quiet; and that's the only way with them; for they are too quiet and smart, as it is, naturally. Teach them to read and write, and it's just adding fuel to fire—fire to gunpowder, sir. Teach them any thing, and directly you set them up: now it's our business to keep them down, unless, sir, you'd wish to have your throat cut. Education, sir! Lord bless your soul, sir! they have a great deal too much; they know too much already, which makes them so refractory to the laws, and so idle. I will go no farther than New-town-Hardcastle, to prove all this. So, my good sir," concluded he, triumphantly, "education, I grant you, is necessary for the rich; but tell me, if you can, what's the use of education to the poor?"

"Much the same, I apprehend, as to the rich," answered M'Leod. "The use of education, as I understand it, is to teach men to see clearly, and to follow steadily, their real interests. All morality, you know, is comprised in this definition; and—"

"Very true, sir; but all this can never apply to the poor in Ireland."

"Why, sir; are they not men?"

"Men, to be sure; but not like men in Scotland. The Irish know nothing of their interests; and as to morality, that's out of the question: they know nothing about it, my dear sir."

"That is the very thing of which I complain," said M'Leod. "They know nothing, because they have been taught nothing."

"They cannot be taught, sir."

"Did you ever try?"

"I did, sir, no later than last week. A fellow that I caught stealing my turf, instead of sending him to jail, I said to him, with a great deal of lenity, My honest fellow, did you never hear of the eighth commandment, 'Thou shalt not steal?' He confessed he had; but did not know it was the eighth. I showed it to him, and counted it to him myself; and set him, for a punishment, to get his whole catechism. Well, sir, the next week I found him stealing my turf again! and when I caught him by the wrist in the fact, he said, it was because the priest would not let him learn the catechism I gave him, because it was a Protestant one. Now you see, sir, there's a bar for ever to all education."

Mr. M'Leod smiled, said something about time and patience, and observed, "that one experiment was not conclusive against a whole nation." Any thing like a general argument Mr. Hardcastle could not comprehend. He knew every blade of grass within the reach of his tether, but could not reach an inch beyond. Any thing like an appeal to benevolent feelings was lost upon him; for he was so frank in his selfishness, that he did not even pretend to be generous. By sundry self-complacent motions he showed whilst his adversary spoke, that he disdained to listen almost as much as to read: but, as soon as M'Leod paused, he said, "What you observe, sir, may possibly be very true; but I have made up my mind." Then he went over and over again his assertions, in a louder and a louder voice, ending with a tone of interrogation that seemed to set all answer at defiance, "What have you to answer to me now, sir?— Can any man alive doubt this, sir?"

M'Leod was perfectly silent. The company broke up; and, as we were going out of the room, I maliciously asked M'Leod, why he, who could say so much in his own defence, had suffered himself to be so completely silenced? He answered me, in his low, deliberate voice, in the words of Moiré— "'Qu'est-ce que la raison avec un filet de voix contre une gueule comme celle-là?' At some other time," added Mr. M'Leod, "my sentiments shall be at your lordship's disposal."

Indolent persons love positive people, when they are of their own opinion; because they are saved the trouble of developing their thoughts, or supporting their assertions: but the moment the positive differs in sentiment from the indolent man, there is an end of the friendship. The indolent man then hates his pertinacious adversary as much as he loved his sturdy friend. So it happened between Mr. Hardcastle and me. This gentleman was a prodigious favourite with me, so long as his opinions were not in opposition to my own; but an accident happened, which brought his love of power and mine into direct competition, and then I found his peremptory mode of reasoning and his ignorance absurd and insufferable.

Before I can do justice to my part of this quarrel, I must explain the cause of the interest which I took in behalf of the persons aggrieved. During the time that my first hot fit of benevolence was on me, I was riding home one evening after dining with Mr. Hardcastle, and I was struck with the sight of a cabin, more wretched than any I had ever before beheld: the feeble light of a single rush-candle through the window revealed its internal misery.

"Does any body live in that hovel?" said I

"Ay, sure, does there: the Noonans, plase your honour," replied a man on the road. Noonans! I recollected the name to be that of the pugilist, who had died in consequence of the combat at which I had been present in London; who had, with his dying breath, besought me to convey his only half-guinea and his silk handkerchief to his poor father and sister. I alighted from my horse, asking the man, at the same time, if the son of this Noonan had not died in England.

"He had, sir, a son in England, Mick Noonan, who used to send him odd guineas, I mind, and was a good lad to his father, though wild; and there's been no account of him at-all-at-all this long while: but the old man has another boy, a sober lad, who's abroad with the army in the East Indies; and it's he that is the hope of the family. And there's the father—and old as he is, and poor, and a cripple, I'd engage there is not a happier man in the three counties at this very time speaking: for it is just now I seen young Jemmy Riley, the daughter's bachelor, go by with a letter. What news? says I. 'Great news!' says he: 'a letter from Tom Noonan to his father; and I'm going in to read it for him.'"

By the time my voluble informant had come to this period, I had reached the cabin door. Who could have expected to see smiles and hear exclamations of joy under such a roof?

I saw the father, with his hands clasped in ecstasy, and looking up to heaven, with the strong expression of delight in his aged countenance. I saw every line of his face; for the light of the candle was full upon it. The daughter, a beautiful girl, kneeling beside him, held the light for the young man, who was reading her brother's letter. I was sorry to interrupt them.

"Your honour's kindly welcome," said the old man, making an attempt to rise.

"Pray, don't let me disturb you."

"It was only a letter from a boy of mine that's over the seas, we was reading," said the old man. "A better boy to an ould father, that's good for nothing now in this world, never was, plase your honour. See what he has sent me: a draft here for ten guineas out of the little pay he has. God for ever bless him!—as he surely will."

After a few minutes' conversation, the old man's heart was so much opened towards me, that he talked as freely as if he had known me for years. I led to the subject of his other son Michael, who was mentioned in the letter as a wild chap. "Ah! your honour, that's what lies heaviest on my heart, and will, to my dying day, that Mick, before he died, which they say he did surely a twelvemonth ago, over there in England, never so much as sent me one line, good or bad, or his sister a token to remember him by even!"

"Had he but sent us the least bit of a word, or the least token in life, I had been content," said the sister, wiping her eyes: "we don't so much as know how he died."

I took this moment to relate the circumstances of Michael Noonan's death; and when I told them of his dying request about the half-guinea and the silk handkerchief, they were all so much touched, that they utterly forgot the ten-guinea draft, which I saw on the ground, in the dirt, under the old man's feet, whilst he contemplated the half-guinea which his poor Michael had sent him: repeating, "Poor fellow! poor fellow! 'twas all he had in the world. God bless him!—Poor Michael! he was a wild chap! but none better to his parents than he while the life was in him. Poor Michael!"

In no country have I found such strong instances of filial affection as in Ireland. Let the sons go where they may, let what will befall them, they never forget their parents at home: they write to them constantly the most affectionate letters, and send them a share of whatever they earn.

When I asked the daughter of this Noonan, why she had not married? the old man answered, "That's her own fault—if it be a fault to abide by an old father. She wastes her youth here, in the way your honour sees, tending him who has none other to mind him."

"Oh! let alone that," said the girl, with a cheerful smile; "we be too poor to think of marrying yet, by a great deal! so, father dear, you're no hinderance any way. For don't I know, and doesn't Jemmy there know, that it's a sin and a shame, as my mother used to say, for them that have nothing, to marry and set up house-keeping, like the rogue that ruined my father?"

"That's true," said the young man, with a heavy sigh; "but times will mend, or we'll strive and mend them, with the blessing of God."

I left this miserable but in admiration of the generosity of its inhabitants. I desired the girl to come to Glenthorn Castle the next day, that I might give her the silk handkerchief which her poor brother had sent her. The more I inquired into the circumstances of this family, the more cause I found for pity and approbation. The old man had been a good farmer in his day, as the traditions of the aged, and the memories of the young, were ready to witness; but he was unfortunately joined in co-partnership with a drunken rogue, who ran away, and left an arrear of rent, which ruined Noonan. Mr. Hardcastle, the agent, called upon him to pay it, and sold all that the old man possessed; and this being insufficient to discharge the debt, he was forced to give up his farm, and retire, with his daughter, to this hovel; and soon afterwards he lost the use of his side by a paralytic stroke.

I was so much pleased with the goodness of these poor people, that, in despite of my indolent disposition, I bestirred myself the very next day to find a better habitation for them on my own estate. I settled them, infinitely to their satisfaction, in a small farm; and the girl married her lover, who undertook to manage the farm for the old man. To my utter surprise, I found that Mr. Hardcastle was affronted by the part I took in this affair. He complained that I had behaved in a very ungentlemanlike manner, and had spirited the tenants away from Lady Ormsby's estate, against the regulation which he had laid down for all the tenants not to emigrate from the estate. Jemmy Riley, it seems, was one of the cotters on the Ormsby estate, a circumstance with which I was unacquainted; indeed I scarcely at that time understood what was meant by a cotter. Mr. Hardcastle's complaint, in matter and manner, was unintelligible to me; but I was quite content to leave off visiting him, as he left off visiting me—but here the matter did not stop. This over-wise and over-busy gentleman took upon him, amongst other offices, the regulation of the markets in the town of Ormsby; and as he apprehended, for reasons best and only known to himself, a year of scarcity, he thought fit to keep down the price of oats and potatoes. He would allow none to be sold in the market of Ormsby but at the price which he stipulated. The poor people grumbled, and, to remedy the injustice, made private bargains with each other. He had information of this, and seized the corn that was selling above the price he had fixed. Young Riley, Noonan's son-in-law, came to me to complain, that his little oats were seized and detained. I remonstrated. Hardcastle resented the appeal to me, and bid him wait and be damned. The young man, who was rather of a hasty temper, and who did not much like either to wait or be damned, seized his own oats, and was marching off, when they were recaptured by Hardcastle's bailiff, whom young Riley knocked down; and who, as soon as he got up again, went straight and swore examinations against Riley. Then I was offended, as I had a right to be, by the custom of the country, with the magistrate who took an examination against my tenant, without writing first to me. Then there was a race between the examinations of my justice of peace and his justice of peace. My indolence was conquered by my love of power: I supported the contest; the affair came before our grand jury: I conquered, and Mr. Hardcastle was ever after, of course, my enemy. To English ears the possessive pronouns my and his may sound extraordinary, prefixed to a justice of peace; but, in many parts of Ireland, this language is perfectly correct. A great man talks of making a justice of the peace with perfect confidence; a very great man talks with as much certainty of making a sheriff; and a sheriff makes the jury; and the jury makes the law. We must not forget, however, that in England, during the reign of Elizabeth, a member of parliament defined a justice of peace to be "an animal, who for half a dozen chickens will dispense with half a dozen penal statutes." Time is necessary to enforce the sanctions of legislation and civilization— But I am anticipating reflections which I made at a much later period of my life. To return to my history.

My benevolence was soon checked by slight disappointments. Ellinor's cottage, which I had taken so much pains to build, became a source of mortification to me. One day I found my old nurse sitting at her wheel, in the midst of the wreck and litter of all sorts of household furniture, singing her favourite song of

"There was a lady loved a swine:
Honey! says she,
I'll give ye a silver trough.
Hunk! says he!"

Ellinor seemed, alas! to have as little taste for the luxuries with which I had provided her as the pig had for the silver trough. What I called conveniences were to her incumbrances: she had not been used to them; she was put out of her way; and it was a daily torment to one of her habits, to keep her house clean and neat.

There may be, as some philosophers assure us that there is, an innate love of order in the human mind; but of this instinctive principle my poor Ellinor was totally destitute. Her ornamented farm-house became, in a wonderfully short time, a scene of dirt, rubbish, and confusion. There was a partition between two rooms, which had been built with turf or peat, instead of bricks, by the wise economy I had employed. Of course, this was pulled down to get at the turf. The stairs also were pulled down and burned, though there was no scarcity of firing. As the walls were plastered and papered before they were quite dry, the paper grew mouldy, and the plaster fell off. In the hurry of finishing, some of the woodwork had but one coat of paint. In Ireland they have not faith in the excellent Dutch proverb, "Paint costs nothing." I could not get my workmen to give a second coat of paint to any of the sashes, and the wood decayed: divers panes of glass in the windows were broken, and their places filled up with shoes, an old hat, or a bundle of rags. Some of the slates were blown off one windy night: the slater lived at ten miles distance, and before the slates were replaced, the rain came in, and Ellinor was forced to make a bedchamber of the parlour, and then of the kitchen, retreating from corner to corner as the rain pursued, till, at last, when "it would come every way upon her bed," she petitioned me to let her take the slates off and thatch the house; for a slated-house, she said, was never so warm as a tatched cabin; and as there was no smoke, she was kilt with the cowld.

In my life I never felt so angry. I was ten times more angry than when Crawley ran away with my wife. In a paroxysm of passion, I reproached Ellinor with being a savage, an Irish-woman, and an ungrateful fool.

"Savage I am, for any thing I know; and fool I am, that's certain; but ungrateful I am not," said she, bursting into tears. She went home and took to her bed; and the next thing I heard from her son was, "that she was lying in the rheumatism, which had kept her awake many a long night, before she would come to complain to my honour of the house, in dread that I should blame myself for sending of her into it afore it was dry."

The rheumatism reconciled me immediately to Ellinor; I let her take her own way, and thatch the house, and have as much smoke as she pleased, and she recovered. But I did not entirely recover my desire to do good to my poor tenants. After forming, in the first enthusiasm of my benevolence, princely schemes for their advantage, my ardour was damped, and my zeal discouraged, by a few slight disappointments.

I did not consider, that there is often, amongst uncultivated people, a mixture of obstinate and lazy content, which makes them despise the luxuries of their richer neighbours; like those mountaineers, who, proud of their own hard fare, out of a singular species of contempt, call the inhabitants of the plains mange-rotis, "eaters of roast meat." I did not consider that it must take time to change local and national habits and prejudices; and that it is necessary to raise a taste for comforts, before they can be properly enjoyed.

In the pettishness of my disappointment, I decided that it was in vain to attempt to improve and civilize such people as the Irish. I did not recollect, perhaps at that time I did not know, that even in the days of the great Queen Elizabeth, "the greatest part of the buildings in the cities and good towns of England consisted only of timber, cast over with thick clay to keep out the wind. The new houses of the nobility were indeed either of brick or stone; and glass windows were then beginning to be used in England:" and clean rushes were strewed over the dirty floors of the royal palace. In the impatience of my zeal for improvement, I expected to do the work of two hundred years in a few months: and because I could not accelerate the progress of refinement in this miraculous manner, I was out of humour with myself and with a whole nation. So easily is the humanity of the rich and great disgusted and discouraged! as if any people could be civilized in a moment, and at the word of command of ignorant pride or despotic benevolence!

CHAPTER IX

*"He saw—and but that admiration*
*Had been too active, too like passion,*
*Or had he been to ton less true,*
*Cupid had shot him through and through."*

I have not thought it necessary to record every visit that I received from all my country neighbours; but I must now mention one, which led to important consequences; a visit from Sir Harry Ormsby, a very young dashing man of fortune, who, in expectation of the happy moment when he should be of age, resided with his mother, the dowager Lady Ormsby. Her ladyship had heard that there had been some disagreement between her agent, Mr. Hardcastle, and my people; but she took the earliest opportunity of expressing her wishes, that our families should be on an amicable footing.

Lady Ormsby was just come to the country, with a large party of her fashionable friends—some Irish, some English: Lord and Lady Kilrush; my Lady Kildangan, and her daughter the Lady Geraldine —; the knowing widow O'Connor; the English dasher, Lady Hauton; the interesting Mrs. Norton, separated but not parted from her husband; the pleasant Miss Bland; the three Miss Ormsbys, better known by the name of the Swanlinbar Graces; two English aides-de-camp from the Castle, and a brace of brigadiers; besides other men of inferior note.

I perceived that Sir Harry Ormsby took it for granted that I must be acquainted with the pretensions of all these persons to celebrity; his talkativeness and my taciturnity favoured me so fortunately, that he never discovered the extent of my ignorance. He was obligingly impatient to make me personally acquainted "with those of whom I must have heard so much in England." Observing that Ormsby Villa was too far from Glenthorn Castle for a morning visit, he pressed me to waive ceremony, and to do Lady Ormsby and him the honour of spending a week with them, as soon as I could make it convenient. I accepted this invitation, partly from a slight emotion of curiosity, and partly from my habitual inability to resist any reiterated importunity.

Arrived at Ormsby Villa, and introduced to this crowd of people, I was at first disappointed by seeing nothing extraordinary. I expected that their manners would have been as strange to me as some of their names appeared: but whether it was from my want of the powers of discrimination, or from the real sameness of the objects, I could scarcely, in this fashionable flock, discern any individual marks of distinction. At first view, the married ladies appeared much the same as those of a similar class in England, whom I had been accustomed to see. The young ladies I thought, as usual, "best distinguished by black, brown, and fair:" but I had not yet seen Lady Geraldine —; and a great part Of the conversation, the first day I was at Ormsby Villa, was filled with lamentations on the unfortunate tooth-ache, which prevented her ladyship from appearing. She was talked of so much, and as a person of such importance, and so essential to the amusement of society, that I could not help feeling a slight wish to see her. The next day at breakfast she did not appear; but, five minutes before dinner, her ladyship's humble companion whispered, "Now Lady Geraldine is coming, my lord." I was always rather displeased to be called upon to attend to any thing or any body, yet as Lady Geraldine entered, I gave one involuntary glance of curiosity. I saw a tall, finely-shaped woman, with the commanding air of a woman of rank; she moved well; not with feminine timidity, but with ease, promptitude, and decision. She had fine eyes and a fine complexion, yet no regularity of feature. The only thing that struck me as really extraordinary was her indifference when I was introduced to her. Every body had seemed extremely desirous that I should see her ladyship, and that her ladyship should see me; and I was rather surprised by her unconcerned air. This piqued me, and fixed my attention. She turned from me, and began to converse with others. Her voice was agreeable: she did not speak with the Irish accent; but, when I listened maliciously, I detected certain Hibernian inflections; nothing of the vulgar Irish idiom, but something that was more interrogative, more exclamatory, and perhaps more rhetorical, than the common language of English ladies, accompanied with much animation of countenance and demonstrative gesture. This appeared to me peculiar and unusual, but not affected. She was uncommonly eloquent, and yet, without action, her words were not sufficiently rapid to express her ideas. Her manner appeared foreign, yet it was not quite French. If I had been obliged to decide, I should, however, have pronounced it rather more French than English. To determine what it was, or whether I had ever seen any thing similar, I stood considering her ladyship with more attention than I had ever bestowed on any other woman. The words striking—fascinating—bewitching, occurred to me as I looked at her and heard her speak. I resolved to turn my eyes away, and shut my ears; for I was positively determined not to like her, I dreaded so much the idea of a second Hymen. I retreated to the farthest window, and looked out very soberly upon a dirty fish-pond. Dinner was announced. I observed Lady Kildangan manoeuvring to place me beside her daughter Geraldine, but Lady Geraldine counteracted this movement. I was again surprised and piqued. After yielding the envied position to one of the Swanlinbar Graces, I heard Lady Geraldine whisper to her next neighbour, "Baffled, mamma!"

It was strange to me to feel piqued by a young lady's not choosing to sit beside me. After dinner, I left the gentlemen as soon as possible, because the conversation wearied me. Lord Kilrush, the chief orator, was a courtier, and could talk of nothing but Dublin Castle, and my lord lieutenant's levees. The moment that I went to the ladies, I was seized upon by the officious Miss Bland: she could not speak of any thing but Lady Geraldine, who sat at so great a distance, and who was conversing with such animation herself, that she could not hear her prôneuse, Miss Bland, inform me, that "her friend, Lady Geraldine, was extremely clever; so clever, that many people were at first a little afraid of her; but that there was not the least occasion; for that, where she liked, nobody could be more affable and engaging." This judicious friend, a minute afterwards, told me, as a very great secret, that Lady Geraldine was an admirable mimic; that she could draw or speak caricatures; that she was also wonderfully happy in the invention of agnomens and cognomens, so applicable to the persons, that they could scarcely be forgotten or forgiven. I was a little anxious to know whether her ladyship would honour me with an agnomen. I could not learn this from Miss Bland, and I was too prudent to betray my curiosity: I afterwards heard it, however. Pairing me and Mr. M'Leod, whom she had seen together, her ladyship observed, that Sawney and Yawney were made for each other; and she sketched, in strong caricature, my relaxed elongation of limb, and his rigid rectangularity. A slight degree of fear of Lady Geraldine's powers kept my attention alert. In the course of the evening, Lady Kildangan summoned her daughter to the music-room, and asked me to come and hear an Irish song. I exerted myself so far as to follow immediately; but though summoned, Lady Geraldine did not obey. Miss Bland tuned the harp, and opened the music-books on the piano; but no Lady Geraldine appeared. Miss Bland was sent backwards and forwards with messages; but Lady Geraldine's ultimatum was, that she could not possibly sing, because she was afraid of the tooth-ache. God knows, her mouth had never been shut all the evening. "Well, but," said Lady Kildangan, "she can play for us, cannot she?" No; her ladyship was afraid of the cold in the music-room. "Do, my Lord Glenthorn, go and tell the dear capricious creature, that we are very warm here."

Very reluctantly I obeyed. The Lady Geraldine, with her circle round her, heard and answered me with the air of a princess.

"Do you the honour to play for you, my lord! Excuse me: I am no professor—I play so ill, that I make it a rule never to play but for my own amusement. If you wish for music, there is Miss Bland; she plays incomparably, and I dare say will think herself happy to oblige your lordship." I never felt so silly, or so much abashed, as at this instant. "This comes," thought I, "of acting out of character. What possessed me to exert myself to ask a lady to play? I, that have been tired to death of music! Why did I let myself be sent ambassador, when I had no interest in the embassy?"

To convince myself and others of my apathy, I threw myself on a sofa, and never stirred or spoke the remainder of the night. I presume I appeared fast asleep, else Lady Geraldine would not have said, within my hearing, "Mamma wants me to catch somebody, and to be caught by somebody; but that will not be; for, do you know, I think somebody is nobody."

I was offended as much as it was in my nature to be offended, and I began to meditate apologies for shortening my visit at Ormsby Villa: but, though I was shocked by the haughtiness of Lady Geraldine, and accused her, in my own mind, of want of delicacy and politeness, yet I could not now suspect her of being an accomplice with her mother in any matrimonial designs upon me. From the moment I was convinced of this, my conviction was, I suppose, visible to her ladyship's penetrating eyes, and from that instant she showed me that she could be polite and agreeable. Now, soothed to a state of ease and complacency, I might have sunk to indifference and ennui, but fresh singularities in this lady struck me, and kept my attention awake and fixed upon her character. If she had treated me with tolerable civility at first, I never should have thought about her. High-born and high-bred, she seemed to consider more what she thought of others than what others thought of her. Frank, candid, and affable, yet opinionated, insolent, and an egotist, her candour and affability appeared the effect of a naturally good temper, her insolence and egotism only those of a spoiled child. She seemed to talk of herself purely to oblige others, as the most interesting possible topic of conversation; for such it had always been to her fond mother, who idolized her ladyship as an only daughter, and the representative of an ancient house. Confident of her talents, conscious of her charms, and secure of her station, Lady Geraldine gave free scope to her high spirits, her fancy, and her turn for ridicule. She looked, spoke, and acted, like a person privileged to think, say, and do, what she pleased. Her raillery, like the raillery of princes, was without fear of retort. She was not ill-natured, yet careless to whom she gave offence, provided she produced amusement; and in this she seldom failed; for, in her conversation, there was much of the raciness of Irish wit, and the oddity of Irish humour. The singularity that struck me most about her ladyship was her indifference to flattery. She certainly preferred frolic. Miss Bland was her humble companion; Miss Tracey her butt. Her ladyship appeared to consider Miss Bland as a necessary appendage to her rank and person, like her dress or her shadow; and she seemed to think no more of the one than of the other. She suffered Miss Bland to follow her; but she would go in quest of n Miss Tracey. Miss Bland was allowed to speak; but her ladyship listened to Miss Tracey. Miss Bland seldom obtained an answer; but Miss Tracey never opened her lips without a repartee.

In describing Miss Tracey, Lady Geraldine said, "Poor simpleton! she cannot help imitating all she sees us do; yet, would you believe it, she really has starts of common sense, and some tolerable ideas of her own. Spoiled by bad company! In the language of the bird-fanciers, she has a few notes nightingale, and all the rest rubbish."

It was one of Lady Geraldine's delights to humour Miss Tracey's rage for imitating the fashions of fine people.

"Now you shall see Miss Tracey appear at the ball to-morrow, in every thing that I have sworn to her is fashionable. Nor have I cheated her in a single article: but the tout ensemble I leave to her better judgment; and you shall see her, I trust, a perfect monster, formed of every creature's best: Lady Kilrush's feathers, Mrs. Moore's wig, Mrs. O'Connor's gown, Mrs. Lighton's sleeves, and all the necklaces of all the Miss Ormsbys. She has no taste, no judgment; none at all, poor thing! but she can imitate as well as those Chinese painters, who, in their drawings, give you the flower of one plant stuck on the stalk of another, and garnished with the leaves of a third."

Miss Tracey's appearance the ensuing night justified all Lady Geraldine's predictions, and surpassed her ladyship's most sanguine hopes. Even I, albeit unused to the laughing mood, could not forbear smiling at the humour and ease with which her ladyship played off this girl's credulous vanity.

At breakfast the next morning, Lord Kilrush, in his grave manner (always too solemn by half for the occasion), declared, "that no man was more willing than himself to enter into a jest in proper time, and season, and measure, and so forth; but that it was really, positively, morally unjustifiable, in his apprehension, the making this poor girl so publicly ridiculous."

"My good lord," replied Lady Geraldine, "all the world are ridiculous some way or other: some in public, some in private. Now," continued she, with an appealing look to the whole company, "now, after all, what is there more extravagant in my Miss Tracey's delighting, at sixteen, in six yards of pink riband, than in your courtier sighing, at sixty, for three yards of blue riband? or what is there more ridiculous in her coming simpering into a ball-room, fancying herself the mirror of fashion, when she is a figure for a print-shop, than in the courtier rising solemnly in the House of Lords, believing himself an orator, and expecting to make a vast reputation, by picking up, in every debate, the very worst arguments that every body else let fall? There would be no living in this world, if we were all to see and expose one another's ridicules. My plan is much the best—to help my friends to expose themselves, and then they are infinitely obliged to me."

Satisfied with silencing all opposition, and seeing that the majority was with her, Lady Geraldine persisted in her course; and I was glad she was incorrigible, because her faults entertained me. As to love, I thought I was perfectly safe; because, though I admired her quickness and cleverness, yet I still, at times, perceived, or fancied I perceived, some want of polish, and elegance, and tact. She was not exactly cut out according to my English pattern of a woman of fashion; so I thought I might amuse myself without danger, as it was partly at her ladyship's expense. But about this time I was alarmed for myself by a slight twinge of jealousy. As I was standing lounging upon the steps at the hall-door, almost as ennuyé as usual, I saw a carriage at a distance, between the trees, driving up the approach; and, at the same instant, I heard Lady Geraldine's eager voice in the hall, "Oh! they are coming; he is coming; they are come. Run, Miss Bland, run, and give Lord Craiglethorpe my message before he gets out of the carriage—before any body sees him."

Afraid of hearing what I should not hear, I walked down the steps deliberately, and turned into a shrubbery-walk, to leave the coast clear. Out ran Miss Bland: and then it was that I felt the twinge—very slight, however. "Who is this Lord Craiglethorpe, with whom Lady Geraldine is on such favourable terms? I wonder what kind of looking man he is; and what could the message mean?—but, at all events, it cannot concern me; yet I am curious to see this Lord Craiglethorpe. I wonder any woman can like a man with so strange a name: but does she like him, after all?—Why do I plague myself about it?"

As I returned from my saunter, I was met by Miss Bland.

"A charming day, ma'am," said I, endeavouring to pass on.

"A charming day, my lord! But I must stop your lordship a moment. Oh, I am so out of breath—I went the wrong way—"

"The wrong way! Indeed! I am sorry. I am concerned you should have had so much trouble."

"No trouble in the world. Only I want to beg you'll keep our secret—my Lady Geraldine's secret."

"Undoubtedly, madam—a man of honour—Lady Geraldine cannot doubt—her ladyship's secret is perfectly safe."

"But do you know it? You don't know it yet, my lord."

"Pardon me; I was on the steps just now. I thought you saw me."

"I did, my lord—but I don't understand—"

"Nor I, neither," interrupted I, half laughing; for I began to think I was mistaken in my suspicions; "pray explain yourself, my dear Miss Bland: I was very rude to be so quick in interrupting you."

Miss Bland then made me the confidant of a charming scheme of Lady Geraldine's for quizzing Miss Tracey.

"She has never in her life seen Lord Craiglethorpe, who is an English lord travelling through Ireland," continued Miss Bland. "Now, you must know, that Miss Tracey is passionately fond of lords, let them be what they may. Now, Lord Craiglethorpe, this very morning, sent his groom with a note and excuse to Lady Ormsby, for not coming to us to-day; because, he said, he was bringing down in the chaise with him a surveyor, to survey his estate near here; and he could not possibly think of bringing the surveyor, who is a low man, to Ormsby Villa. But Lady Ormsby would take no apology, and wrote by the groom to beg that Lord Craiglethorpe would make no scruple of bringing the surveyor; for you know she is so polite and accommodating, and all that. Well, the note was scarcely gone, before Lady Geraldine thought of her charming scheme, and regretted, of all things, she had not put it into it."

"It into it!" repeated I to myself. "Ma'am," said I, looking a little bewildered.

"But," continued my clear narrator, "I promised to remedy all that, by running to meet the carriage, which was what I ran for when you saw me, my lord, in such a hurry."

I bowed—and was as wise as ever.

"So, my lord, you comprehend, that the surveyor, whose name, whose odious name, is Gabbitt, is to be my Lord Craiglethorpe, and my Lord Craiglethorpe is to be passed for Mr. Gabbitt upon Miss Tracey; and, you will see, Miss Tracey will admire Mr. Gabbitt prodigiously, and call him vastly genteel, when she thinks him a lord. Your lordship will keep our secret; and she is sure Lord Craiglethorpe will do any thing to oblige her, because he is a near connexion of hers. But, I assure you, it is not every body could get Lord Craiglethorpe to join in a joke; for he is very stiff, and cold, and high. Of course your lordship will know which is the real lord at first sight. He is a full head taller than Gabbitt."

Never was explanation finally more satisfactory: and whether the jest was really well contrived and executed, or whether I was put into a humour to think so, I cannot exactly determine; but, I confess, I was amused with the scenes that followed, though I felt that they were not quite justifiable even in jest.

The admiration of Miss Tracey for the false Craiglethorpe, as Lady Geraldine called Mr. Gabbitt; the awkwardness of Mr. Gabbitt with his title, and the awkwardness of Lord Craiglethorpe without it, were fine subjects of her ladyship's satirical humour.

In another point of view, Lord Craiglethorpe afforded her ladyship amusement; as an English traveller, full of English prejudices against Ireland and every thing Irish. Whenever Miss Tracey was out of the room, Lady Geraldine allowed Lord Craiglethorpe to be himself again; but he did not fare the better for this restoration to his honours. Lady Geraldine contrived to make him as ridiculous in his real as in his assumed character. Lord Craiglethorpe was, as Miss Bland had described him, very stiff, cold, and high. His manners were in the extreme of English reserve, and his ill-bred show of contempt for the Irish was sufficient provocation and justification of Lady Geraldine's ridicule. He was much in awe of his fair and witty cousin: she could easily put him out of countenance, for he was extremely bashful.

His lordship had that sort of bashfulness which makes a man surly and obstinate in his taciturnity; which makes him turn upon all who approach him, as if they were going to assault him; which makes him answer a question as if it were an injury, and repel a compliment as if it were an insult. Once, when he was out of the room, Lady Geraldine exclaimed, "That cousin Craiglethorpe of mine is scarcely an agreeable man: the awkwardness of mauvaise honte might be pitied and pardoned, even in a nobleman," continued her ladyship, "if it really proceeded from humility; but here, when I know it is connected with secret and inordinate arrogance, 'tis past all endurance. Even his ways of sitting and standing provoke me, they are so self-sufficient. Have you observed how he stands at the fire? Oh, the caricature of 'the English fire-side' outdone! Then, if he sits, we hope that change of posture may afford our eyes transient relief: but worse again; bolstered up, with his back against his chair, his hands in his pockets, and his legs thrown out, in defiance of all passengers and all decorum, there he sits, in magisterial silence, throwing a gloom upon all conversation. As the Frenchman said of the Englishman, for whom even his politeness could not find another compliment, 'Il faut avouer que ce monsieur a un grand talent pour le silence;' he holds his tongue, till the people actually believe that he has something to say; a mistake they could never fall into if he would but speak."

Some of the company attempted to interpose a word or two in favour of Lord Craiglethorpe's timidity, but the vivacious and merciless lady went on.

"I tell you, my good friends, it is not timidity—it is all pride. I would pardon his dulness, and even his ignorance; for one, as you say, might be the fault of his nature, and the other of his education: but his self-sufficiency is his own fault, and that I will not, and cannot pardon. Somebody says, that nature may make a fool, but a coxcomb is always of his own making. Now, my cousin—(as he is my cousin, I may say what I please of him)—my cousin Craiglethorpe is a solemn coxcomb, who thinks, because his vanity is not talkative and sociable, that it's not vanity. What a mistake! his silent superciliousness is to me more intolerable than the most garrulous egotism that ever laid itself open to my ridicule."

Miss Bland and Miss Ormsby both confessed that Lord Craiglethorpe was vastly too silent.

"For the honour of my country," continued Lady Geraldine, "I am determined to make this man talk, and he shall say all that I know he thinks of us poor Irish savages. If he would but speak, one could answer him: if he would find fault, one might defend: if he would laugh, one might perhaps laugh again: but here he comes to hospitable, open-hearted Ireland; eats as well as he can in his own country; drinks better than he can in his own country; sleeps as well as he can in his own country; accepts all our kindness without a word or a look of thanks, and seems the whole time to think, that, 'Born for his use, we live but to oblige him.' There he is at this instant: look at him, walking in the park, with his note-book in his hand, setting down our faults, and conning them by rote. We are even with him. I understand, Lady Kilrush, that my bright cousin Craiglethorpe means to write a book, a great book, upon Ireland."

Lady Kilrush replied, that she understood Lord Craiglethorpe had it in contemplation to publish a Tour through Ireland, or a View of Ireland, or something of that nature.

"He! with his means of acquiring information!" exclaimed Lady Geraldine. "Posting from one great man's house to another, what can he see or know of the manners of any rank of people but of the class of gentry, which in England and Ireland is much the same? As to the lower classes, I don't think he ever speaks to them; or, if he does, what good can it do him? for he can't understand their modes of expression, nor they his: if he inquire about a matter of fact, I defy him to get the truth out of them, if they don't wish to tell it; and, for some reason or other, they will, nine times in ten, not wish to tell it to an Englishman. There is not a man, woman, or child, in any cabin in Ireland, who would not have wit and 'cuteness enough to make my lard believe just what they please. So, after posting from Dublin to Cork, and from the Giants' Causeway to Killarney; after travelling east, west, north, and south, my wise cousin Craiglethorpe will know just as much of the lower Irish as the cockney who has never been out of London, and who has never, in all his born days, seen an Irishman but on the English stage; where the representations are usually as like the originals, as the Chinese pictures of lions, drawn from description, are to the real animal."

"Now! now! look at his lordship!" cried Miss Bland; "he has his note-book out again."

"Mercy on us!" said Miss Callwell, "how he is writing!"

"Yes, yes, write on, my good cousin Craiglethorpe," pursued Lady Geraldine, "and nil the little note-book, which will soon turn to a ponderous quarto. I shall have a copy, bound in morocco, no doubt, from the author, if I behave myself prettily; and I will earn it, by supplying valuable information. You shall see, my friends, how I'll deserve well of my country, if you'll only keep my counsel and your own countenances."

Presently Lord Craiglethorpe entered the room, walking very pompously, and putting his note-book up as he advanced.

"Oh, my dear lord, open the book again; I have a bull for you."

Lady Geraldine, after putting his lordship in good humour by this propitiatory offering of a bull, continued to supply him, either directly or indirectly, by some of her confederates, with the most absurd anecdotes, incredible facts, stale jests, and blunders, such as were never made by true-born Irishmen; all which my Lord Craiglethorpe took down with an industrious sobriety, at which the spectators could scarcely refrain from laughing. Sometimes he would pause, and exclaim, "A capital anecdote! a curious fact! May I give my authority? may I quote your ladyship?"

"Yes, if you'll pay me a compliment in the preface," whispered Lady Geraldine: "and now, dear cousin, do go up stairs and put it all in ink."

When she had despatched the noble author, her ladyship indulged her laughter. "But now," cried she, "only imagine a set of sober English readers studying my cousin Craiglethorpe's New View of Ireland, and swallowing all the nonsense it will contain!"

When Lord Kilrush remonstrated against the cruelty of letting the man publish such stuff, and represented it as a fraud upon the public, Lady Geraldine laughed still more, and exclaimed, "Surely you don't think I would use the public and my poor cousin so ill. No, I am doing him and the public the greatest possible service. Just when he is going to leave us, when the writing-box is packed, I will step up to him, and tell him the truth. I will show him what a farrago of nonsense he has collected as materials for his quarto; and convince him at once how utterly unfit he is to write a book, at least a book on Irish affairs. Won't this be deserving well of my country and of my cousin?"

Neither on this occasion, nor on any other, were the remonstrances of my Lord Kilrush of power to stop the course of this lady's flow of spirits and raillery.

Whilst she was going on in this manner with the real Lord Craiglethorpe, Miss Tracey was taking charming walks in the park with Mr. Gabbitt, and the young lady began to be seriously charmed with her false lord. This was carrying the jest farther, than Lady Geraldine had intended or foreseen; and her good-nature would probably have disposed her immediately to dissolve the enchantment, had she not been provoked by the interference of Lord Kilrush, and the affected sensibility of Miss Clementina

Ormsby, who, to give me an exalted opinion of her delicacy, expostulated incessantly in favour of the deluded fair one. "But, my dear Lady Geraldine, I do assure you, it really hurts my feelings. This is going too far—when it comes to the heart. I can't laugh, I own—the poor girl's affections will be engaged—she is really falling in love with this odious surveyor."

"But now, my dear Clementina, I do assure you, it really hurts my feelings to hear you talk so childishly. 'When it comes to the heart!' 'affections engaged!' You talk of falling in love as if it were a terrible fall: for my part, I should pity a person much more for falling down stairs. Why, my dear, where is the mighty height from which Miss Tracey could fall? She does not live in the clouds, Clementina, as you do. No ladies live there now; for the best of all possible reasons, because there are no men there. So, my love, make haste and come down, before you are out of your teens, or you may chance to be left there till you are an angel or an old maid. Trust me, my dear, I, who have tried, tell you, there is no such thing as falling in love, now-a-days: you may slip, slide, or stumble; but to fall in love, I defy you."

I saw Lady Kildangan's eyes fix upon me as her daughter pronounced the last sentence.

"Geraldine, my dear, you do not know what you are talking about," said her ladyship. "Your time may come, Geraldine. Nobody should be too courageous. Cupid does not like to be defied."

Lady Kildangan walked away as she spoke, with a very well-satisfied air, leaving a party of us young people together. Lady Geraldine looked haughtily vexed. When in this mood, her wit gave no quarter; spared neither sex nor age.

"Every body says," whispered she, "that mamma is the most artful woman in the world; and I should believe it, only that every body says it: now, if it were true, nobody would know it."

Lady Geraldine's air of disdain towards me was resumed. I did not quite understand. Was it pride? was it coquetry? She certainly blushed deeply, and for the first time that I ever saw her blush, when her mother said, "Your time may come, Geraldine."

My week being now at an end, I resolved to take my leave. When I announced this resolution, I was assailed with the most pressing entreaties to stay a few days longer—one day longer. Lady Ormsby and Sir Harry said every thing that could be said upon the occasion: indeed, it seemed a matter of general interest to all, except to Lady Geraldine. She appeared wholly indifferent, and I was not even gratified by any apparent affectation of desiring my departure. Curiosity to see whether this would be sustained by her ladyship to the last, gave me resolution sufficient to resist the importunities of Sir Harry; and I departed, rejoicing that my indifference was equal to her ladyship's. As Tasso said of some fair one, whom he met at the carnival of Mantua, I ran some risk of falling in love. I had been so far roused from my habitual apathy that I actually made some reflections. As I returned home, I began to perceive that there was some difference between woman and woman, besides the distinctions of rank, fortune, and figure. I think I owe to Lady Geraldine my first relish for wit, and my first idea that a woman might be, if not a reasonable, at least a companionable animal. I compared her ladyship with the mere puppets and parrots of fashion, of whom I had been wearied; and I began to suspect that one might find, in a lady's "lively nonsense," a relief from ennui. These reflections, however, did not prevent me from sleeping the greatest part of the morning on my way home; nor did I dream of any thing that I can remember.

At the porter's lodge I saw Ellinor sitting at her spinning-wheel; and my thoughts took up my domestic affairs just where I had left them the preceding week.

## CHAPTER X

In vain I attempted to interest myself in my domestic affairs; the silence and solitude of my own castle appeared to me intolerably melancholy, after my return from Ormsby Villa. There was a blank in my existence during a week, in which I can remember nothing that I did, said, or thought, except what passed during one ride, which Mr. McLeod compelled my politeness to take with him. He came with the same face to see me, and the same set of ideas, as those he had before I went to Ormsby Villa. He began to talk of my schemes for improving my tenantry, and of my wish that he should explain his notions relative to the education of the poor of Ireland, which, he said, as I now seemed to be at leisure, he was ready to do as concisely as possible. As concisely as possible were the only words of his address that I heard with satisfaction; but of course I bowed, said I was much obliged, and I should be happy to have the advantage of Mr. M'Leod's opinions and sentiments. What these were I cannot recollect, for I settled myself in a reverie soon after his voice began to sound upon my ear; but I remember at last he wakened me, by proposing that I should ride with him to see a school-house and some cottages, which he had built on a little estate of his own in my neighbourhood: "for," said he, "'tis better, my lord, to show you what can be done with these people, than to talk of what might be effected."

"Very true," said I, agreeing readily; because I wanted to finish a conversation that wearied me, and to have a refreshing ride. It was a delightful evening; and when we came on M'Leod's estate, I really could not help being pleased and interested. In an unfavourable situation, with all nature, vegetable and animal, against him, he had actually created a paradise amid the wilds. There was nothing wonderful in any thing I saw around me; but there was such an air of neatness and comfort, order and activity, in the people and in their cottages, that I almost thought myself in England; and I could not forbear exclaiming,—"How could all this be brought about in Ireland!"

"Chiefly by not doing and not expecting too much at first," said M'Leod. "We took time, and had patience. We began by setting them the example of some very slight improvements, and then, lured on by the sight of success, they could make similar trials themselves. My wife and I went among them, and talked to them in their cottages, and took an interest in their concerns, and did not want to have every thing our own way; and when they saw that, they began to consider which way was best; so by degrees we led where we could not have driven; and raised in them, by little and little, a taste for conveniences and comforts. Then the business was done; for the moment the taste and ambition were excited; to work the people went to gratify them; and according as they exerted themselves, we helped them. Perhaps it was best for them and for us, that we were not rich; for we could not do too much at a time, and were never tempted to begin grand schemes that we could not finish. There," said McLeod, pointing to a cottage with a pretty porch covered with woodbine, and a neat garden, in which many children were busily at work, "that house and that garden were the means of doing all the rest; that is our school-house. We could not expect to do much with the old, whose habits were fixed; but we tried to give the young children better notions, and it was a long time before we could bring that to bear. Twenty-six years we have been at this work; and in that time if we have done any thing, it was by beginning with the children: a race of our own training has now grown up, and they go on in the way they were taught, and prosper to our hearts' content, and, what is better still, to their hearts' content."

McLeod, habitually grave and taciturn, seemed quite enlivened and talkative this day; but I verily believe that not the slightest ostentation or vanity inspired him, for I never before or since heard him talk or allude to his own good deeds: I am convinced his motive was to excite me to persevere in my benevolent projects, by showing what had been done by small means. He was so truly in earnest that he never perceived how tired I was; indeed he was so little in the habit of expecting sympathy or applause, that he never missed even the ordinary expressions of concurrent complaisance.

"Religion," continued he, "is the great difficulty in Ireland. We make no difference between Protestants and Catholics; we always have admitted both into our school. The priest comes on Saturday morning, and the parish minister on Saturday evening, to hear the children belonging to each church their catechisms, and to instruct them in the tenets of their faith. And as we keep to our word, and never attempt making proselytes, nor directly or indirectly interfere with their religious opinions, the priests are glad to let us instruct the catholic children in all other points, which they plainly see must advance their temporal interests."

Mr. McLeod invited me to go in and look at the school. "In a hedge or ditch school," said he, "which I once passed on this road, and in which I saw a crowd of idle children, I heard the schoolmaster cry out, 'Rehearse! rehearse! there's company going by; and instantly all the boys snatched up their books, and began gabbling as fast as ever they could, to give an idea to the passenger of their diligence in repeating their lessons. But here, my lord," continued M'Leod, "you will not see any exhibitions got up for company. I hate such tricks. Walk in, my lord, if you please."

I walked in; but am ashamed to say, that I observed only that every thing looked as if it had been used for many years, and yet not worn out; and the whole school appeared as if all were in their places, and occupied and intent upon their business: but this general recollection is all I have retained. The enthusiasm for improvement had subsided in my mind; and though I felt a transient pleasure in the present picture of the happiness of these poor people and their healthy children, yet, as I rode home, the images faded away like a dream. I resolved, indeed, at some future period, to surpass all that Mr. M'Leod had done, or all that with his narrow income he could ever accomplish; and to this resolution I was prompted by jealousy of this man, rather than by benevolence. Before I had arranged, even in imagination, my plans, young Ormsby came one morning, and pressed me to return with him to Ormsby Villa. I yielded to his solicitations and to my own wishes. When I arrived, the ladies were all at their toilettes, except Miss Bland, who was in the book-room with the gentlemen, ready to receive me with her perpetual smile. Wherever Miss Bland went, she was always l'amie de la maison, accustomed to share with the lady of the house the labour of entertaining her guests. This double of Lady Ormsby talked to me most courteously of all the nothings of the day, and informed me of the changes which had taken place in the ever-varying succession of company at Ormsby Villa. The two brigadiers and one of the aides-de-camp were gone; but Captain Andrews, another castle aide-de-camp, was come, and my Lord O'Toole had arrived. Then followed a by-conversation between Miss Bland and some of the gentlemen, about the joy and sorrow which his lordship's arrival would create in the hearts of two certain ladies; one of whom, as I gathered from the innuendoes, was Lady Hauton, and the other Lady O'Toole. As I knew nothing of Dublin intrigues and scandal, I was little attentive to all this. Miss Bland, persisting in entertaining me, proceeded to inform me, that my Lord O'Toole had brought down with him Mr. Cecil Devereux, who was a wit and a poet, very handsome and gallant, and one of the most fashionable young men in Dublin. I determined not to like him—I always hated a flourish of trumpets; whoever enters, announced in this parading manner, appears to disadvantage. Mr. Cecil Devereux entered just as the flourish ceased. He was not at all the sort of person I was prepared to see: though handsome, and with the air of a man used to good company, there was nothing of a coxcomb in his manner; on the contrary, there was such an appearance of carelessness about himself, and deference towards others, that, notwithstanding the injudicious praise that had been bestowed on him, and my consequent resolution to dislike him, I was pleased and familiar with him before I had been ten minutes in his company. Lord Kilrush introduced him to me, with great pomposity, as a gentleman of talents, for whom he and his brother O'Toole interested themselves much. This air of patronage, I saw, disgusted Mr. Devereux; and instead of suffering himself to be shown off, he turned the conversation from his own poems to general subjects. He asked me some questions about a curious cavern, or subterraneous way, near Glenthorn Castle, which stretched from the sea-shore to a considerable distance under the rock, and communicated with an old abbey near the castle. Mr. Devereux said that such subterraneous places had been formerly used in Ireland as granaries by the ancient inhabitants; but a gentleman of the neighbourhood who was present observed, that the caverns on this coast had, within his memory, been used as hiding-places by smugglers: on this hint Lord Kilrush began a prosing dissertation upon smugglers and contraband traders, and talked to me a prodigious deal about exports and imports, and bounties, and the balance of trade. Not one word he said did I comprehend, and I question whether his lordship understood the subjects upon which he spoke so dictatorially; but he thought he succeeded in giving me an opinion of his wisdom and information. His brother O'Toole appeared next: he did not look like a man of gallantry, as I had been taught to expect from the hints thrown out respecting Lady Hauton; his lordship's whole soul seemed devoted to ambition, and he talked so much of great men, and state affairs, and court intrigues, and honours and preferments, that I began to fancy I had been buried alive, because I knew little of these things. I was tired of hearing him, yet mortified that I could not speak exactly in the same manner, and with the same air of being the best possible authority. I began to wish that I also had some interest at court. The cares and troubles of the ambitious man, so utterly repugnant to the indolence of my disposition, vanished in this moment of infatuation from my view, and I thought only of the pleasures of power. Such is the infectious nature of ambition!

Mr. Devereux helped me to throw off this dangerous contagion, before it did me any injury. He happened to stay in the room with me a quarter of an hour after the other gentlemen went to dress. Though not often disposed to conversation with a stranger, yet I was won by this gentleman's easy address: he politely talked of the English fashionable world, with which he knew that I was well acquainted; I, with equal politeness, recurred to the Irish great world: we fastened together upon Lord O'Toole, who took us to Dublin Castle; and I began to express my regret that I had not yet been at the Irish court, and that I had not earlier in life made myself of political consequence.

"Ambition," said I, "might help to keep a man awake and alive; all common pleasures have long since ceased to interest me—they really cannot make me stir."

"My lord," said Mr. Devereux, "you would do better to sit or lie still all your life than to toil for such vain objects.

'Full little knowest thou that hast not tried,
What hell it is in sueing long to bide;'

Your lordship may remember Spenser's description of that hell?"

"Not exactly," said I, unwilling to lower the good opinion this gentleman seemed to have taken for granted of my literature. He took Spenser's poems out of the book-case, and I actually rose from my seat to read the passage; for what trouble will not even the laziest of mortals take to preserve the esteem of one by whom he sees that he is over-valued. I read the following ten lines without yawning!

"Full little knowest thou that hast not tried,

What hell it is in sueing long to bide;
To lose good days, that might be better spent,
To waste long nights in pensive discontent,
To speed to-day, to be put back to-morrow,
To feed on hope, to pine with fear and sorrow,
To fret thy soul with crosses and with cares,
To eat thy heart through comfortless despairs,
To fawn, to crouch, to wait, to ride, to run,
To spend, to give, to want, to be undone."

"Very strong, indeed," said I, with a competent air, as if used to judge of poetry.

"And it comes with still greater force, when we consider by whom it was written. A man, you know, my lord, who had been secretary to a lord lieutenant."

I felt my nascent ambition die away within me. I acknowledged it was better to spend an easy life. My determination was confirmed at this instant by the appearance of Lady Geraldine. Ambition and love, it is said, are incompatible passions. Neither of them had yet possession of my heart; but love and Lady Geraldine had perhaps a better chance than ambition and Lord O'Toole. Lady Geraldine appeared in high spirits; and, though I was not a vain man, I could not help fancying that my return to Ormsby Villa contributed to her charming vivacity. This gratified me secretly and soberly, as much as it visibly delighted her mother. Miss Bland, to pay her court to Lady Kildangan, observed that Lady Geraldine was in uncommonly fine spirits this evening. Lady Geraldine threw back a haughty frown over her left shoulder: this was the only time I ever saw her notice, in any manner, any thing that fell from her obsequious friend. To avert the fair one's displeasure, I asked for Miss Tracey and Mr. Gabbitt.

"Mr. Gabbitt," said her ladyship, resuming her good-humour instantly; "Mr. Gabbitt is gone off the happiest man in Ireland, with the hopes of surveying my Lord O'Toole's estate; a good job, which I was bound in honour to obtain for him, as a reward for taking a good joke. After mocking him with the bare imagination of a feast, you know the Barmecide in the Arabian Tales gave poor Shakabac a substantial dinner, a full equivalent for the jest."

"And Miss Tracey." said I, "what did your ladyship do for her?"

"I persuaded her mamma that the sweet creature was falling into an atrophy. So she carried the forlorn damsel post haste to the Black Rock for the recovery of her health, or her heart. Clementina, my dear, no reproachful looks; in your secret soul do not you know, that I could not do a young lady a greater favour than to give her a plausible excuse for getting away from home?"

I was afraid that Lady Geraldine would feel the want of her butt; however, I found that Miss Tracey's place was supplied by Captain Andrews, one of the Castle's aides-de-camp; and when Captain Andrews was out of the way, Lord Kilrush and his brother O'Toole were good marks. High and mighty as these personages thought themselves, and respectfully, nay obsequiously, as they were treated by most others, to this lady their characters appeared only a good study; and to laugh at them seemed only a good practice.

"Perhaps, my lord," said she to me, "you do not yet know my Lord O'Toole?"

"I have had the honour to be introduced to him."

"That's well; for he thinks that,
'Not to know him, argues yourself unknown.'

But as your lordship is a stranger in this country, you may be pardoned; and I will make you better acquainted with him. I suppose you know there are many Tooles in Ireland; some very ancient, respectable, and useful: this, however, is but a mere political tool, and the worst of all tools, a cat's paw. There's one thing to the credit of these brothers, they agree vastly well; for one delights in being always on the stage, and the other always behind the scenes. These brothers, with Captain Andrews—I hope they are none of them within hearing—form a charming trio, all admirable in their way. My Lord O'Toole is—artifice without art. My Lord Kilrush—importance without power. And Captain Andrews—pliability without ease. Poor Andrews! he's a defenceless animal—safe in impenetrable armour. Give him but time—as a man said, who once showed me a land-tortoise—give him but time to draw his head into his shell, and a broad-wheeled waggon may go over him without hurting him. Lord Glenthorn, did you ever observe Captain Andrews's mode of conversation?"

"No; I never heard him converse."

"Converse! nor I indeed; but you have heard him talk." "I have heard him say—Very true—and Of course."

"Lord Glenthorn is quite severe this evening," said Mrs. O'Connor.

"But though your lordship," continued Lady Geraldine, "may have observed Captain Andrews's wonderful economy of words, do you know whence it arises? Perhaps you think from his perception of his own want of understanding."

"Not from his perception of the want," said I.

"Again! again!" said Mrs. O'Connor, with an insulting tone of surprise; "Lord Glenthorn's quite witty this evening."

Lady Geraldine looked as if she were fully sensible of the want of politeness in Mrs. O'Connor's mode of praising. "But, my lord," pursued she, "you wrong Captain Andrews, if you attribute his monosyllabic replies either to stupidity or timidity. You have not guessed the reason why he never gives on any subject more than half an opinion."

"It was in the diplomatic school he was taught that art," said Mr. Devereux.

"You must know," pursued Lady Geraldine, "that Captain Andrews is only an aide-de-camp till a diplomatic situation can be found for him; and to do him justice, he has been so well trained in the diplomatic school, that he will not hazard an assertion on any subject; he is not certain of any thing, not even of his own identity."

"He assuredly wants," said Devereux, "the only proof of existence which Descartes would admit—I think, therefore I am."

"He has such a holy horror of committing himself," continued Lady Geraldine, "that if you were to ask him if the sun rose this morning, he would answer, with his sweet smile—So I am told—or—So I am informed."

"Begging your ladyship's pardon," cried Mr. Devereux, "that is much too affirmative. In the pure diplomatic style, impersonal verbs must ever be used in preference to active or passive. So I am told, lays him open to the dangerous questions, Who told you? or, By whom were you informed? Then he is forced into the imprudence of giving up his authorities; whereas he is safe in the impersonality of So it is said, or So it is reported."

"How I should like to see a meeting between two perfectly finished diplomatists!" cried Lady Geraldine.

"That is demonstrably impossible," said Mr. Devereux; "for in certain political, as well as in certain geometrical lines, there is a continual effort to approach, without a possibility of meeting."

Lady Geraldine's raillery, like all other things, would, perhaps, soon have become tiresome to me; but that there was infinite variety in her humour. At first I had thought her merely superficial, and intent solely upon her own amusement; but I soon found that she had a taste for literature, beyond what could have been expected in one who lived so dissipated a life; a depth of reflection that seemed inconsistent with the rapidity with which she thought; and, above all, a degree of generous indignation against meanness and vice, which seemed incompatible with the selfish character of a fine lady, and which appeared quite incomprehensible to the imitating tribe of her fashionable companions.

I mentioned a Mrs. Norton and Lady Hauton amongst the company of Ormsby Villa. These two English ladies, whom I had never met in any of the higher circles in London, who were persons of no consequence, and of no marked character in their own country, made, it seems, a prodigious sensation when they came over to Ireland, and turned the heads of half Dublin by the extravagance of their dress, the impertinence of their airs, and the audacity of their conduct. Fame flew before them to the remote parts of the country; and when they arrived at Ormsby Villa, all the country gentlemen and ladies were prepared to admire these celebrated fashionable belles. All worshipped them present, and abused them absent, except Lady Geraldine, who neither joined in the admiration nor inquired into the scandal. One morning Mrs. Norton and Lady Hauton had each collected her votaries round her: one group begging patterns of dress from Lady Hauton, who stood up in the midst of them, to have everything she wore examined and envied; the other group sat on a sofa apart, listening to Mrs. Norton, who, sotto voce, was telling interesting anecdotes of an English crim. con., which then occupied the attention of the fashionable world. Mrs. Norton had letters from the best authorities in London, which she was entreated by her auditors to read to them. Mrs. Norton went to look for the letters, Lady Hauton to direct her woman to furnish some patterns of I know not what articles of dress; and, in the mean time, all the company joined in canvassing the merits and demerits of the dress and characters of the two ladies who had just left the room. Lady Geraldine, who had kept aloof, and who was examining some prints at the farther end of the room, at this instant laid down her book, and looked upon the whole party with an air of magnanimous disdain; then smiling, as in scorn, she advanced towards them, and, in a tone of irony, addressing one of the Swanlinbar graces, "My dear Theresa," said her ladyship, "you are absolutely ashamed, I see, of not being quite naked; and you, my good Bess, will, no doubt, very soon be equally scandalized, at the imputation of being a perfectly modest woman. Go on, my friends; go on, and prosper; beg and borrow all the patterns and precedents you can collect of the newest fashions of folly and vice. Make haste, make haste; they don't reach our remote island fast enough. We Irish might live in innocence half a century longer, if you didn't expedite the progress of profligacy; we might escape the plague that rages in neighbouring countries, if we didn't, without any quarantine, and with open arms, welcome every suspected stranger; if we didn't encourage the importation of whole bales of tainted fineries, that will spread the contagion from Dublin to Cork, and from Cork to Galway!"

"La!" said Miss Ormsby, "how severe your ladyship is; and all only for one's asking for a pattern!"

"But you know," pursued Mrs. O'Connor, "that Lady Geraldine is too proud to take pattern from any body."

"Too proud am I? Well, then, I'll be humble; I'll abase myself—shall I?

'Proud as I am, I'll put myself to school;'

and I'll do what the ladies Hauton and Norton shall advise, to heighten my charms and preserve my reputation. I must begin, must not I, Mrs. O'Connor, by learning not to blush? for I observed you were ashamed for me yesterday at dinner, when I blushed at something said by one of our fair missionaries. Then, to whatever lengths flirtations and gallantry may go between unmarried or married people, I must look on. I may shut my eyes, if I please, and look down; but not from shame—from affectation I may as often as I please, or to show my eyelashes. Memorandum—to practise this before Clementina Ormsby, my mirror of fashion. So far, so good, for my looks; but now for my language. I must reform my barbarous language, and learn from Mrs. Norton, with her pretty accommodating voice, to call an intrigue an arrangement, and a crim. con. an affair in Doctors' Commons, or that business before the Lords.

'We never mention Hell to ears polite.'
How virtuous we shall be when we have no name for vice! But stay, I must mind my lessons—I have more, much more to learn. From the dashing Lady Hauton I may learn, if my head be but strong, and my courage intrepid enough, 'to touch the brink of all we hate,' without tumbling headlong into the gulf; and from the interesting Mrs. Norton, as I hear it whispered amongst you ladies, I may learn how, with the assistance of a Humane-society, to save a half-drowned reputation. It is, I understand, the glory of one class of fashionable females, to seem worse than they are; and of another class the privilege, to be worse than they seem."

Here clamorous voices interrupted Lady Geraldine—some justifying, some attacking, Lady Hauton and Mrs. Norton.

"Oh! Lady Geraldine, I assure you, notwithstanding all that was said about General — and Mrs. Norton, I am convinced there was nothing in it."

"And, my dear Lady Geraldine, though Lady Hauton does go great lengths in coquetting with a certain lord, you must see that there's nothing wrong; and that she means nothing, but to provoke his lady's jealousy. You know his lordship is not a man to fall in love with."

"So, because Lady Hauton's passion is hatred instead of love, and because her sole object is to give pain to a poor wife, and to make mischief in families, all her sins are to be forgiven! Now, if I were forced to forgive any ill-conducted female, I would rather excuse the woman who is hurried on by love than she who is instigated by hatred."

Miss Bland now began to support her ladyship's opinion, that "Lady Hauton was much the worst of the two;" and all the scandal that was in circulation was produced by the partisans of each of these ladies.

"No matter, no matter, which is the worst," cried Lady Geraldine; "don't let us waste our time in repeating or verifying scandalous stories of either of them. I have no enmity to these ladies; I only despise them, or rather, their follies and their faults. It is not the sinner, but the sin we should reprobate. Oh! my dear countrywomen," cried Lady Geraldine, with increasing animation of countenance and manner—"Oh! my dear countrywomen, let us never stoop to admire and imitate these second-hand airs and graces, follies and vices. Let us dare to be ourselves!"

My eyes were fixed upon her animated countenance, and, I believe, I continued gazing even after her voice ceased. Mrs. O'Connor pointed this out, and I was immediately embarrassed. Miss Bland accounted for my embarrassment by supposing, that what Lady Geraldine had said of English crim. cons, had affected me. From a look and a whisper among the ladies, I guessed this; but Lady Geraldine was too well-bred to suppose I could suspect her of ill-breeding and ill-nature, or that I could apply to myself what evidently was not intended to allude to my family misfortunes. By an openness of manner and sweetness of expression, which I cannot forget, she, in one single look, conveyed all this to me: and then resuming her conversation, "Pray, my lord," said she, "you who have lived so much in the great world in England, say, for you can, whether I am right or wrong in my suspicion, that these ladies, who have made such a noise in Ireland, have been little heard of in England?"

I confirmed her ladyship's opinion by my evidence. The faces of the company changed. Thus, in a few seconds, the empire of Lady Hauton and of Mrs. Norton seemed shaken to the foundation, and never recovered from this shock.

The warmth of Lady Geraldine's expressions, on this and many other occasions, wakened dormant feelings in my heart, and made me sensible that I had a soul, and that I was superior to the puppets with whom I had been classed.

One day Lady Kilrush, in her mixed mode, with partly the graces of a fine lady and partly the airs of a bel esprit, was talking of Mr. Devereux, whom she affected to patronise and produce.

"Here, Devereux!" cried she; "Cecil Devereux! What can you be thinking of? I am talking to you. Here's this epitaph of Francis the First upon Petrarch's Laura, that you showed me the other day: do you know, I dote upon it. I must have it translated: nobody can do it so well as you. I have not time; but I shall not sleep to-night if it is not done: and you are so quick: so sit down here, there's a dear man, and do it in your elegant way for me, whilst I go to my toilette. Perhaps you did not know that my name was Laura," said she, leaving the room with a very sentimental air.

"What will become of me!" cried Devereux. "Never was a harder task set by cruel patroness. I would rather 'turn a Persian tale for half-a-crown.' Read this, my lord, and tell me whether it will be easy to turn my Lady Kilrush into Petrarch's Laura."

"This sonnet, to be sure, is rather difficult to translate, or at least to modernize, as bespoke," said Lady Geraldine, after she had perused the sonnet; "but I think, Mr. Devereux, you brought this difficulty upon yourself. How came you to show these lines to such an amateur, such a fetcher and carrier of bays as Lady Kilrush? You might have been certain that, had they been trash, with the name of Francis the First, and with your fashionable approbation, and something to say about Petrarch and Laura, my Lady Kilrush would talk for ever, et se pâmerait d'affectation."

"Mr. Devereux," said I, "has only to abide by the last lines, as a good and sufficient apology to Lady Kilrush for his silence:

'Qui te pourra louer qu'en se taisant?
Car la parole est toujours réprimée
Quand le sujet surmonte le disant.'"

"There is no way to get out of my difficulties," said Mr. Devereux, with a very melancholy look; and with a deep sigh he sat down to attempt the translation of the poem. In a few minutes, however, he rose and left the room, declaring that he had the bad habit of not being able to do any thing in company.

Lady Geraldine now, with much energy of indignation, exclaimed against the pretensions of rich amateurs, and the mean and presumptuous manner in which some would-be great people affect to patronise genius.

"Oh! the baseness, the emptiness of such patronising ostentation!" cried she. "I am accused of being proud myself; but I hope—I believe—I am sure, that my pride is of another sort. Persons of any elevation or generosity of mind never have this species of pride; but it is your mean, second-rate folk, who imagine that people of talent are a sort of raree-show for their entertainment. At best, they consider men of genius only as artists formed for their use, who, if not in a situation to be paid with money, are yet to be easily recompensed by praise—by their praise—their praise! Heavens! what conceit! And these amateur-patrons really think themselves judges, and presume to advise and direct genius, and employ it to their petty purposes! Like that Pietro de Medici, who, at some of his entertainments, set Michael Angelo to make a statue of snow. My lord, did you ever happen to meet with Les Mémoires de Madame de Staël?"

"No: I did not know that they were published."

"You mistake me: I mean Madame de Staël of Louis the Fourteenth and the Regent's time, Mademoiselle de Launay."

I had never heard of such a person, and I blushed for my ignorance.

"Nay, I met with them myself only yesterday," said Lady Geraldine: "I was struck with the character of the Duchess de la Ferté, in which this kind of proud patronising ignorance is admirably painted from the life. It is really worth your while, my lord, to look at it. There's the book on that little table; here is the passage. You see, this Duchess de la Ferté is showing off to a sister-duchess a poor girl of genius, like a puppet or an ape.

"'Allons, mademoiselle, parlez—Madame, vous allez voir comme elle parle—Elle vit que j'hésitois à répondre, et pensa qu'il falloit m'aider comme une chanteuse à qui l'on indique ce qu'on désire d'entendre—Parlez un peu de religion, mademoiselle, vous direz ensuite autre chose.'

"This speech, Mr. Devereux tells me, has become quite proverbial in Paris," continued Lady Geraldine; "and it is often quoted, when any one presumes in the Duchess de la Ferte's style."

"Ignorance, either in high or low life, is equally self-sufficient, I believe," said I, exerting myself to illustrate her ladyship's remarks. "A gentleman of my acquaintance lately went to buy some razors at Packwood's. Mrs. Packwood alone was visible. Upon the gentleman's complimenting her on the infinite variety of her husband's ingenious and poetical advertisements, she replied, 'La! sir, and do you think husband has time to write them there things his-self? Why, sir, we keeps a poet to do all that there work.'"

Though Lady Geraldine spoke only in general of amateur-patrons and of men of genius, yet I could not help fancying, from the warmth with which she expressed herself, and from her dwelling on the subject so long, that her feelings were peculiarly interested for some individual of this description. Thus I discovered that Lady Geraldine had a heart; and I suspected that her ladyship and Mr. Devereux had also made the same discovery. This suspicion was strengthened by a slight incident, which occurred the following evening.

Lady Geraldine and Cecil Devereux, as we were drinking coffee, were in a recessed window, while some of the company stood round them, amused by their animated conversation. They went on, repartee after repartee, as if inspired by each other's spirits.

"You two," said a little girl of six years old, who was playing in the window, "go on singing to one another like two nightingales; and this shall be your cage," added she, drawing the drapery of the window-curtains across the recessed window. "You shall live always together in this cage: will you, pretty birds?"

"No, no; some birds cannot live in a cage, my dear," cried Lady Geraldine, playfully struggling to get free, whilst the child held her prisoner.

"Mr. Devereux seems tolerably quiet and contented in his cage," said the shrewd Mrs. O'Connor.

"I can't get out! I can't get out!" cried Devereux, in the melancholy tone of the starling in the Sentimental Journey.

"What is all this?" said my Lady Kildangan, sailing up to us.

"Only two birds," the child began.

"Singing-birds," interrupted Lady Geraldine, catching the little girl up in her arms, and stopping her from saying more, by beginning to sing most charmingly.

Lady Kildangan returned to the sofa without comprehending one word of what had passed. For my part, I now felt almost certain of the justice of my suspicions: I was a little vexed, but not by any means in that despair into which a man heartily in love would have been thrown by such a discovery.

Well, thought I, it is well it is no worse: it was very lucky that I did not fall quite in love with this fair lady, since it seems that she has given her heart away. But am I certain of this? I was mistaken once. Let me examine more carefully.

Now I had a new motive to keep my attention awake.

## CHAPTER XI

To preserve the continuity of my story, and not to fatigue the reader with the journals of my comings and goings from Ormsby Villa to Glenthorn Castle, and from Glenthorn Castle to Ormsby Villa, I must here relate the observations I made, and the incidents that occurred, during various visits at Sir Harry Ormsby's in the course of the summer.

After the incident of the birds and cage, my sagacity was for some time at fault. I could not perceive any further signs of intelligence between the parties: on the contrary, all communication seemed abruptly to cease. As I was not well versed in such affairs, this quieted my suspicions, and I began to think that I had been entirely mistaken. Cecil Devereux spent his days shut up in his own apartment, immersed, as far as I could understand, in the study of the Persian language. He talked to me of nothing but his hopes of an appointment which Lord O'Toole had promised to procure for him in India. When he was not studying, he was botanizing or mineralogizing with O'Toole's chaplain. I did not envy him his new mode of life. Lady Geraldine took no notice of it. When they did meet, which happened as seldom as possible, there was an air of haughty displeasure on her part; on his, steady and apparently calm respect and self-satisfaction. Her spirits were exuberant, but variable; and, at times, evidently forced: his were not high, but even and certain. Towards me, her ladyship's manners were free from coquetry, yet politely gratifying, as she marked, by the sort of conversation she addressed to me, her opinion that I was superior in ability and capability to what she had at first thought me, and to what I had always thought myself.

Mr. Devereux, though with more effort, treated me with distinction, and showed a constant desire to cultivate my friendship. On every occasion he endeavoured to raise my opinion of myself: to give me ambition and courage to cultivate my mind. Once, when I was arguing in favour of natural genius, and saying that I thought no cultivation could make the abilities of one man equal to those of another, he, without seeming to perceive that I was apologizing at once for my own indolence and my intellectual inferiority, answered in general terms, "It is difficult to judge what are the natural powers of the mind, they appear so different in different circumstances. You can no more judge of a mind in ignorance than of a plant in darkness. A philosophical friend told me, that he once thought he had discovered a new and strange plant growing in a mine. It was common sage; but so degenerated and altered, that he could not know it: he planted it in the open air and in the light, and gradually it resumed its natural appearance and character."

Mr. Devereux excited, without fatiguing, my mind by his conversation; and I was not yet sufficiently in love to be seriously jealous. I was resolved, however, to sound him upon the subject of Lady Geraldine, I waited for a good opportunity: at length, as we were looking together over the prints of Bürger's Lenore, he led to the sort of conversation that I desired, by telling me an anecdote relative to the poet, which he had lately heard from a German baron.

Burger was charmed with a sonnet, which an unknown fair one addressed to him, in praise of his poetry; he replied in equal strains; and they went on flattering one another, till both believed themselves in love: without ever having met, they determined to marry: they at length met, and married: they quarrelled and parted: in other words, the gentleman was terribly disappointed in his unknown mistress; and she consoled herself by running away from him with another lover.

The imprudence of this poetic couple led us to reflections on love and marriage in general. Keeping far away from all allusion to Lady Geraldine, I rallied Mr. Devereux about the fair Clementina, who was evidently a romantic admirer of his.

"Who, except Cupid, would barter his liberty for a butterfly?" said he; "and Cupid was a child. Men now-a-days are grown too wise to enslave themselves for women. Love occupies a vast space in a woman's thoughts, but fills a small portion in a man's life. Women are told, that 'The great, th' important business of their life, is love;' but men know that they are born for something better than to sing mournful ditties to a mistress's eyebrow. As to marriage, what a serious, terrible thing! Some quaint old author says, that man is of too smooth and oily a nature to climb up to heaven, if, to make him less slippery, there be not added to his composition the vinegar of marriage. This may be; but I will keep as long as possible from the vinegar."

"Really, Devereux," said I, smiling, "you talk so like a cynic and an old bachelor, and you look so little like either, that it is quite ridiculous."

"A man must be ridiculous sometimes," said he, "and bear to be thought so. No man ever distinguished himself, who could not bear to be laughed at."

Mr. Devereux left the room singing,

"No more for Amynta fresh garlands I wove;
Ambition, I said, will soon cure me of love."

I was uncertain what to think of all this. I inclined to believe that ambition was his ruling passion, notwithstanding the description of that Hell which he showed me in Spenser. His conduct to his patron-lords, by which a surer judgment of his character could be formed than by his professions, was not, however, that of a man merely intent upon rising in the world.

I remember once hearing Lord O'Toole attack a friend of this gentleman's, calling him, in a certain tone, a philosopher. Mr. Devereux replied, "that he could not consider that as a term of reproach; that where a false or pretended philosopher was meant, some other name should be used, equivalent to the Italian term of reproach, filosofastro."

Lord O'Toole would by no means admit of this Italianism: he would make no distinctions: he deemed philosophers altogether a race of beings dangerous and inimical to states.

"For states read statesmen," said Devereux, who persisted in the vindication of his friend till Lord O'Toole grew pale with anger, while Captain Andrews smiled with ineffable contempt at the political bévue: Lady Geraldine glowed with generous indignation.

Afterwards, in speaking to me of Lord O'Toole, Devereux said, "His lordship's classification of men is as contracted as the savage's classification of animals: he divides mankind into two classes, knaves and fools; and when he meets with an honest man, he does not know what to make of him."

My esteem for Mr. Devereux was much increased by my daily observations upon his conduct: towards Lady Geraldine, I thought it particularly honourable: when her displeasure evidently merged in esteem, when her manners again became most winning and attractive, his continued uniformly the same; never passing the bounds of friendly respect, or swerving, in the slightest degree, from the line of conduct which he had laid down for himself. I thought I now understood him perfectly. That he liked Lady Geraldine I could scarcely doubt; but I saw that he refrained from aiming at the prize which he knew he ought not to obtain; that he perceived her ladyship's favourable disposition towards him, yet denied himself not only the gratification of his vanity, but the exquisite pleasure of conversing with her, lest he should stand in the way of her happier prospects. He frequently spoke to me of her ladyship in terms of the warmest approbation. He said, that all the world saw and admired her talents and beauty, but that he had had opportunities, as a relation, of studying her domestic life. "With all her vivacity, she has a heart formed for tenderness," said he; "a high sense of duty, the best security for a woman's conduct; and in generosity and magnanimity, I never found her superior in either sex. In short, I never saw any woman whose temper and disposition were more likely to make a man of sense and feeling supremely happy."

I could not forbear smiling, and asking Cecil Devereux how all this accorded with his late professions of hatred to marriage. "My professions were sincere," said he. "It would be misery to me to marry any inferior woman, and I am not in circumstances to marry as I could wish. I could not think of Lady Geraldine without a breach of trust, of which your lordship, I hope, cannot suspect me. Her mother places confidence in me. I am not only a relation, but treated as a friend of the family. I am not in love with Lady Geraldine. I admire, esteem, respect her ladyship; and I wish to see her united to a man, if such a man there be, who may deserve her. We understand one another now. Your lordship will have the goodness never more to speak to me on this subject." He spoke with much emotion, but with steadiness, and left me penetrated with feelings that were entirely new to me.

Much as I admired his conduct, I was yet undecided as to my own: my aversion to a second marriage was not yet conquered:—I was amused, I was captivated by Lady Geraldine; but I could not bring myself to think of making a distinct proposal. Captain Andrews himself was not more afraid of being committed than I was upon this tender subject. To gain time, I now thought it necessary to verify all the praises Mr. Devereux had bestowed on her ladyship. Magnanimity was a word that particularly struck my ear as extraordinary when applied to a female. However, by attending carefully to this lady, I thought I discovered what Mr. Devereux meant. Lady Geraldine was superior to manoeuvring little arts and petty stratagems to attract attention: she would not stoop, even to conquer. From gentlemen she seemed to expect attention as her right, as the right of her sex; not to beg or accept of it as a favour: if it were not paid, she deemed the gentleman degraded, not herself. Far from being mortified by any preference shown to other ladies, her countenance betrayed only a sarcastic sort of pity for the bad taste of the men, or an absolute indifference and look of haughty absence. I saw that she beheld with disdain the paltry competitions of the young ladies her companions: as her companions, indeed, she hardly seemed to consider them; she tolerated their foibles, forgave their envy, and never exerted any superiority, except to show her contempt of vice and meanness. To be in any degree excepted from the common herd; to be in any degree distinguished by a lady so proud, and with so many good reasons to be proud, was flattering to my self-love. She gave me no direct encouragement; but I never advanced far enough to require encouragement, much less to justify repulse. Sometimes I observed, or I fancied, that she treated me with more favour when Mr. Devereux was present than at other times; perhaps—for she was a woman, not an angel—to pique Devereux, and try if she could move him from the settled purpose of his soul. He bore it all with surprising constancy: his spirits, however, and his health, began visibly to decline.

"If I do not intrude too much on your valuable time, Mr. Devereux," said her ladyship to him one evening, in her most attractive manner, "may I beg you to read to us some of these beautiful poems of Sir William Jones?"

There was a seat beside her ladyship on the sofa: the book was held out by the finest arm in the world.

"Nay," said Lady Geraldine, "do not look so respectfully miserable; if you have any other engagements, you have only to say so: or if you cannot speak you may bow: a bow, you know, is an answer to every thing. And here is my Lord Glenthorn ready to supply your place: pray, do not let me detain you prisoner. You shall not a second time say, I can't get out."

Devereux made no further effort to escape, but took the book and his dangerous seat. He remained with us, contrary to his custom, the whole evening. Afterwards, as if he felt that some apology was necessary to me for the pleasure in which he had indulged himself, "Perhaps, my lord," said he, "another man in my situation, and with my feelings, would think it necessary to retreat, and prudent to secure his safety by flight; but flight is unworthy of him who can combat and conquer: the man who is sure of himself does not skulk away to avoid danger, but advances to meet it, armed secure in honesty."

This proud and rash security in his own courage, strength of mind, and integrity, was the only fault of Cecil Devereux. He never prayed not to be led into temptation, he thought himself so sure of avoiding evil. Unconscious of his danger, even though his disease was at its height, he now braved it most imprudently: he was certain that he should never pass the bounds of friendship; he had proved this to himself, and was satisfied: he told me that he could with indifference, nay, with pleasure, see Lady Geraldine mine. In the mean time, upon the same principle that he deemed flight inglorious, he was proud to expose himself to the full force of Love's artillery. He was with us now every day, and almost all day, and Lady Geraldine was more charming than ever. The week was fixed for her departure. Still I could not decide. I understood that her ladyship would pass the ensuing winter in Dublin, where she would probably meet with new adorers; and even if Mr. Devereux should not succeed, some adventurous knight might win and wear the prize. This was an alarming thought. It almost decided me to hazard the fatal declaration; but then I recollected that I might follow her ladyship to town the next winter, and that if the impression did not, as might be hoped, wear off during the intervening autumn, it would be time enough to commit myself when I should meet my fair one in Dublin. This was at last my fixed resolution. Respited from the agonies of doubt, I now waited very tranquilly for that moment to which most lovers look forward with horror, the moment of separation. I was sensible that I had accustomed myself to think about this lady so much, that I had gradually identified my existence with hers, and I thus found my spirit of animation much increased. I dreaded the departure of Lady Geraldine less than the return of ennui.

In this frame of mind I was walking one morning in the pleasure grounds with Lady Geraldine, when a slight accident made me act in direct contradiction to all my resolutions, and, I think, inconsistently with my character. But such is the nature of man! and I was doomed to make a fool of myself, even in the very temple of Minerva. Among the various ornamental buildings in the grounds at Ormsby Villa, there was a temple dedicated to this goddess, from which issued a troop of hoyden young ladies, headed by the widow O'Connor and Lady Kilrush, all calling to us to come and look at some charming discovery which they had just made in the temple of Minerva. Thither we proceeded, accompanied by the merry troop. We found in the temple only a poetical inscription of Lady Kilrush's, pompously engraved on a fine marble tablet. We read the lines with all the attention usually paid to a lady's poetry in the presence of the poetess. Lady Geraldine and I turned to pay some compliments on the performance, when we found that Lady Kilrush and all her companions were gone.

"Gone! all gone!" said Lady Geraldine; "and there they are, making their way very fast down to the temple of Folly! Lady Kilrush, you know, is so ba-a-ashful, she could not possibly stay to receive nos hommages. I love to laugh at affectation. Call them back, do, my lord, and you shall see the fair author go through all the evolutions of mock humility, and end by yielding quietly to the notion that she is the tenth Muse. But run, my lord, or they will be out of our reach."

I never was seen to run on any occasion; but to obey Lady Geraldine I walked as fast as I could to the door, and, to my surprise, found it fastened.

"Locked, I declare! Some of the witty tricks of the widow O'Connor, or the hoyden Miss Callwells!"

"How I hate hoydens!" cried Lady Geraldine: "but let us take patience; they will be back presently. If young ladies must perform practical jokes, because quizzing is the fashion, I wish they would devise something new. This locking-up is so stale a jest. To be sure it has lately to boast the authority of high rank in successful practice: but these bungling imitators never distinguish between cases the most dissimilar imaginable. Silly creatures! We have only to be wise and patient."

Her ladyship sat down to re-peruse the tablet. I never saw her look so beautiful.—The dignified composure of her manner charmed me; it was so unlike the paltry affectation of some of the fashionable ladies by whom I had been disgusted. I recollected the precedent to which she alluded. I recollected that the locking-up ended in matrimony; and as Lady Geraldine made some remarks upon the verses, I suppose my answers showed my absence of mind.

"Why so grave, my lord? why so absent? I assure you I do not suspect your lordship of having any hand in this vulgar manoeuvre. I acquit you honourably; therefore you need not stand any longer like a criminal."

What decided me at this instant I cannot positively tell: whether it was the awkwardness of my own situation, or the grace of her ladyship's manner: but all my prudential arrangements were forgotten, all my doubts vanished. Before I knew that the words passed my lips, I replied, "That her ladyship did me justice by such an acquittal; but that though I had no part in the contrivance, yet I felt irresistibly impelled to avail myself of the opportunity it afforded of declaring my real sentiments." I was at her ladyship's feet, and making very serious love, before I knew where I was. In what words my long-delayed declaration was made, I cannot recollect, but I well remember Lady Geraldine's answer.

"My lord, I assure you that you do not know what you are saying: you do not know what you are doing. This is all a mistake, as you will find half an hour hence. I will not be so cruelly vain as to suppose you serious."

"Not serious! no man ever was more serious."

"No, no—No, no, no."

I swore, of course, most fervently.

"Oh! rise, rise, I beseech you, my lord, and don't look so like a hero; though you have done an heroical action, I grant. How you ever brought yourself to it, I cannot imagine. But now, for your comfort, you are safe—Vous voilà quitte pour la peur! Do not, however, let this encourage you to venture again in the same foolish manner. I know but few, very few young ladies to whom Lord Glenthorn could offer himself with any chance or reasonable hope of being refused. So take warning: never again expect to meet with such another as my whimsical self."

"Never, never can I expect to meet with any thing resembling your charming self," cried I. This was a new text for a lover's rhapsody. It is not necessary, and might not be generally interesting to repeat all the ridiculous things I said, even if I could remember them.

Lady Geraldine listened to me, and then very calmly replied, "Granting you believe all that you are saying at this minute, which I must grant from common gratitude, and still more common vanity; nevertheless, permit me to assure you, my lord, that this is not love; it is only a fancy—only the nettle-rash, not the plague. You will not die this time. I will insure your life. So now jump out of the window as fast as you can, and unlock the door—you need not be afraid of breaking your neck—you know your life is insured. Come, take the lover's leap, and get rid of your passion at once."

I grew angry.

"Only a cloud," said Lady Geraldine—"it will blow over."

I became more passionate—I did not know the force of my own feelings, till they met with an obstacle; they suddenly rose to a surprising height.

"Now, my lord," cried Lady Geraldine with a tone and look of comic vexation, "this is really the most provoking thing imaginable; you have no idea how you distress me, nor of what exquisite pleasures you deprive me—all the pleasures of coquetry; legitimate pleasures, in certain circumstances, as I am instructed to think them by one of the first moral authorities. There is a case—I quote from memory, my lord; for my memory, like that of most other people, on subjects where I am deeply interested, is tolerably tenacious—there is a case, says the best of fathers, in his Legacy to the best of daughters—there is a case, where a woman may coquet justifiably to the utmost verge which her conscience will allow. It is where a gentleman purposely declines making his addresses, till such time as he thinks himself perfectly sure of her consent. Now, my lord, if you had had the goodness to do so, I might have made this delightful case my own; and what charming latitude I might have allowed my conscience! But now, alas! it is all over, and I must be as frank as you have been, under pain of forfeiting what I value more even than admiration—my own good opinion."

She paused, and was silent for a few moments; then suddenly changing her manner, she exclaimed, in a serious, energetic tone, "Yes, I must, I will be sincere; let it cost me what it may. I will be sincere. My lord, I never can be yours. My lord, you will believe me, even from the effort with which I speak:" her voice softened, and her face suffused with crimson, as she spoke. "I love another—my heart is no longer in my own possession; whether it will ever be in my power, consistently with my duty and his principles, to be united with the man of my choice, is doubtful—more than doubtful—but this is certain, that with such a prepossession, such a conviction in my mind, I never could nor ought to think of marrying any other person."

I pleaded, that however deserving of her preference the object of her favour might be, yet that if there were, as her own prudence seemed to suggest, obstacles, rendering the probability of her union with that person more than doubtful, it might be possible that her superior sense and strength of mind, joined to the persevering affection of another lover, who would spare no exertions to render himself worthy of her, might, perhaps, in time—

"No, no," said she, interrupting me; "do not deceive yourself. I will not deceive you. I give you no hopes that my sentiments may change. I know my own mind—it will not change. My attachment is founded on the firm basis of esteem; my affection has grown from the intimate knowledge of the principles and conduct of the man I love. No other man, let his merits be what they may, could have these advantages in my opinion. And when I say that the probability of our being united is more than doubtful, I do not mean to deny that I have distant hope that change of circumstances might render love and duty compatible. Without hope I know love cannot long exist. You see I do not talk romantic nonsense to you. All that you say of prudence, and time, and the effect of the attentions of another admirer, would be perfectly just and applicable, if my attachment were a fancy of yesterday—if it were a mere young lady's commonplace first love; but I am not a very young lady, nor is this, though a first love, commonplace. I do not, you see, in the usual style, tell you that the man I adore is an angel, and that no created form ever did, or ever can, resemble this angel in green and gold; but, on the contrary, do justice to your lordship's merit: and believing, as I do, that you are capable of a real love; still more, believing that such an attachment would rouse you to exertion, and bring to life and light a surprising number of good qualities; yet I should deceive you unpardonably, fatally for my own peace of mind, if not for yours, were I not frankly and decidedly to assure you, that I never could reward or return your affection. My attachment to—I trust entirely where I trust at all—my attachment to Mr. Devereux is for life."

"He deserves it—deserves it all," cried I, struggling for utterance; "that is as much as a rival can say."

"Not more than I expected from you, my lord."

"But your ladyship says there is a hope of duty and love being compatible. Would Lady Kildangan ever consent?"

She looked much disturbed.

"No, certainly; not unless—Lord O'Toole has promised—not that I depend on courtiers' promises—but Lord O'Toole is a relation of ours, and he has promised to obtain an appointment abroad, in India, for Mr. Devereux. If that were done, he might appear of more consequence in the eyes of the world. My mother might then, perhaps, be propitious. My lord, I give you the strongest proof of my esteem, by speaking with such openness. I have had the honour of your lordship's acquaintance only a few months; but without complimenting my own penetration, I may securely trust to the judgment of Mr. Devereux, and his example has taught me to feel confidence in your lordship. Your conduct now will, I trust, justify my good opinion, by your secrecy; and by desisting from useless pursuit you will entitle yourself to my esteem and gratitude. These, I presume, you will think worth securing."

My soul was so completely touched, that I could not articulate.

"Mr. Devereux is right—I see, my lord, that you have a soul that can be touched."

"Kissing hands, I protest!" exclaimed a shrill voice at the window. We turned, and saw Mrs. O'Connor and a group of tittering faces peeping in. "Kissing hands, after a good hour's tête-à-tête! Oh, pray, Lady Kildangan, make haste here," continued Mrs. O'Connor; "make haste, before Lady Geraldine's blushes are over."

"Were you ever detected in the crime of blushing, in your life, Mrs. O'Connor?" said I.

"I never was found out locked up with so fine a gentleman," replied Mrs. O'Connor.

"Then it hurts your conscience only to be found out, like all the rest of the vast family of the Surfaces," said Lady Geraldine, resuming her spirit.

"Found out!—Locked up!—bless me! bless me! What is all this?" cried Lady Kildangan, puffing up the hill. "For shame! young ladies; for shame!" continued her ladyship, with a decent suppression of her satisfaction, when she saw, or thought she saw, how matters stood. "Unlock the door, pray. Don't be vexed, my Geraldine. Fie! fie! Mrs. O'Connor. But quizzing is now so fashionable—nobody can be angry with any body. My Geraldine, consider we are all friends."

The door unlocked, and as we were going out, Lady Geraldine whispered to me—"For mercy's sake, my lord, don't break my poor mother's heart! Never let her know that a coronet has been within my grasp, and that I have not clutched it."

Lady Kildangan, who thought that all was now approaching that happy termination she so devoutly wished, was so full of her own happy presentiments, that it was impossible for me to undeceive her ladyship. Even when I announced before her, to Sir Harry Ormsby, that I was obliged to return home immediately, on particular business, she was, I am sure, persuaded that I was going to prepare matters for marriage-settlements. When I mounted my horse, Mr. Devereux pressed through a crowd assembled on the steps at the hall-door, and offered me his hand, with a look and manner that seemed to say— Have you sufficient generosity to be still my friend? "I know the value of your friendship, Mr. Devereux," said I, "and I hope to deserve it better every year that I live."

For the effort which it cost me to say this I was rewarded. Lady Geraldine, who had retired behind her companions, at this instant approached with an air of mingled grace and dignity, bowed her head, and gave me a smile of grateful approbation. This is the last image left on my mind, the last look of the charming Geraldine—I never saw her again.

After I got home I did not shave for two days, and scarcely ever spoke. I should have taken to my bed to avoid seeing any human creature; but I knew that if I declared myself ill, no power would keep my old nurse Ellinor from coming to moan over me; and I was not in a humour to listen to stories of the Irish Black Beard, or the ghost of King O'Donoghoe; nor could I, however troublesome, have repulsed the simplicity of her affection. Instead of going to bed, therefore, I continued to lie stretched upon a sofa, ruminating sweet and bitter thoughts, after giving absolute orders that I should not be disturbed on any account whatever. Whilst I was in this state of reverie, one of my servants—an odd Irish fellow, who, under pretence of being half-witted, took more liberties than his companions—bolted into my presence.

"Plase your lordship, I thought it my duty, in spite of 'em all below, to come up to advertise to your lordship of the news that's going through the country. That they are all upside down at Ormsby Villa, all mad entirely—fighting and setting off through the kingdom, every one their own way; and, they say, it's all on account of something that Miss Clemmy Ormsby told, that Lady Geraldine said about my Lord O'Toole's being no better than a cat's paw, or something that way, which made his lordship quite mad; and he said, in the presence of Captain Andrews, and my Lady Kildangan, and Lady Geraldine, and all that were in it, something that vexed Lady Geraldine, which made Mr. Cecil Devereux mad next; and he said something smart in reply, that Lord O'Toole could not digest, he said, which made his lordship madder than ever, and he discharged Mr. Devereux from his favour, and he is not to get that place that was vacant, the lord-lieutenancy of some place in the Indies that he was to have had; this made Lady Geraldine mad, and it was found out she was in love with Mr. Devereux, which made her mother mad, the maddest of all, they say, so that none can hold her, and she is crying night and day how her daughter might have had the first coronet in the kingdom, maning you, my lard, if it had not been that she preferred a beggar-man, maning Mr. Cecil Devereux, who is as poor, they say, as a Connaughtman—and he's forbid to think of her, and she's forbid, under pain of bread and water, ever to set her eyes upon him the longest day ever she lives; so the horses and coaches are ordered, and they are all to be off with the first light for Dublin: and that's all, my lard; and all truth, not a word of lies I'm telling."

I was inclined not to credit a story so oddly told; but, upon inquiry, I found it true in its material points. My own words to Mr. Devereux, and the parting look of Lady Geraldine, were full in my recollection; I was determined, by an unexpected, exertion, to surprise both the lovers, and to secure for ever their esteem and gratitude. The appointment, which Mr. Devereux desired, was not yet given away; the fleet was to sail in a few days. I started up from my sofa—ordered my carriage instantly—shaved myself—sent a courier on before to have horses ready at every stage to carry me to Dublin—got there in the shortest time possible—found Lord O'Toole but just arrived. Though unused to diplomatic language and political negotiation, I knew pretty well on what they all hinge. I went directly to the point, and showed that it would be the interest of the party concerned to grant my request. By expressing a becoming desire that my boroughs, upon a question where a majority was required, should strengthen the hands of government, I obtained for my friend the favour he deserved. Before I quitted Lord O'Toole, his secretary, Captain Andrews, was instructed to write a letter, announcing to Mr. Devereux his appointment. A copy of the former letter of refusal now lay before me; it was in his lordship's purest diplomatic style—as follows:

"Private.

"Lord O'Toole is concerned to inform Mr. Devereux that he cannot feel himself justified in encouraging Mr. D., under the existing circumstances, to make any direct application relative to the last conversation his lordship had the honour to hold with Mr. Devereux."

"To Cecil Devereux, Esq. &c. Thursday —"

The letter which I obtained, and of which I took possession, ran as follows:

"Private.

"Lord O'Toole is happy to have it in command to inform Mr. Devereux, that his lordship's representations on the subject of their last conversation have been thought sufficient, and that an official notification of the appointment to India, which Mr. D. desired, will meet the wishes of Mr. Devereux.

"Captain Andrews has the honour to add his congratulations."

"To Cecil Devereux, Esq. &c. Thursday —"

Having despatched this business with a celerity that surprised all the parties concerned, and most myself, I called at the lodgings of Mr. Devereux, delivered the letter to his servant, and left town. I could not bear to see either Mr. Devereux or Lady Geraldine. I had the pleasure to hear, that the obtaining this appointment was followed by Lady Kildangan's consent to their marriage. Soon after my return to Glenthorn Castle, I received a letter of warm thanks from Devereux, and a polite postscript from Lady Geraldine, declaring that, though she felt much pleasure, she could feel no surprise in seeing her opinion of Lord Glenthorn justified; persuaded, as she and Mr. Devereux had always been, that only motive and opportunity were wanting to make his lordship's superior qualities known to the world, and, what was still more difficult, to himself. They left Ireland immediately afterwards in consequence of their appointment in India.

I was raised in my own estimation—I revelled a short time in my self-complacent reflections; but when nothing more remained to be done, or to be said—when the hurry of action, the novelty of generosity, the glow of enthusiasm, and the freshness of gratitude, were over, I felt that, though large motives could now invigorate my mind, I was still a prey to habitual indolence, and that I should relapse into my former state of apathy and disease.

## CHAPTER XII

I remember to have heard, in some epilogue to a tragedy, that the tide of pity and of love, whilst it overwhelms, fertilizes the soul. That it may deposit the seeds of future fertilization, I believe; but some time must elapse before they germinate: on the first retiring of the tide, the prospect is barren and desolate. I was absolutely inert, and almost imbecile for a considerable time, after the extraordinary stimulus, by which I had been actuated, was withdrawn. I was in this state of apathy when the rebellion broke out in Ireland; nor was I roused in the least by the first news of the disturbances. The intelligence, however, so much alarmed my English servants, that, with one accord, they left me; nothing could persuade them to remain longer in Ireland. The parting with my English gentleman affected my lethargic selfishness a little. His loss would have been grievous to such a helpless being as I was, had not his place been immediately supplied by that half-witted Irishman, Joe Kelly, who had ingratiated himself with me by a mixture of drollery and simplicity, and by suffering himself to be continually my laughing-stock; for, in imitation of Lady Geraldine, I thought it necessary to have a butt. I remember he first caught my notice by a strange answer to a very simple question. I asked, "What noise is that I hear?" "My lard," said he, "it is only the singing in my ears; I have had it these six months." Another time, when I reproached him for having told me a lie, he answered, "Why, now indeed, and plase your honour, my lard, I tell as few lies as possibly I can." This fellow, the son of a bricklayer, had originally been intended for a priest, and he went, as he told me, to the College of Maynooth to study his humanities; but, unluckily, the charms of some Irish Heloise came between him and the altar. He lived in a cabin of love, till he was weary of his smoke-dried Heloise, and then thought it convanient to turn sarving man, as he could play on the flute, and brush a coat remarkably well, which he larned at Maynooth, by brushing the coats of the superiors. Though he was willing to be laughed at, Joe Kelly could in his turn laugh; and he now ridiculed, without mercy, the pusillanimity of the English renegadoes, as he called the servants who had just left my service; He assured me that, to his knowledge, there was no manner of danger, excepted a man preferred being afraid of his own shadow, which some did, rather than have nothing to talk of, or enter into resolutions about, with some of the spirited men in the chair.

Unwilling to be disturbed, I readily believed all that lulled me in my security. I would not be at the trouble of reading the public papers; and when they were read to me, I did not credit any paragraph that militated against my own opinion. Nothing could awaken me. I remember, one day, lying yawning on my sofa, repeating to Mr. M'Leod, who endeavoured to open my eyes to the situation of the country, "Pshaw, my dear sir; there is no danger, be assured—none at all—none at all. For mercy's sake! talk to me of something more diverting, if you would keep me awake; time enough to think of these things when they come nearer to us."

Evils that were not immediately near me had no power to affect my imagination. My tenantry had not yet been contaminated by the epidemic infection, which broke out soon after with such violence as to threaten the total destruction of all civil order. I had lived in England—I was unacquainted with the causes and the progress of the disease, and I had no notion of my danger; all I knew was, that some houses had been robbed of arms, and that there was a set of desperate wretches called defenders; but I was annoyed only by the rout that was now made about them. Having been used to the regular course of justice which prevailed in England, I was more shocked at the summary proceedings of my neighbours than alarmed at the symptoms of insurrection. Whilst my mind was in this mood, I was provoked by the conduct of some of the violent party, which wounded my personal pride, and infringed upon my imagined consequence. My foster-brother's forge was searched for pikes, his house ransacked, his bed and bellows, as possible hiding places, were cut open; by accident, or from private malice, he received a shot in his arm; and, though not the slightest cause of suspicion could be found against him, the party left him with a broken arm, and the consolation of not being sent to jail as a defender. Without making any allowance for the peculiar circumstances of the country, my indignation was excited in the extreme, by the injury done to my foster-brother; his sufferings, the tears of his mother, the taunts of Mr. (now Captain) Hardcastle, and the opposition made by his party, called forth all the faculties of my mind and body. The poor fellow, who was the subject of this contest, showed the best disposition imaginable: he was excessively grateful to me for interesting myself to get him justice; but as soon as he found that parties ran high against me, he earnestly dissuaded me from persisting.

"Let it drop, and plase your honour; my lord, let it drop, and don't be making of yourself inimies for the likes of me. Sure, what signifies my arm? and, before the next assizes, sha'n't I be as well as ever, arm and all?" continued he, trying to appear to move the arm without pain. "And there's the new bellows your honour has give me; it does my heart good to look at 'em, and it won't be long before I will be blowing them again as stout as ever; and so God bless your honour, my lord, and think no more about it—let it drop entirely, and don't be bringing yourself into trouble."

"Ay, don't be bringing yourself into trouble, dear," added Ellinor, who seemed half distracted between her feelings for her son and her fears for me; "it's a shame to think of the way they've treated Christy— but there's no help now, and it's best not to be making bad worse; and so, as Christy says, let the thing drop, jewel, and don't be bringing yourself into trouble; you don't know the natur of them people, dear—you are too innocent for them entirely, and myself does not know the mischief they might do yees."

"True for ye," pursued Christy; "I wouldn't for the best cow ever I see that your honour ever larnt a sentence about me or my arm; and it is not for such as we to be minding every little accident—so God lend you long life, and don't be plaguing yourself to death! Let it drop, and I'll sleep well the night, which I did not do the week, for thinking of all the trouble you got, and would get, God presarve ye!"

This generous fellow's eloquence produced an effect directly contrary to what was intended; both my feelings and my pride were now more warmly interested in his cause. I insisted upon his swearing examinations before Mr. M'Leod, who was a justice of the peace. Mr. M'Leod behaved with the utmost steadiness and impartiality; and in this trying moment, when "it was infamy to seem my friend," he defended my conduct calmly, but resolutely, in private and in public, and gave his unequivocal testimony, in few but decided words, in favour of my injured tenant. I should have respected Mr. M'Leod more, if I had not attributed this conduct to his desire of being returned for one of my boroughs at the approaching election. He endeavoured, with persevering goodness, to convince me of the reality of the danger in the country. My eyes were with much difficulty forced open so far as to perceive that it was necessary to take an active part in public affairs to vindicate my loyalty, and to do away the prejudices that were entertained against me; nor did my incredulity, as to the magnitude of the peril, prevent me from making exertions essential to the defence of my own character, if not to that of the nation. How few act from purely patriotic and rational motives! At all events I acted, and acted with energy; and certainly at this period of my life I felt no ennui. Party spirit is an effectual cure for ennui; and perhaps it is for this reason that so many are addicted to its intemperance. All my passions were roused, and my mind and body kept in continual activity. I was either galloping, or haranguing, or fearing, or hoping, or fighting; and so long as it was said that I could not sleep in my bed, I slept remarkably well, and never had so good an appetite as when I was in hourly danger of having nothing to eat. The rebels were up, and the rebels were down—and Lord Glenthorn's spirited conduct in the chair, and indefatigable exertions in the field, were the theme of daily eulogium amongst my convivial companions and immediate dependants. But, unfortunately, my sudden activity gained me no credit amongst the violent party of my neighbours, who persisted in their suspicions; and my reputation was now still more injured, by the alternate charge of being a trimmer or a traitor. Nay, I was further exposed to another danger, of which, from my ignorance of the country, I could not possibly be aware. The disaffected themselves, as I afterwards found, really believed, that, as I had not begun by persecuting the poor, I must be a favourer of the rebels; and all that I did to bring the guilty to justice, they thought was only to give a colour to the thing, till the proper moment should come for my declaring myself. Of this absurd and perverse mode of judging I had not the slightest conception; and I only laughed when it was hinted to me. My treating the matter so lightly confirmed suspicion on both sides. At this time all objects were so magnified and distorted by the mist of prejudice, that no inexperienced eye could judge of their real proportions. Neither party could believe the simple truth, that my tardiness to act arose from the habitual inertia of my mind and body.

Whilst prepossessions were thus strong, the time, the important time, in Ireland the most important season of the year, the assizes, arrived. My foster-brother's cause, or, as it was now generally called, Lord Glenthorn's cause, came on to be tried. I spared no expense, I spared no exertions; I fee'd the ablest counsel; and not content with leaving them to be instructed by my attorney, I explained the affair to them myself with indefatigable zeal. One of the lawyers, whom I had seen, or by whom I had been seen, in my former inert state of existence, at some watering-place in England, could not refrain from expressing his astonishment at my change of character; he could scarcely believe that I was the same Lord Glenthorn, of whose indolence and ennui he had formerly heard and seen so much.

Alas! all my activity, all my energy, on the present occasion, proved ineffectual. After a dreadful quantity of false swearing, the jury professed themselves satisfied; and, without retiring from the box, acquitted the persons who had assaulted my foster-brother. The mortification of this legal defeat was not all that I had to endure; the victorious party mobbed me, as I passed some time afterwards through a neighbouring town, where Captain Hardcastle and his friends had been carousing. I was hooted, and pelted, and narrowly escaped with my life—I who, but a few months ago, had imagined myself possessed of nearly despotic power: but opinions had changed; and on opinion almost all power is founded. No individual, unless he possess uncommon eloquence, joined to personal intrepidity, can withstand the combination of numbers, and the force of prejudice.

Such was the result of my first public exertions! Yet I was now happier and better satisfied with myself than I had ever been before. I was not only conscious of having acted in a manly and generous manner, but the alarms of the rebels, and of the French, and of the loyalists, and the parading, and the galloping, and the quarrelling, and the continual agitation in which I was kept, whilst my character and life were at stake, relieved me effectually from the intolerable burden of ennui.

## CHAPTER XIII

*"And, for the book of knowledge fair,*
*Presented with an universal blank*
*Of Nature's works, to me expunged and rased."*

Unfortunately for me, the rebellion in Ireland was soon quelled; the nightly scouring of our county ceased; the poor people returned to their duty and their homes; the occupation of upstart and ignorant associators ceased, and their consequence sunk at once. Things and persons settled to their natural level. The influence of men of property, and birth, and education, and character, once more prevailed. The spirit of party ceased to operate: my neighbours wakened, as if from a dream, and wondered at the strange injustice with which I had been treated. Those who had lately been my combined enemies were disunited, and each was eager to assure me that he had always been privately my friend, but that he was compelled to conceal his sentiments: each exculpated himself, and threw the blame on others: all apologized to me, and professed to be my most devoted humble servants. My popularity, my power, and my prosperity were now at their zenith, unfortunately for me; because my adversity had not lasted long enough to form and season my character. I had been driven to exertion by a mixture of pride and generosity; my understanding being uncultivated, I had acted from the virtuous impulse of the moment, but never from rational motive, which alone can be permanent in its operation. When the spur of the occasion pressed upon me no longer, I relapsed into my former inactivity. When the great interests and strong passions, by which I had been impelled to exertion, subsided, all other feelings, and all less objects, seemed stale, flat, and unprofitable. For the tranquillity which I was now left to enjoy I had no taste; it appeared to me a dead calm, most spiritless and melancholy.

I remember hearing, some years afterwards, a Frenchman, who had been in imminent danger of been guillotined by Robespierre, and who at last was one of those who arrested the tyrant, declare, that when the bustle and horror of the revolution were over, he could hardly keep himself awake; and that he thought it very insipid to live in quiet with his wife and family. He further summed up the catalogue of Robespierre's crimes, by exclaiming, "D'ailleurs c'étoit un grand philanthrope!" I am not conscious of any disposition to cruelty, and I heard this man's speech with disgust; yet upon a candid self-examination, I must confess, that I have felt, though from different causes, some degree of what he described. Perhaps ennui may have had a share in creating revolutions. A French author pronounces ennui to be "a moral indigestion, caused by a monotony of situations!"

I had no wife or family to make domestic life agreeable: nor was I inclined to a second marriage, my first had proved so unfortunate, and the recollection of my disappointment with Lady Geraldine was so recent. Even the love of power no longer acted upon me: my power was now undisputed. My jealousy and suspicions of my agent, Mr. M'Leod, were about this time completely conquered, by his behaviour at a general election. I perceived that he had no underhand design upon my boroughs; and that he never attempted or wished to interfere in my affairs, except at my particular desire. My confidence in him became absolute and unbounded; but this was really a misfortune to me, for it became the cause of my having still less to do. I gave up all business, and from all manner of trouble I was now free: yet I became more and more unhappy, and my nervous complaints returned. I was not aware that I was taking the very means to increase my own disease. The philosophical Dr. Cullen observes, that "whatever aversion to application of any kind may appear in hypochondriacs, there is nothing more pernicious to them than absolute idleness, or a vacancy from all earnest pursuit. It is owing to wealth admitting of indolence, and leading to the pursuit of transitory and unsatisfying amusements, or exhausting pleasures only, that the present times exhibit to us so many instances of hypochondriacism."

I fancied that change of air and change of place would do me good; and, as it was fine summer weather, I projected various parties of pleasure. The Giants' Causeway, and the Lake of Killarney, were the only things I had ever heard mentioned as worth seeing in Ireland. I suffered myself to be carried into the county of Antrim, and I saw the Giants' Causeway. From the description given by Dr. Hamilton of some of these wonders of nature, the reader may judge how much I ought to have been astonished and delighted.

In the bold promontory of Bengore, you behold, as you look up from the sea, a gigantic colonnade of basaltes, supporting a black mass of irregular rock, over which rises another range of pillars, "forming altogether a perpendicular height of one hundred and seventy feet, from the base of which the promontory, covered over with rock and grass, slopes down to the sea, for the space of two hundred feet more: making, in all, a mass of near four hundred feet in height, which, in the beauty and variety of its colouring, in elegance and novelty of arrangement, and in the extraordinary magnificence of its objects, cannot be rivalled."

Yet I was seized with a fit of yawning, as I sat in my pleasure-boat, to admire this sublime spectacle. I looked at my watch, observed that we should be late for dinner, and grew impatient to be rowed back to the place where we were to dine; not that I was hungry, but I wanted to be again set in motion. Neither science nor taste expanded my view; and I saw nothing worthy of my admiration, or capable of giving me pleasure. The watching a straw floating down the tide was the only amusement I recollect to have enjoyed upon this excursion.

I was assured, however, by Lady Ormsby, that I could not help being enchanted with the Lake of Killarney. The party was arranged by this lady, who, having the preceding summer seen me captivated by Lady Geraldine, and pitying my disappointment, had formed the obliging design of restoring my spirits, and marrying me to one of her near relatives. She calculated, that as I had been charmed by Lady Geraldine's vivacity, I must be enchanted with the fine spirits of Lady Jocunda Lawler. So far were the thoughts of marriage from my imagination, that I only was sorry to find a young lady smuggled into our party, because I was afraid she would be troublesome: but I resolved to be quite passive upon all occasions, where attentions to the fair sex are sometimes expected. My arm, or my hand, or my assistance, in any manner, I was determined not to offer: the lounging indifference which some fashionable young men affect towards ladies, I really felt; and, besides, nobody minds unmarried women! This fashion was most convenient to my indolence. In my state of torpor I was not, however, long left in peace. Lady Jocunda was a high-bred romp, who made it a rule to say and do whatever she pleased. In a hundred indirect ways I was called upon to admire her charming spirits: but the rattling voice, loud laughter, flippant wit, and hoyden gaiety, of Lady Jocunda, disgusted me beyond expression. A thousand times on my journey I wished myself quietly asleep in my own castle. Arrived at Killarney, such blowing of horns, such boating, such seeing of prospects, such prosing of guides, all telling us what to admire! Then such exclamations, and such clambering! I was walked and talked till I was half-dead. I wished the rocks, and the hanging-woods, and the glens, and the water-falls, and the arbutus, and the myrtles, and the upper and lower lakes, and the islands, and Mucruss, and Mucruss Abbey, and the purple mountain, and the eagle's nest, and the Grand Turk, and the lights and the shades, and the echoes, and, above all, the Lady Jocunda, fairly at the devil.

A nobleman in the neighbourhood had the politeness to invite us to see a stag-hunt upon the water. The account of this diversion, which I had met with in my Guide to the Lakes, promised well. I consented to stay another day: that day I really was revived by this spectacle, for it was new. The sublime and the beautiful had no charms for me: novelty was the only power that could waken me from my lethargy; perhaps there was in this spectacle something more than novelty. The Romans had recourse to shows of wild beasts and gladiators to relieve their ennui. At all events, I was kept awake this whole morning, though I cannot say that I felt in such ecstasies as to be in any imminent danger of jumping out of the boat.

Of our journey back from Killarney I remember nothing, but my being discomfited by Lady Jocunda's practical jests and overpowering gaiety. When she addressed herself to me, my answers were as constrained and as concise as possible; and, as I was afterwards told, I seemed, at the close of my reply to each interrogative of her ladyship's, to answer with Odin's prophetess,

"Now my weary lips I close;
Leave me, leave me to repose."

This she never did till we parted; and, at that moment, I believe, my satisfaction appeared so visible, that Lady Ormsby gave up all hopes of me. Arrived at my own castle, I threw myself on my bed quite exhausted. I took three hours' additional sleep every day for a week, to recruit my strength, and rest my nerves, after all that I had been made to suffer by this young lady's prodigious animal spirits.

CHAPTER XIV

I could now boast that I had travelled all over Ireland, from north to south; but, in fact, I had seen nothing of the country or of its inhabitants. In these commodious parties of pleasure, every thing had been provided to prevent the obstacles that roused my faculties. Accustomed by this time to the Hibernian tone, I fancied that I knew all that could be known of the Irish character; familiarized with the comic expressions of the lower class of people, they amused me no longer. On this journey, however, I recollect making one observation, and once laughing at what I thought a practical bull. We saw a number of labourers at work in a bog, on a very hot day, with a fire lighted close to them. When I afterwards mentioned, before Mr. M'Leod, this circumstance, which I had thought absurd, he informed me that the Irish labourers often light fires, that the smoke may drive away or destroy those myriads of tiny flies, called midges, by which they are often tormented so much, that without this remedy, they would, in hot and damp weather, be obliged to abandon their work. Had I been sufficiently active during my journey to pen a journal, I should certainly, without further inquiry, have noted down, that the Irish labourers always light fires in the hottest weather to cool themselves; and thus I should have added one more to the number of cursory travellers, who expose their own ignorance, whilst they attempt to ridicule local customs, of which they have not inquired the cause, or discovered the utility.

A foreigner, who has lately written Letters on England, has given a laughable instance of this promptitude of misapprehension. He says, he had heard much of the venality of the British parliament, but he had no idea of the degree to which it extended, till he actually was an eye-witness of the scene. The moment the minister entered the House, all the members ran about exclaiming, "Places! places!" which means, Give us places—give us places.

My heavy indolence fortunately preserved me from exposing myself, like these volatile tourists. I was at least secure from the danger of making mistakes in telling what I never saw.

As to the mode of living of the Irish, their domestic comforts or grievances, their habits and opinions, their increasing or decreasing ambition to better their condition, the proportion between the population and the quantity of land cultivated or capable of cultivation, the difference between the profits of the husbandman and the artificer, the relation between the nominal wages of labour and the actual command over the necessaries of life;—these were questions wholly foreign to my thoughts, and, at this period of my life, absolutely beyond the range of my understanding. I had travelled through my own country without making even a single remark upon the various degrees of industry and civilization visible in different parts of the kingdom. In fact, it never occurred to me that it became a British nobleman to have some notion of the general state of that empire, in the legislation of which he has a share; nor had I the slightest suspicion that political economy was a study requisite or suitable to my rank in life or situation in society. Satisfied with having seen all that is worth seeing in Ireland, the Giants' Causeway and the Lake of Killarney, I was now impatient to return to England. During the rebellion, I could not, with honour, desert my post; but now that tranquillity was apparently restored, I determined to quit a country of which my partial knowledge had in every respect been unfortunate. This resolution of mine to leave Ireland threw Ellinor into despair, and she used all her eloquence to dissuade me from the journey. I was quite surprised by the agony of grief into which she was thrown by the dread of my departure. I felt astonished that one human being could be so attached to another, and I really envied her sensibility. My new man, Joe Kelly, also displayed much reluctance at the thoughts of leaving his native country; and this sentiment inclined Ellinor to think more favourably of him, though she could not quite forgive him for being a Kelly of Ballymuddy.

"Troth," said she to him one day, in my presence, "none of them Kellys of Ballymuddy but what are a bad clan! Joey, is not there your own broder's uncle lying in the jail of — at this present time for the murder of a woman?"—"Well," replied Joe, "and if he was so unfortunate to be put up, which was not asy done neither, is it not better and more creditabler to lie in a jail for a murder than a robbery, I ask you?" This new scale of crimes surprised me; but Joe spoke what was the sense of many of his countrymen at that period.

By various petty attentions, this man contrived to persuade me of the sincerity of his attachment: chiefly by the art of appearing to be managed by me in all things, he insensibly obtained power over my pride; and, by saving me daily trouble, secured considerable influence over my indolence. More than any one whom I had ever seen, he had the knack of seeming half-witted—too simple to overreach, and yet sufficiently acute and droll to divert his master. I liked to have him about me, as uncultivated kings like to have their fools. One of our ancient monarchs is said to have given three parishes to his joculator; I gave only three farms to mine. I had a sort of mean pride in making my favourite an object of envy: besides, I fell into the common mistake of the inexperienced great, who fancy that attachment can be purchased, and that gratitude can be secured, by favours disproportioned to deserts. Joe Kelly, by sundry manoeuvres too minute for description, contrived to make me delay, from day to day, the preparations for my journey to England. From week to week it was put off till the autumn was far advanced. At length Kelly had nothing left to suggest, but that it would be best to wait for answers from my English steward to the letters that had been written to inquire whether every thing was ready for my reception. During this interval, I avoided every human creature (except Joe Kelly), and was in great danger of becoming a misanthrope from mere indolence. I did not hate my fellow-creatures, but I dreaded the trouble of talking to them. My only recreation, at this period, was sauntering out in the evening beside the sea-shore. It was my regular practice to sit down upon a certain large stone, at the foot of a rock, to watch the ebbing of the tide. There was something in the contemplation of the sea and of the tides which was fascinating to my mind. I could sit and look at the ocean whole hours together; for, without any exertion of my own, I beheld a grand operation of nature, accompanied with a sort of vast monotony of motion and sound, which lulled me into reverie.

Late one evening, as I was seated on my accustomed stone, my attention was slightly diverted from the sea by the sight of a man descending the crag above me, in rather a perilous manner. With one end of a rope coiled round his body, and the other fastened to a stake driven into the summit of the rock, he let himself half-way down the terrible height. One foot now rested on a projecting point, one hand held the rope, and hanging thus midway in the air, he seemed busy searching in the crevices of the rock, for the eggs of water-fowl. This dangerous trade I had seen frequently plied on this coast, so that I should scarcely have regarded the man if he had not turned, from time to time, as if to watch me. When he saw that he had fixed my eye, he threw down, as I thought, a white stone, which fell nearly at my feet. I stooped to examine it; the man waited till he saw it in my hands, then coiled himself swiftly up his rope to the summit of the rock, and disappeared. I found a paper tied round the stone, and on this paper, in a hand-writing that seemed to be feigned, were written these words:—

"Your life and caracter, one or t'other—say both, is in danger. Don't be walking here any more late in the evening, near them caves, nor don't go near the old abbey, any time—And don't be trusting to Joe Kelly any way—Lave the kingdom entirely; the wind sarves.

"So prays your true well-wisher.

"P.S. Lave the castle the morrow, and say nothing of this to Joe Kelly, or you'll repent when it's all over wid you."

I was startled a little by this letter at first, but in half an hour I relapsed into my apathy. Many gentlemen in the country had received anonymous letters: I had been tired of hearing of them during the rebellion. This, I thought, might be only a quiz, or a trick to hurry me out of the kingdom, contrived by some of those who desired my absence. In short, the labour of thinking about the matter fatigued me. I burned the letter as soon as I got home, and resolved not to puzzle or plague myself about it any more. My steward's answer came the next morning from England; Kelly made no difficulty, when I ordered him to be ready to set out in three days. This confirmed me in my opinion that the letter was malicious, or a jest. Mr. M'Leod came to take leave of me. I mentioned the circumstance to him slightly, and in general terms: he looked very serious, and said, "All these things are little in themselves, but are to be heeded, as marking the unsettled minds of the people—straws that show which way the wind blows. I apprehend we shall have a rough winter again, though we have had so still a summer. The people about us are too hush and too prudent—it is not their natures—there's something contriving among them: they don't break one another's heads at fairs as they used to do; they keep from whiskey; there must be some strong motive working this change upon them—good or bad, 'tis hard to say which. My lord, if we consider the condition of these poor people, and if we consider the causes—"

"Oh! for Heaven's sake, do not let us consider any more about it now; I am more than half asleep already," said I, yawning; "and our considering about it can do no good, to me at least; for you know I am going out of the kingdom; and when I am gone, M'Leod, you, in whom I have implicit confidence, must manage as you always used to do, you know, and as well as you can."

"True," said M'Leod, calmly, "that is what I shall do, indubitably; for that is my duty, and since your lordship has implicit confidence in me, my pleasure. I wish your lordship a good night and a good journey."

"I shall not set out in the morning; not till the day after to-morrow, I believe," said I; "for I feel consumedly tired to-night: they have plagued me about so many things to-day; so much business always before one can get away from a place; and then Joe Kelly has no head."

"Have a care he has not too much head, my lord, as your anonymous correspondent hints—he may be right there: I told you from the first I would not go security for Joe Kelly's honesty; and where there is not strict honesty, I conceive there ought not to be implicit confidence."

"Oh, hang it! as to honesty, they are none of them honest; I know that: but would you have me plague myself till I find a strictly honest servant? Joe's as honest as his neighbours, I dare say: the fellow diverts me, and is attached to me, and that's all I can expect. I must submit to be cheated, as all men of large fortunes are, more or less."

Mr. M'Leod listened with stubborn patience, and replied, that if I thought it necessary to submit to be cheated he could make no objection, except where it might come under his cognizance, and then he must take the liberty to remonstrate, or to give up his agency to some of the many, who could play better than he could the part of the dog in the fable, pretending to guard his master's meat.

The cold ungracious integrity of this man, even in my own cause, at once excited my spleen and commanded my respect. After shaking my leg, as I sat for two minutes in silence, I called after M'Leod, who moved towards the door, "Why, what can I do, Mr. M'Leod? What would you have me do? Now, don't give me one of your dry answers, but let me have your notions as a friend: you know, M'Leod, I cannot help having the most perfect confidence in you."

He bowed, but rather stiffly.

"I am proud to hear you cannot help that, my lord," said he. "As to a friend, I never considered myself upon that footing till now: but, as you at present honour me so far as to ask my counsel, I am free to give it. Part with Joe Kelly to-night; and whether you go or stay, you are safer without him. Joe's a rogue: he can do no good, and may do harm."

"Then," said I, "you are really frightened by this anonymous letter?"

"Cannot a man take prudent precautions without being frightened?" said M'Leod.

"But have you any particular reason to believe—in short to—to think, there can be any real danger for my life?"

"No particular reason, my lord; but the general reasons I have mentioned, the symptoms among the common people lead me to apprehend there may be fresh risings of the people soon; and you, as a man of fortune and rank, must be in danger. Captain Hardcastle says that he has had informations of seditious meetings; but, he being a prejudiced man, I don't trust altogether to what he says."

"Trust altogether to what he says!" exclaimed I; "no, surely; for my part, I do not trust a word he says; and his giving it as his opinion that the people are ill-inclined would decide me to believe the exact contrary."

"It would hardly be safe to judge that way either," said M'Leod; "for that method of judging by contraries might make another's folly the master of one's own sense."

"I don't comprehend you now. Safe way of judging or not, Captain Hardcastle's opinion shall never lead mine. When I asked for your advice, Mr. M'Leod, it was because I have a respect for your understanding; but I cannot defer to Captain Hardcastle's. I am now decided in my own opinion, that the people in this neighbourhood are perfectly well-disposed; and as to this anonymous letter, it is a mere trick, depend upon it, my good sir. I am surprised that a man of your capacity should be the dupe of such a thing; I should not be surprised if Hardcastle himself, or some of his people, wrote it."

"I should," said M'Leod, coolly.

"You should!" cried I, warmly. "Why so? And why do you pronounce so decidedly, my good friend? Have not I the same means of judging as you have? unless, indeed, you have some private reason with which I am unacquainted. Perhaps," cried I, starting half up from the sofa on which I lay, charmed with a bright idea, which had just struck me, "perhaps, M'Leod, you wrote the letter yourself for a jest. Did you?"

"That's a question, my lord," said M'Leod, growing suddenly red, and snatching up his hat with a quicker motion than I ever saw from him before, "that's a question, my lord, which I must take leave not to answer; a question, give me leave to add, my Lord Glenthorn," continued he, speaking in a broader Scotch accent than I had ever heard from him before, "which I should knock my equal doon for putting to me. A M'Leod, my lord, in jest or in earnest, would scorn to write to any man breathing that letter to which he would not put his name; and more, a M'Leod would scorn to write or to say that thing, to which he ought not to put his name. Your humble servant, my Lord Glenthorn," said he, and, making a hasty bow, departed.

I called after him, and even followed him to the head of the stairs, to explain and apologize; but in vain: I never saw him angry before.

"It's very weel, my lord, it's very weel; if you say you meant nothing offensive, it's very weel; but if you think fit, my lord, we will sleep upon it before we talk any more. I am a wee bit warmer than I could wish, and your lordship has the advantage of me, in being cool. A M'Leod is apt to grow warm, when he's touched on the point of honour; and there's no wisdom in talking when a man's not his own master."

"My good friend," said I, seizing his hand as he was buttoning up his coat, "I like you the better for this warmth; but I won't let you sleep upon your wrath: you must shake hands with me before that hall-door is opened to you."

"Then so I do, for there's no standing against this frankness; and, to be as frank with you, my lord, I was wrong myself to be so testy—I ask pardon, too. A M'Leod never thought it a disgrace to crave a pardon when he was wrong."

We shook hands, and parted better friends than ever. I spoke the exact truth when I said that I liked him the better for his warmth: his anger wakened me, and gave me something to think of, and some emotion for a few minutes. Joe Kelly presently afterwards came, with the simplest face imaginable, to inquire what I had determined about the journey.

"To put it off till the day after to-morrow," said I. "Light me to bed."

He obeyed; but observed, that "it was not his fault now if there was puttings-off; for his share, every thing was ready, and he was willing and ready to follow me, at a moment's warning, to the world's end, as he had a good right to do, let alone inclination; for, parting me, he could never be right in himself: and though loth to part his country, he had rather part that nor me."

Then, without dwelling upon these expressions of attachment, he changed to a merry mood, and by his drolleries diverted me all the time I was going to bed, and at last fairly talked me asleep.


CHAPTER XV

When the first grey light of morning began to make objects indistinctly visible, I thought I saw the door of my apartment open very softly. I was broad awake, and kept my eyes fixed upon it—it opened by very slow degrees; my head was so full of visions, that I expected a ghost to enter—but it was only Ellinor.

"Ellinor!" cried I; "is it you at this time in the morning?"

"Hush! hush!" said she, shutting the door with great precaution, and then coming on tiptoe close to my bedside; "for the love of God, speak softly, and make no stir to awake them that's asleep near and too near you. It's unknown to all that I come up; for may be, when them people are awake and about, I might not get the opportunity to speak, or they might guess I knew something by my looks."

Her looks were full of terror—I was all amazement and expectation. Before she would say a word more, she searched the closets carefully, and looked behind the tapestry, as if she apprehended that she might be overheard: satisfied that we were alone, she went on speaking, but still in a voice that, with my utmost strained attention, I could but just hear.

"As you hope to live and breathe," said she, "never go again after night-fall any time walking in that lone place by the sea-shore. It's a mercy you escaped as you did; but if you go again you'll never come back alive—for never would they get you to do what they want, and to be as wicked as themselves the wicked villains!"

"Who?" said I. "What wicked villains? I do not understand you; are you in your right senses?"

"That I am, and wish you was as much in yours; but it's time yet, by the blessing of God! What wicked villains am I talking of? Of three hundred that have sworn to make you their captain, or, in case you refuse, to have your life this night. What villains am I talking of? Of him, the wickedest of all, who is now living in the very house with you, that is now lying in the very next room to you."

"Joe Kelly?"

"That same. From the first minute I saw him in the castle, I should have hated him, but for his causing you for to put off the journey to England. I never could abide him; but that blinded me, or I am sure I would have found him out long ago."

"And what have you found out concerning him?"

"That he is (speaking very low) a united-man, and stirring up the rubbles again here; and they have their meetings at night in the great cave, where the smugglers used to hide formerly, under the big rock, opposite the old abbey—and there's a way up into the abbey, that you used to be so fond of walking to, dear."

"Good Heavens! can this be true?"

"True it is, and too true, dear."

"But how did you find all this out, Ellinor?"

"It was none of I found it, nor ever could any such things have come into my head—but it pleased God to make the discovery of all by one of the childer—my own grandson—the boy you gave the gun to, long and long ago, to shoot them rabbits. He was after a hare yesterday, and it took him a chase over that mountain, and down it went and took shelter in the cave, and in went the boy after it, and as he was groping about, he lights on an old great coat; and he brought it home with him, and was showing it, as I was boiling the potatoes for their dinner yesterday, to his father forenent me; and turning the pockets inside out, what should come up but the broken head of a pipe; then he sarches in the other pocket, and finds a paper written all over—I could not read it—thank God, I never could read none of them wicked things, nor could the boy—by very great luck he could not, being no scholar, or it would be all over the country before this."

"Well, well! but what was in the paper after all? Did any body read it?"

"Ay, did they—that is, Christy read it—none but Christy—but he would not tell us what was in it—but said it was no matter, and he'd not be wasting his time reading an old song—so we thought no more, and he sent the boy up to the castle with a bill for smith's work, as soon as we had eat the potatoes, and I thought no more about any thing's being going wrong, no more than a child; and in the evening Christy said he must go to the funeral of a neighbour, and should not be home till early in the morning, may be; and it's not two hours since he came home and wakened me, and told me where he had been, which was not to the funeral at all, but to the cave where the coat was found; and he put the coat and the broken head of the pike, and the papers all in the pockets, just as we found it, in the cave—and the paper was a list of the names of them rubbles that met there, and a letter telling how they would make Lord Glenthorn their captain, or have his life; this was what made Christy to try and find out more—so he hid hisself in a hole in the side of the cave, and built hisself up with rubbish, only just leaving a place for hisself to breathe—and there he stayed till nightfall; and then on till midnight, God help us! so sure enough, them villains all come filling fast into the cave. He had good courage, God bless him for it—but he always had—and there he heard and saw all—and this was how they were talking:—First, one began by saying, how they must not be delaying longer to show themselves; they must make a rising in the country—then named the numbers in other parts that would join, and that they would not be put down so asy as afore, for they would have good leaders—then some praised you greatly, and said they was sure you favoured them in your heart, by all the ill-will you got in the county the time of the last 'ruction. But, again, others said you was milk and water, and did not go far enough, and never would, and that it was not in you, and that you was a sleepy man, and not the true thing at all, and neither beef nor vael. Again, thim that were for you spoke and said you would show yourself soon—and the others made reply, and observed you must now spake out, or never spake more; you must either head 'em, or be tramped under foot along with the rest, so it did not signify talking, and Joey Kelly should not be fribbling any more about it; and it was a wonder, said they, he was not the night at the meeting. And what was this about your being going off for England—what would they do when you was gone with M'Leod the Scotchman, to come in over them again agent, who was another guess sort of man from you, and never slept at all, and would scent 'em out, and have his corps after 'em, and that once M'Leod was master, there would be no making any head again his head; so, not to be tiring you too much with all they said, backward and forward, one that was a captain, or something that way, took the word, and bid 'em all hold their peace, for they did not know what they was talking on, and said that Joey Kelly and he had settled it all, and that the going to England was put off by Joe, and all a sham, and that when you would be walking out to-morrow at nightfall, in those lone places by the sea-side or the abbey, he and Joe was to seize upon you, and when you would be coming back near the abbey, to have you down through the trap-door into the cave, and any way they would swear you to join and head them, and if you would not, out with you, and shove you into the sea, and no more about it, for it would be give out you drown' yourself in a fit of the melancholy lunacy, which none would question, and it would be proved too you made away wid yourself, by your hat and gloves lying on the bank—Lord save us! What are you laughing at in that, when it is truth every word, and Joe Kelly was to find the body, after a great search. Well, again, say you would swear and join them, and head them, and do whatever they pleased, still that would not save you in the end; for they would quarrel with you at the first turn, because you would not be ruled by them as captain, and then they would shoot or pike you (God save the mark, dear), and give the castle to Joe Kelly, and the plunder all among 'em entirely. So it was all laid out, and they are all to meet in the cave to-morrow evening—they will go along bearing a funeral, seemingly to the abbey-ground. And now you know the whole truth, and the Lord preserve you! And what will be done? My poor head has no more power to think for you no more than an infant's, and I'm all in a tremble ever since I heard it, and afraid to meet any one lest they should see all in my face. Oh, what will become of yees now—they will be the death of you, whatever you do!"

By the time she came to these last words, Ellinor's fears had so much overpowered her, that she cried and sobbed continually, repeating—"What will be done now! What will be done! They'll surely be the death of you, whatever you do." As to me, the urgency of the danger wakened my faculties: I rose instantly, wrote a note to Mr. M'Leod, desiring to see him immediately on particular business. Lest my note should by any accident be intercepted or opened, I couched it in the most general and guarded terms; and added a request, that he would bring his last settlement of accounts with him; so that it was natural to suppose my business with him was of a pecuniary nature. I gradually quieted poor Ellinor by my own appearance of composure: I assured her, that we should take our measures so as to prevent all mischief—thanked her for the timely warning she had given me—advised her to go home before she was observed, and charged her not to speak to any one this day of what had happened. I desired that as soon as she should see Mr. M'Leod coming through the gate, she would send Christy after him to the castle, to get his bill paid; so that I might then, without exciting suspicion, talk to him in private, and we might learn from his own lips the particulars of what he saw and heard in the cavern.

Ellinor returned home, promising to obey me exactly, especially as to my injunction of secrecy—to make sure of herself she said "she would go to bed straight, and have the rheumatism very bad all day; so as not to be in a way to talk to none who would call in." The note to M'Leod was despatched by one of my grooms, and I, returning to bed, was now left at full leisure to finish my morning's nap.

Joe Kelly presented himself at the usual hour in my room; I turned my head away from him, and, in a sleepy tone, muttered that I had passed a bad night, and should breakfast in my own apartment.

Some time afterwards Mr. M'Leod arrived, with an air of sturdy pride, and produced his accounts, of which I suffered him to talk, till the servant who waited upon us had left the room; I then explained the real cause of my sending for him so suddenly. I was rather vexed, that I could not produce in him, by my wonderful narrative, any visible signs of agitation or astonishment. He calmly observed—"We are lucky to have so many hours of daylight before us. The first thing we have to do is to keep the old woman from talking."

I answered for Ellinor.

"Then the next thing is for me, who am a magistrate, to take the examinations of her son, and see if he will swear to the same that he says."

Christy was summoned into our presence, and he came with his bill for smith's work done; so that the servants could have no suspicion of what was going forward. His examinations were taken and sworn to in a few minutes: his evidence was so clear and direct, that there was no possibility of doubting the truth. The only variation between his story and his mother's report to me was as to the numbers he had seen in the cavern—her fears had turned thirteen into three hundred.

Christy assured us that there were but thirteen at this meeting, but that they said there were three hundred ready to join them.

"You were a very bold fellow, Christy," said I, "to hazard yourself in the cave with these villains; if you had been found out in your hiding-place, they would have certainly murdered you."

"True for me." said Christy; "but a man must die some way, please your honour; and where's the way I could die better? Sure, I could not but remember how good you was to me that time I was shot, and all you suffered for it! It would have been bad indeed if I would stay quiet, and let 'em murder you after all. No, no, Christy O'Donoghoe would not do that—any way. I hope, if there's to be any fighting, your honour would not wrong me so much as not to give me a blunderbush, and let me fight a bit along wid de rest for yees."

"We are not come to that yet, my good fellow," said Mr. M'Leod, who went on methodically; "if you are precipitate, you will spoil all. Go home to your forge, and work as usual, and leave the rest to us; and I promise that you shall have your share, if there is any fighting."

Very reluctantly Christy obeyed. Mr. M'Leod then deliberately settled our plan of operations. I had a fishing-lodge at a little distance, and a pleasure-boat there: to this place M'Leod was to go, as if on a fishing-party with his nephew, a young man, who often went there to fish. They were to carry with them some yeomen in coloured clothes, as their attendants, and more were to come as their guests to dinner. At the lodge there was a small four-pounder, which had been frequently used in times of public rejoicing; a naval victory, announced in the papers of the day, afforded a plausible pretence for bringing it out. We were aware that the rebels would be upon the watch, and therefore took every precaution to prevent their suspecting that we had made any discovery. Our fishing-party was to let the mock-funeral pass them quietly, to ask some trifling questions, and to give money for pipes and tobacco. Towards evening the boat, with the four-pounder on board, was to come under shore, and at a signal given by me was to station itself opposite to the mouth of the cave.

At the same signal a trusty man on the watch was to give notice to a party hid in the abbey, to secure the trap-door above. The signal was to be my presenting a pistol to the captain of the rebels, who intended to meet and seize me on my return from my evening's walk. Mr. M'Leod at first objected to my hazarding a meeting with this man; but I insisted upon it, and I was not sorry to give a public proof of my loyalty, and my personal courage. As to Joe Kelly, I also undertook to secure him.

Mr. M'Leod left me, and went to conduct his fishing-party. As soon as he was gone, I sent for Joe Kelly to play on the flute to me. I guarded my looks and voice as well as I could, and he did not see or suspect any thing—he was too full of his own schemes. To disguise his own plots he affected great gaiety; and to divert me, alternately played on the flute, and told me good stories all the morning. I would not let him leave me the whole day. Towards evening I began to talk of my journey to England, proposed setting out the next morning, and sent Kelly to look for some things in what was called the strong closet—a closet with a stout door and iron-barred windows, out of which no mortal could make his escape. Whilst he was busy searching in a drawer, I shut the door upon him, locked it, and put the key into my pocket. As I left the castle, I said in a jesting tone to some of the servants who met me—"I have locked Joe Kelly up in the strong room; if he calls to you to let him out never mind him; he will not get out till I come home from my walk—I owe him this trick." The servants thought it was some jest, and I passed on with my loaded pistols in my pocket. I walked for some time by the sea-shore, without seeing any one. At last I espied our fishing-boat, just peering out, and then keeping close to the shore. I was afraid that the party would be impatient at not seeing my signal, and would come out to the mouth of the cave, and show themselves too soon. If Mr. M'Leod had not been their commander, this, as I afterwards learned, would have infallibly happened; but he was so punctual, cool, and peremptory, that he restrained the rest of the party, declaring that, if it were till midnight, he would wait till the signal agreed upon was given. At last I saw a man creeping out of the cave—I sat down upon my wonted stone, and yawned as naturally as I could; then began to describe figures in the sand with my stick, as I was wont to do, still watching the image of the man in the water as he approached. He was muffled up in a frieze great coat; he sauntered past, and went on to a turn in the road, as if looking for some one. I knew well for whom he was looking. As no Joe Kelly came to meet him, he returned in a few minutes towards me. I had my hand upon the pistol in my pocket.

"You are my Lard Glenthorn, I presume," said he.

"I am."

"Then you will come with me, if you plase, my lard," said he.

"Make no resistance, or I will shoot you instantly," cried I, presenting my pistol with one hand, and seizing him by the collar with the other. I dragged him (for I had force enough, now my energy was roused) to the spot appointed for my signal. The boat appeared opposite the mouth of the cave. Every thing answered my expectation.

"There," said I, pointing to the boat, "there are my armed friends; they have a four-pounder—the match is ready lighted—your plot is discovered. Go in to your confederates in that cave; tell them so. The trap-door is secured above; there is no escape for them: bid them surrender: if they attempt to rush out, the grape shot will pour upon them, and they are dead men."

I cannot say that my rebel captain showed himself as stout as I could have wished, for the honour of my victory. The surprise disconcerted him totally: I felt him tremble under my grasp. He obeyed my orders—went into the cave to bring his associates to submission. His parley with them, however, was not immediately successful: I suppose there were some braver fellows than he amongst them, whose counsel might be for open war. In the mean time our yeomen landed, and surrounded the cave on all sides, so that there was no possibility of escape for those within. At last they yielded themselves our prisoners. I am sorry I have no bloody battle for the entertainment of such of my readers as like horrors; but so it was, that they yielded without a drop of blood being spilled, or a shot fired. We let them out of their hiding-place one by one, searching each as he issued forth, to be secure that they had no concealed weapons. After they had given up the arms which were concealed in the cave, the next question was, what to do with our prisoners. As it was now late, and they could not all be examined and committed with due legal form to the county gaol, Mr. M'Leod advised that we should detain them in the place they had chosen for themselves till morning. Accordingly, in the cave we again stowed them, and left a guard at each entrance to secure them for the night. We returned to the castle. I stopped at the gate to tell Ellinor and Christy that I was safe. They were sitting up watching for the news. The moment Ellinor saw me, she clasped her hands in an ecstasy of joy, but could not speak. Christy was voluble in his congratulations; but, in the midst of his rejoicing, he could not help reproaching me with forgetting to give him the blunderbush, and to let him have a bit of the fighting. "Upon my honour," said I, "there was none, or you should have been there."

"Oh, don't be plaguing and gathering round him now," said Ellinor: "sure he is tired, and look how hot—no wonder—let him get home and to bed: I'll run and warm it with the pan myself, and not be trusting them."

She would not be persuaded that I did not desire to have my bed warmed, but, by some short cut, got in before us. On entering the castle-hall, I found her, with the warming-pan in her hand, held back by the inquisitive servants, who were all questioning her about the news, of which she was the first, and not very intelligible enunciator.

I called for bread and water for my prisoner in the strong-room, and then I heard various exclamations of wonder.

"Ay, it is all true! it is no jest! Joe is at the bottom of all. I never liked Joe Kelly—I always knew Joe was not the right thing—and I always said so; and I, and I, and I. And it was but last week I was saying so: and it was but yesterday I said so and so."

I passed through the gossiping crowd with bread and water for my culprit. McLeod instantly saw and followed me.

"I will make bold to come with you," said he; "a pent rat's a dangerous animal."—I thanked him, and acquiesced; but there was no need for the precaution. When we opened the door, we found the conscience or terror-struck wretch upon his knees, and in the most abject terms he implored for mercy. From the windows of the room, which looked into the castle-yard, he had heard enough to guess all that had happened. I could not bear to look at him. After I had set down his food, he clung to my knees, crying and whining in a most unmanly manner. McLeod, with indignation, loosened him from me, threw him back, and locked the door.

"Cowardice and treachery," said he, "usually go together."

"And courage and sincerity," said I. "And now we'll go to supper, my good friends. I hope you are all as hungry as I am."

I never did eat any meal with so much appetite.

"Tis a pity, my lord," said McLeod, "but that there was a conspiracy against you every day of your life, it seems to do you so much good."

## CHAPTER XVI

"What new wonders? What new misfortunes, Ellinor?" said I, as Ellinor, with a face of consternation, appeared again in the morning in my room, just as I was going down to breakfast: "what new misfortunes, Ellinor?"

"Oh! the worst that could befall me!" cried she, wringing her hands; "the worst, the very worst!—to be the death of my own child!" said she, with inexpressible horror. "Oh! save him! save him! for the love of heaven, dear, save him! If you don't save him, 'tis I shall be his death."

She was in such agony, that she could not explain herself farther for some minutes.

"It was I gave the information against them all to you. But how could I ever have thought Owen was one of them? My son, my own son, the unfortunate cratur; I never thought but what he was with the militia far away. And how could it ever come into my head that Owen could have any hand in a thing of the kind?"

"But I did not see him last night," interrupted I.

"Oh! he was there! One of his own friends, one of the military that went with you, saw him among the prisoners, and came just now to tell me of it. That Owen should be guilty of the like!—Oh! what could have come over him! He must have been out of his rason. And against you to be plotting! That's what I never will believe, if even I'd hear it from himself. But he's among them that were taken last night. And will I live to see him go to gaol?—and will I live to see—No, I'd rather die first, a thousand and a thousand times over. Oh! for mercy's sake!" said she, dropping on her knees at my feet, "have pity on me, and don't let the blood of my own child be upon me in my old days."

"What would you have me do, Ellinor?" said I, much moved by her distress.

"There is but one thing to do," said she. "Let him off: sure a word from you would be enough for the soldiers that are over them on guard. And Mr. McLeod has not yet seen him; and if he was just let escape, there would be no more about it; and I'd I engage he shall fly the country, the unfortunate cratur! and never trouble you more. This is all I ask: and sure, dear, you can't refuse it to your own Ellinor; your old nurse, that carried ye in her arms, and fed ye with her milk, and watched over ye many's the long night, and loved ye; ay, none ever loved, or could love ye so well."

"I am sensible of it; I am grateful," interrupted I; "but what you ask of me, Ellinor, is impossible—I cannot let him escape; but I will do my utmost."

"Troth, nothing will save him, if you would not say the word for him now. Ah! why cannot you let him off, then?"

"I should lose my honour; I should lose my character. You know that I have been accused of favouring the rebels already—you saw the consequences of my protecting your other son, though he was innocent and injured, and bore an excellent character."

"Christy; ay, true: but poor Owen, unlucky as he is, and misguided, has a better claim upon you."

"How can that be? Is not the other my foster-brother, in the first place?"

"True for him."

"And had not I proofs of his generous conduct and attachment to me?"

"Owen is naturally fonder of you by a great deal," interrupted she; "I'll answer for that."

"What! when he has just been detected in conspiring against my life?"

"That's what I'll never believe," cried Ellinor, vehemently: "that he might be drawn in, may be, when out of his rason—he was always a wild boy—to be a united-man, and to hope to get you for his captain, might be the case, and bad enough that; but, jewel, you'll find he did never conspire against you: I'd lay down my life upon that."

She threw herself again at my feet, and clung to my knees.

"As you hope for mercy yourself in this world, or the world to come, show some now, and do not be so hard-hearted as to be the death of both mother and son."

Her supplicating looks and gestures, her words, her tears, moved me so much, that I was on the point of yielding; but recollecting what was due to justice and to my own character, with an effort of what I thought virtuous resolution, I repeated, "It is impossible: my good Ellinor, urge me no farther: ask any thing else, and it shall be granted, but this is impossible."

As I spoke, I endeavoured to raise her from the ground; but with the sudden force of angry despair, she resisted.

"No, you shall not raise me," cried she. "Here let me lie, and break my heart with your cruelty! 'Tis a judgment upon me—it's a judgment, and it's fit I should feel it as I do. But you shall feel too, in spite of your hard heart. Yes, your heart is harder than the marble: you want the natural touch, you do; for your mother has knelt at your feet, and you have denied her prayer."

"My mother!"

"And what was her prayer?—to save the life of your brother."

"My brother! Good heavens! what do I hear?"

"You hear the truth: you hear that I am your lawful mother. Yes, you are my son. You have forced that secret from me, which I thought to have carried with me to my grave. And now you know all: and now you know how wicked I have been, and it was all for you; for you that refused me the only thing ever I asked, and that, too, in my greatest distress, when my heart was just breaking: and all this time too, there's Christy—poor good Christy; he that I've wronged, and robbed of his rightful inheritance, has been as a son, a dutiful good son to me, and never did he deny me any thing I could ask; but in you I have found no touch of tenderness. Then it's fit I should tell you again, and again, and again, that he who is now slaving at the forge, to give me the earnings of his labour; he that lives, and has lived all his days, upon potatoes and salt, and is content; he who has the face and the hands so disguised with the smoke and the black, that yourself asked him t'other day did he ever wash his face since he was born—I tell ye, he it is who should live in this castle, and sleep on that soft bed, and be lord of all here—he is the true and real Lord Glenthorn, and to the wide world I'll make it known. Ay, be pale and tremble, do; it's your turn now: I've touched you now: but it's too late. In the face of day I shall confess the wrong I've done; and I shall call upon you to give back to him all that by right is his own."

Ellinor stopped short, for one of my servants at this instant came into the room.

"My lord, Mr. McLeod desires me to let you know the guard has brought up the prisoners, and he is going to commit them to gaol, and would be glad to know if you choose to see them first, my lord."

Stupified by all I had just heard, I could only reply, that I would come presently. Ellinor rushed past the servant,—"Are they come?" cried she. "Where will I get a sight of them?" I stayed for a few minutes alone, to decide upon what I ought to say and do. A multitude of ideas, more than had ever come in my mind in a twelvemonth, passed through it in these few minutes.

As I was slowly descending the great staircase, Ellinor came running, as fast as she could run, to the foot of the stairs, exclaiming, "It's a mistake! it's all a mistake, and I was a fool to believe them that brought me the word. Sure Ody's not there at all! nor ever was in it. I've seen them all, face to face; and my son's not one of them, nor ever was: and I was a fool from beginning to end—and I beg your pardon entirely," whispered she, coming close to my ear: "I was out of my reason at the thought of that boy's being to suffer, and I, his mother, the cause of it. Forgive all I said in my passion, my own best jewel: you was always good and tender to me, and be the same still, dear. I'll never say a word more about it to any one living: the secret shall die with me. Sure, when my conscience has borne it so long, it may strive and bear it a little longer for your sake: and it can't be long I have to live, so that will make all easy. Hark! they are asking for you. Do you go your ways into the great parlour, to Mr. McLeod, and think no more of any thing at all but joy. My son's not one of them! I must go to the forge, and tell Christy the good news."

Ellinor departed, quite satisfied with herself, with me, and with all the world. She took it for granted that she left me in the same state of mind, and that I should obey her injunctions, and think of nothing but joy. Of what happened in the great parlour, and of the examinations of the prisoners, I have but a confused recollection. I remember that Mr. McLeod seemed rather surprised by my indifference to what concerned me so nearly; and that he was obliged to do all the business himself. The men were, I believe, all committed to gaol, and Joe Kelly turned king's evidence; but as to any further particulars, I know no more than if I had been in a dream. The discovery which Ellinor had just made to me engrossed all my powers of attention.


CHAPTER XVII

"Le vrai n'est pas toujours vraisemblable," says an acute observer of human affairs. The romance of real life certainly goes beyond all other romances; and there are facts which few writers would dare to put into a book, as there are skies which few painters would venture to put into a picture.

When I had leisure to reflect, I considered, that as yet I had no proof of the truth of Ellinor's strange story, except her own assertions. I sent for her again, to examine her more particularly. I was aware that, if I alarmed her, I should so confuse her imagination, that I should never obtain the truth; therefore I composed myself, and assumed my usual external appearance of nonchalance. I received her lolling upon my sofa, as usual, and I questioned her merely as if to gratify an idle curiosity.

"Troth, dear," said she, "I'll tell you the whole story how it was, to make your mind asy, which, God knows, mine never was, from that minute it first came into my head, till this very time being. You mind the time you got the cut in your head—no, not you, jewel; but the little lord that was then, Christy there below that is.—Well, the cut was a terrible cut as ever you seen, got by a fall on the fender from the nurse's arms, that was drunk, three days after he was born."

"I remember to have heard my father talk of some accident of this sort, which happened to me when I was an infant."

"Ay, sure enough it did, and that was what first put him in the notion of taking the little lord out of the hands of the Dublin nurse-tenders, and them that were about my Lady Glenthom, and did not know how to manage her, which was the cause of her death: and he said he'd have his own way about his son and heir any way, and have him nursed by a wholesome woman in a cabin, and brought up hardy, as he, and the old lord, and all the family, were before him. So with that he sends for me, and he puts the young lord, God bless him, into my arms himself, and a donny thing he was that same time to look at, for he was but just out of the surgeon's hands, the head just healed and scarred over like; and my lord said there should be no more doctors never about him. So I took him, that is, Christy, and you, to a house at the sea, for the salt water, and showed him every justice; and my lord often came to see him whilst he was in the country; but then he was off, after a time, to Dublin, and I was in a lone place, where nobody came, and the child was very sick with me, and you was all the time as fine and thriving a child as ever you see; and I thought, to be sure, one night, that he would die wid me. He was very bad, very bad indeed; and I was sitting up in bed, rocking him backwards and forwards this ways: I thought with myself, what a pity it was, the young lord should die, and he an only son and heir, and the estate to go out of the family the Lord knows where; and then the grief the father would be in: and then I thought how happy he would be if he had such a fine babby as you, dear; and you was a fine babby to be sure: and then I thought how happy it would be for you, if you was in the place of the little lord: and then it came into my head, just like a shot, where would be the harm to change you? for I thought the real lord would surely die; and then, what a gain it would be to all, if it was never known, and if the dead child was carried to the grave, since it must go, as only poor Ellinor O'Donoghoe's, and no more about it. Well, if it was a wicked thought, it was the devil himself put it in my head, to be sure; for, only for him, I should never have had the sense to think of such a thing, for I was always innocent like, and not worldly given. But so it was, the devil put it in my head, and made me do it, and showed me how, and all in a minute. So, I mind, your eyes and hair were both of the very same colour, dear; and as to the rest, there's no telling how those young things alter in a few months, and my lord would not be down from Dublin in a hurry, so I settled it all right; and as there was no likelihood at all the real lord would live, that quieted my conscience; for I argued, it was better the father should have any sort of child at all than none. So, when my lord came down, I carried him the child to see, that is you, jewel. He praised me greatly for all the care I had taken of his boy; and said, how finely you was come on! and I never see a father in greater joy; and it would have been a sin, I thought, to tell him the truth, after he took the change that was put upon him so well, and it made him so happy like. Well, I was afeard of my life he'd pull off the cap to search for the scar, so I would not let your head be touched any way, dear, saying it was tinder and soft still with the fall, and you'd cry if the cap was stirred; and so I made it out indeed, very well; for, God forgive me, I twitched the string under your chin, dear, and made you cry like mad, when they would come to touch you. So there was no more about it, and I had you home to myself, and, all in good time, the hair grew, and fine thick hair it was, God bless you; and so there was no more about it, and I got into no trouble at all, for it all fell out just as I had laid it out, except that the real little young lord did not die as I thought; and it was a wonder but he did, for you never saw none so near death, and backwards and forwards, what turns of sickness he took with me for months upon months, and year after year, so that none could think, no more than me, there was any likelihood at all of rearing him to man's estate. So that kept me easier in my mind concerning what I'd done; for as I kept saying to myself, better the family should have an heir to the estate, suppose not the right, than none at all; and if the father, nor nobody, never found it out, there was he and all the family made happy for life, and my child made a lord of, and none the wiser or the worse. Well, so I down-argued my conscience; and any way I took to little Christy, as he was now to be called—and I loved him, all as one as if he was my own—not that he was ever as well-looking as Ody, or any of the childer I had, but I never made any differ betwixt him and any of my own—he can't say as I did, any how, and he has no reason to complain of my being an unnat'ral mother to him, and being my foster-child I had a right to love him as I did, and I never wronged him in any way, except in the one article of changing him at nurse, which he being an infant, and never knowing, wa" never a bit the worse for, nor never will, now. So all's right^ dear, and make your mind asy, jewel; there's the whole truth of the story, for you."

"But it is a very strange story, Ellinor, after all, and—and I have only your word for it, and may be you are only taking advantage of my regard for you to make me believe you."

"What is it, plase your honour?" said she, stepping forward, as if she did not hear or understand me.

"I say, Ellinor, that after all I have no proof of the truth of this story, except your word."

"And is not that enough? and where's the use of having more? but if it will make you asy, sure I can give you proof—sure need you go farther than the scar on his head? If he was shaved to-morrow, I'd engage you'd see it fast enough. But sure, can't you put your hand up to your head this minute, and feel there never was no scar there, nor if all the hair you have, God save the mark, was shaved this minute, never a bit of a scar would be to be seen: but proof is it you want?—why, there's the surgeon that dressed the cut in the child's head, before he ever came to me; sure he's the man that can't forget it, and that will tell all: so to make your mind asy, see him, dear; but for your life don't let him see your head to feel it, for he'd miss the scar, and might suspect something by your going to question him."

"Where does he live?" interrupted I.

"Not above twelve miles off."

"Is he alive?"

"Ay, if he been't dead since Candlemas."

At first I thought of writing to this man; but afterwards, being afraid of committing myself by writing, I went to him: he had long before this time left off business, and had retired to enjoy his fortune in the decline of life. He was a whimsical sort of character; he had some remains of his former taste for anatomy, and was a collector of curiosities. I found him just returned from a lake which he had been dragging for a moose-deer's horns, to complete the skeleton of a moose-deer, which he had mounted in his hall. I introduced myself, desiring to see his museum, and mentioned to him the thigh-bone of a giant found in ray neighbourhood; then by favour of this bone I introduced the able cure that he had made of a cut in my head, when I was a child.

"A cut in your head, sir? Yes, my lord, I recollect perfectly well, it was a very ugly cut, especially in an infant's head; but I am glad to find you feel no bad effects from it. Have you any cicatrice on the place?—Eleven feet high, did you say? and is the giant's skeleton in your neighbourhood?"

I humoured his fancy, and by degrees he gave me all the information I wanted without in the least suspecting my secret motives. He described the length, breadth, and depth, of the wound to me; showed me just where it was on the head, and observed that it must have left an indelible mark, but that my fine hair covered it. When he seemed disposed to search for it, I defended myself with the giant's thigh-bone, and warded off his attacks most successfully. To satisfy myself upon this point, I affected to think that he had not been paid: he said he had been amply paid, and he showed me his books to prove it. I examined the dates, and found that they agreed with Ellinor's precisely. On my return home, the first thing I did was to make Christy a present of a new wig, which I was certain would induce him to shave his head; for the lower Irish agree with the beaux and belles of London and Paris, in preferring wigs to their own hair. Ellinor told me, that I might safely let his head be shaved, because to her certain knowledge, he had scars of so many cuts which he had received at fairs upon his skull, that there would appear nothing particular in one more or less. As soon as the head was shaved, and the wig was worn, I took an opportunity one day of stopping at the forge to have one of my horse's shoes changed; and whilst this was doing, I took notice of his new wig, and how well it fitted him. As I expected, he took it off to show it me better, and to pay his own compliments to it.

"Sure enough, you are a very fine wig," said he, apostrophising it as he held it up on the end of his hammer; "and God bless him that give it me, and it fits me as if it was nailed to my head."

"You seem to have had a good many nails in your head already, Christy," said I, "if one may judge by all these scars."

"Oh yes, please your honour, my lord," said he, "there's no harm in them neither; they are scratches got when I was no wiser than I should be, at fairs, fighting with the boys of Shrawd-na-scoob."

Whilst he fought his battles o'er again, I had leisure to study his head; and I traced precisely all the boundary lines. The situation, size, and figure of the cicatrice, which the surgeon and Ellinor had described to me, were so visible and exact, that no doubt could remain in my mind of Christy's being the real son of the late Lord and Lady Glenthorn. This conviction was still more impressed upon my mind a few days afterwards. I recollected having seen a file of family pictures in a lumber-room in the castle; and I rummaged them out to see if I could discover amongst them any likeness to Christy: I found one; the picture of my grandfather,—I should say, of his grandfather, to which Christy bore a striking resemblance, when I saw him with his face washed, and in his Sunday clothes.

My mind being now perfectly satisfied of the truth of Ellinor's story, I was next to consider how I ought to act. To be or not to be Lord Glenthorn, or, in other words, to be or not to be a villain, was now the question. I could not dissemble to my conscience this plain state of the case, that I had no right to keep possession of that which I knew to be another's lawful property; yet, educated as I had been, and accustomed to the long enjoyment of those luxuries, which become necessaries to the wealthy; habituated to attendance as I had been; and, even amongst the dissipated and idle, notorious for extravagance the most unbounded and indolence the most inveterate; how was I at once to change my habits, to abdicate my rank and power, to encounter the evils of poverty? I was not compelled to make such sacrifices; for though Ellinor's transient passion had prompted her to threaten me with a public discovery, yet I knew that she would as soon cut off her own right hand as execute her threats. Her affection for me, and her pride in my consequence, were so strong, that I knew I might securely rely upon her secrecy. The horrid idea of being the cause of the death of one of her own children had for a moment sufficient power to balance her love for me; yet there was but little probability that any similar trial should occur, nor had I reason to apprehend that the reproaches of her conscience should induce her to make a voluntary discovery; for all her ideas of virtue depended on the principle of fidelity to the objects of her affection, and no scrupulous notions of justice disturbed her understanding or alarmed her self-complacency. Conscious that she would willingly sacrifice all she had in the world for any body she loved, and scarcely comprehending that any one could be selfish, she, in a confused way, applied the maxim of "Do as you would be done by," and was as generous of the property of others as of her own. At the worst, if a law-suit commenced against me, I knew that possession was nine points of the law. I also knew that Ellinor's health was declining, and that the secret would die with her. Unlawful possession of the wealth I enjoyed could not, however, satisfy my own mind; and, after a severe conflict between my love of ease and my sense of right—between my tastes and my principles—I determined to act honestly and honourably, and to relinquish what I could no longer maintain without committing injustice, and feeling remorse. I was, perhaps, the more ready to do rightly because I felt that I was not compelled to it. The moment when I made this virtuous decision was the happiest I had at that time ever felt: my mind seemed suddenly relieved from an oppressive weight; my whole frame glowed with new life; and the consciousness of courageous integrity elevated me so much in my own opinion, that titles, and rank, and fortune, appeared as nothing in my estimation. I rang my bell eagerly, and ordered that Christy O'Donoghoe should be immediately sent for. The servant went instantly; but it seemed to me an immoderately long time before Christy arrived. I walked up and down the room impatiently, and at last threw myself at full length upon the sofa: the servant returned.

"The smith is below in the hall, my lord."

"Show him up."—He was shown up into the ante-chamber.

"The smith is at the door, my lord."

"Show him in, cannot you? What detains him?"

"My brogues, my lord! I'd be afraid to come in with 'em on the carpet." Saying this, Christy came in, stepping fearfully, astonished to find himself in a splendid drawing-room.

"Were you never in this room before, Christy?" said I.

"Never, my lord, plase your honour, barring the day I mended the bolt."

"It is a fine room, is not it, Christy?"

"Troth, it is the finest ever I see, sure enough."

"How should you like to have such a room of your own, Christy?"

"Is it I, plase your honour?" replied he, laughing; "what should I do with the like?"

"How should you feel if you were master of this great castle?"

"It's a poor figure I should make, to be sure," said he, turning his head over his shoulder towards the door, and resting upon the lock: "I'd rather be at the forge by a great dale."

"Are you sure of that, Christy? Should not you like to be able to live without working any more, and to have horses and servants of your own?"

"What would I do with them, plase your honour, I that have never been used to them? sure they'd all laugh at me, and I'd not be the better o' that, no more than of having nothing to do; I that have been always used to the work, what should I do all the day without it? But sure, my lord," continued he, changing his voice to a more serious tone, "the horse that I shod yesterday for your honour did not go lame, did he?"

"The horse is very well shod, I believe; I have not ridden him since: I know nothing of the matter."

"Because I was thinking, may be, it was that made your honour send for me up in the hurry—I was afeard I'd find your honour mad with me; and I'd be very sorry to disoblige you, my lord; and I'm glad to see your honour looking so well after all the trouble you've been put to by them rubbles, the villains, to be consarting against you under-ground. But, thanks be to God, you have 'em all in gaol now. I thought my mother would have died of the fright she took, when the report came that Ody was one of them. I told her there could not be no truth in it at all, but she would not mind me: it would be a strange unnatural thing, indeed, of any belonging to her to be plotting against your honour. I knew Ody could not be in it, and be a brother of mine; and that's what I kept saying all the time but she never heeded me: for, your honour knows, when the women are frighted, and have taken a thing into their heads, you can't asy get it out again."

"Very true: but to return to what I was saying, should not you like to change places with me, if you could?"

"Your honour, my lord, is a very happy jantleman, and a very good jantleman, there's no doubt, and there's few but would be proud to be like you in any thing at all."

"Thank you for that compliment. But now, in plain English, as to yourself, would you like to be in my place—to change places with me?"

"In your honour's place—I! I would not, my lord; and that's the truth, now," said he, decidedly. "I would not: no offence—your honour bid me to speak the truth; for I've all I want in the world, a good mother, and a good wife, and good childer, and a reasonable good little cabin, and my little pratees, and the grazing of the cow, and work enough always, and not called on to slave, and I get my health, thank God for all; and what more could I have if I should be made a lord to-morrow? Sure, my good woman would never make a lady; and what should I do with her? I'd be grieved to see her the laughing-stock of high and low, besides being the same myself, and my boy after me. That would never answer for me; so I am not like them that would overturn all to get uppermost; I never had any hand, art, or part, in a thing of the kind; I always thought and knew I was best as I am; not but what, if I was to change with any, it is with you, my lord, I would be proud to change; because if I was to be a jantleman at all, I'd wish to be of a ra-al good ould family born."

"You are then what you wish to be?" said I.

"Och!" said he, laughing and scratching his head, "your honour's jesting me about them kings of Ireland, that they say the O'Donoghoes was once: but that's what I never think on, that's all idle talk for the like of me, for sure that's a long time ago, and what use going back to it? One might as well be going back to Adam, that was the father of all, but which makes no differ now."

"But you do not understand me," interrupted I; "I am not going back to the kings of Ireland: I mean to tell you, that you were born a gentleman—nay, I am perfectly serious; listen to me."

"I do, plase your honour, though it is mocking me, I know you are; I would be sorry not to take a joke as well as another."

"This is no joke; I repeat that I am serious. You are not only a gentleman, but a nobleman: to you this castle and this great estate belongs, and to you they shall be surrendered."

He stood astonished; and, his eyes opening wide, showed a great circle of white in his black face.

"Eh!" cried he, drawing that long breath, which astonishment had suppressed. "But how can this be?"

"Your mother can explain better than I can: your mother, did I say? she is not your mother; Lady Glenthorn was your mother."

"I can't understand it at all—I can't understand it at all. I'll lave it all to your honour," said he, making a motion with his hands, as if to throw from him the trouble of comprehending it.

"Did you never hear of such a thing as a child's being changed at nurse?"

"I did, plase your honour; but my mother would never do the like, I'll answer for her, any way; and them that said any thing of the kind, belied her; and don't be believing them, my lord."

"But Ellinor was the person who told me this secret."

"Was she so? Oh, she must have been draaming; she was always too good a mother to me to have sarved me so. But," added he, struggling to clear his intellects, "you say it's not my mother she is; but whose mother is she then? Can it be that she is yours? 'tis not possible to think such a great lord was the son of such as her, to look at you both: and was you the son of my father Johnny O'Donoghoe? How is that again?"

He rubbed his forehead; and I could scarcely forbear laughing at his odd perplexity, though the subject was of such serious importance. When he clearly understood the case, and thoroughly believed the truth, he did not seem elated by this sudden change of fortune; he really thought more of me than of himself.

"Well, I'll tell you what you will do then," continued he, after a pause of deep reflection; "say nothing to nobody, but just keep asy on, even as we are. Don't let there be any surrendering at all, and I'll speak to my mother, that is, Ellinor O'Donoghoe, and settle it so; and let it be so settled, in the name of God, and no more about it: and none need never be the wiser; 'tis so best for all. A good day to your honour, and I'll go shoe the mare."

"Stay," said I; "you may hereafter repent of this sudden determination. I insist upon your taking four-and-twenty hours—no, that would be too little—take a month to consider of it coolly, and then let me know your final determination."

"Oh! plase your honour, I will say the same then as now. It would be a poor thing indeed of me, after all you done for me and mine, to be putting you to more trouble. It would be a poor thing of me to forget how you liked to have lost your life all along with me at the time of the 'ruction. No, I'll not take the fortin from you, any how."

"Put gratitude to me out of the question," said I. "Far be it from me to take advantage of your affectionate temper. I do not consider you as under any obligations to me; nor will I be paid for doing justice."

"Sure enough, your honour desarved to be born a gentleman," said Christy.

"At least I have been bred a gentleman," said I. "Let me see you again this day month, and not till then."

"You shall not—that is, you shall, plase your honour: but for fear any one would suspect any thing, I'd best go shoe the mare, any way."

## CHAPTER XVIII

*"What riches give us, let us then inquire—*
*Meat, fire, and clothes—What more?—Meat, clothes, and fire."*

The philosophy we learn from books makes but a faint impression upon the mind, in comparison with that which we are taught by our own experience; and we sometimes feel surprised to find that what we have been taught as maxims of morality prove true in real life. After having had, for many years, the fullest opportunities of judging of the value of riches, when I reflected upon my past life, I perceived that their power of conferring happiness is limited, nearly as the philosophic poet describes; that all the changes and modifications of luxury must, in the sum of actual physical enjoyment, be reduced to a few elementary pleasures, of which the industrious poor can obtain their share: a small share, perhaps; but then it is enjoyed with a zest that makes it equal in value perhaps to the largest portion offered to the sated palate of ennui. These truths are as old as the world; but they appeared quite new to me, when I discovered them by my own experience.

During the month which I had allowed to my foster-brother for reflection, I had leisure to philosophize, and my understanding made a rapid progress. I foresaw the probability of Christy's deciding to become Earl of Glenthorn; notwithstanding that his good sense had so clearly demonstrated to him in theory, that, with his education and habits, he must be happier working in his forge than he could be as lord of Glenthorn Castle. I was not dismayed by the idea of losing my wealth and rank; I was pleased with myself for my honest conduct, and conscious of a degree of pleasure from my own approbation, superior to what my riches had ever procured.

The day appointed for Christy's final determination arrived. I knew by the first motion of his shoulder as he came into the room, what his decision would be.

"Well, Christy," said I, "you will be Earl of Glenthorn, I perceive. You are glad now that I did not take you at your word, and that I gave you a month's time for consideration."

"Your honour was always considerate; but if I'd wish now to be changing my mind," said he, hesitating, and shifting from leg to leg, "it is not upon my own account, any way, but upon my son Johnny's."

"My good friend," said I, "no apology is necessary. I should be very unjust if I were offended by your decision, and very mean if, after the declarations I have made, I could, for an instant, hesitate to restore to you that property which it is your right and your choice to reclaim."

Christy made a low bow, and seemed much at a loss what he was to say next.

"I hope," continued I, "that you will be as happy when you are Earl of Glenthorn, as you have been as Christy O'Donoghoe."

"May be not, plase your honour; but I trust my childer will be happy after me; and it's them and my wife I'm thinking of, as in duty bound. But it is hard your honour should be astray for want of the fortin you've been bred to; and this weighs with me greatly on the other side. If your honour could live on here, and share with us—But I see your honour's displeased at my naming that. It was my wife thought o' that; I knew it could not do. But then, what I think is, that your honour should name what you would be pleased to keep to live upon: for, to be sure, you have a right to live as a gentleman, that have always lived as one, as every body knows, and none better than I. Would your honour be so kind, then, as just to put down on a bit of paper what you'd wish to keep; and that same, whatever it is, none shall touch but yourself; and I would not own a child for mine that would begrudge it you. I'll step down and wait below while your honour writes what you plase."

The generosity of this man touched me to the heart. I accepted from him three hundred a year; and requested that the annuity I allowed to the unfortunate Lady Glenthorn might be continued; that the house which I had built for Ellinor, and the land belonging to it, might be secured to her rent-free for life; and that all my debts should be paid. I recommended Mr. M'Leod in the strongest manner, as an agent whose abilities and integrity would be to him an invaluable treasure.

Christy, when I gave him the paper on which I had stated these requests, took a pen instantly, and would have signed his name without reading it; but to this I absolutely objected.

"Well, then," said he, "I'll take it home, and read it over, and take time, as you desire, to consider. There's no danger of my changing my mind about this: I hope your honour can't think there is."

The next day, on returning it to me, he observed, that it was making very little of him to put down only such a trifle; and he pressed me to make the hundreds thousands:—this I refused.

"But I hope your honour won't object to what I am going to propose. Is not there a house in London? and is not there another in England, in the country? and, sure, I and mine can't live there and here and every where at once: if you'd just condescend to occupy one of them, you'd do me a great pleasure, and a great sarvice too; for every thing would be right, instead of going wrong, as it might under an agent, and me at a distance, that does not know well how to manage such great estates. I hope you'll not refuse me that, if it's only to show me I don't lose your honour's good-will."

The offer was made with so much earnestness, and even delicacy, that I could not abruptly refuse it at the moment, though one of these magnificent houses could be of no use tome with an income of 300l. per annum.

"As to the annuity," continued Christy, "that shall be paid as punctual as the day: Mr. M'Leod will pay it; and he shall have it all settled right, and put upon a stamp, by the lawyers, in case any thing should happen me. Then, as to Ellinor, sure, she is my mother, for I never can think of her any other way; and, except in that single article of changing me at nurse, was always the best of mothers to me. And even that same trick she played me, though very wicked, to be sure, was very nat'ral—ay, very nat'ral—to prefar her own flesh and blood if she could: and no one could be more sorry for the wrong she did me than she is now: there she is crying at home, ready to break her heart: but as I tell her, there's no use in repenting a thing when once it is done; and as I forgive her, none can ever bring it up against her: and as to the house and farm, she shall surely have that, and shall never want for any thing. So I hope your honour's mind will be asy on that matter; and whatever else you recollect to wish, that shall be done, if in my power."

It is with pleasure that I recollect and record all these instances of goodness of heart in poor Christy, which, notwithstanding the odd mixture of absurdity and sense in his language and ideas, will, I make no doubt, please my readers, though they cannot affect them as much as they affected me. I now prepared for my departure from Glenthorn Castle, never more to return. To spare me from unnecessary mortification, Christy had the wonderful self-command to keep the secret faithfully, so that none of the people in the neighbourhood, nor even my servants, had the slightest idea of the truth. Having long talked of returning to England, the preparations for my journey excited no surprise. Every thing went on as usual, except that Christy, instead of being at the forge, was almost every day at the whiskey-shop.

I thought it proper to speak openly of my affairs to Mr. M'Leod: he was the only person who could make out a correct list of my debts. Besides, I wished to recommend him as agent to the future earl, to whom an honest and able agent would be peculiarly necessary, ignorant, as he was, both of the world and of business; and surrounded, as he must probably be, on his accession to his estate, by a herd of vulgar and designing flatterers.

Albeit not easily moved to surprise, Mr. M'Leod really did, for an instant, look astonished, when I informed him that Christy O'Donoghoe was Earl of Glenthorn. But I must resolve not to stop to describe the astonishment that each individual showed upon this occasion, else I shall never have finished my story.

It was settled that Mr. M'Leod should continue agent; and, for his credit, I must observe that, after he was made acquainted with my loss of rank and fortune, he treated me with infinitely more respect and regard than he had ever shown me whilst he considered me only as his employer. Our accounts were soon settled; and when this was done, and they were all regularly signed, Mr. M'Leod came up to me, and, in a low voice of great emotion, said, "I am not a man of professions; but when I say I am a man's friend, I hope I shall ever be found to be so, as far as can be in my power: and I cannot but esteem and admire the man who has acted so nobly as you have done."

M'Leod wrung my hand as he spoke, and the tears stood in his eyes. I knew that the feeling must indeed be strong, which could extort from him even these few words of praise, and this simple profession of regard; but I did not know, till long afterwards, the full warmth of his affections and energy of his friendship. The very next day, unfortunately for me, he was obliged to go to Scotland, to his mother, who was dying: and at this time I saw no more of him.

In due legal form I now made a surrender of all claim upon the hereditary property of the Earl of Glenthorn, and every thing was in readiness for my journey. During this time poor Ellinor never appeared at the castle. I went to see her, to comfort her about my going away; but she was silent, and seemingly sullen, and would not be comforted.

"I've enough to grieve me," said she: "I know what will be the end of all; I see it as plain as if you'd told me. There's no hiding nothing from a mother: no, there's no use in striving to comfort me." Every method which I tried to console her seemed to grieve her more.

The day before that which was fixed for my departure, I sent to desire to see her. This request I had repeatedly made; but she had, from day to day, excused herself, saying that she was unwell, and that she would be up on the morrow. At last she came; and though but a few days had elapsed since I had seen her, she was so changed in her appearance, that I was shocked the moment I beheld her countenance.

"You don't look well, Ellinor," said I: "sit down."

"No matter whether I sit or stand," said she, calmly; "I'm not long for this world: I won't live long after you are gone, that's one comfort."

Her eyes were fixed and tearless; and there was a dead unnatural tranquillity in her manner.

"They are making a wonderful great noise nailing up the boxes, and I seen them cording the trunks as I came through the hall. I asked them, could I be of any use: but they said I could be of none, and that's true; for, when I put my hand to the cord, to pull it, I had no more strength than an infant. It was seven-and-twenty years last Midsummer-day since I first had you an infant in my arms. I was strong enough then, and you—was a sweet babby. Had I seen that time all that would come to pass this day! But that's over now. I have done a wicked thing; but I'll send for Father Murphy, and get absolution before I die."

She sighed deeply, then went on speaking more quickly.

"But I can do nothing until you go. What time will you go in the morning, dear? It's better go early. Is it in the coach you'll go? I see it in the yard. But I thought you must leave the coach, with all the rest, to the rightful heir. But my head's not clear about it all, I believe—and no matter."

Her ideas rambled from one subject to another in an unconnected manner. I endeavoured in vain to recall her understanding by speaking of her own immediate interests; of the house that was secured to her for life; and of the promise that had been made me, that she should never want for any thing, and that she should be treated with all possible kindness. She seemed to listen to me; but showed that she did not comprehend what I said, by her answers; and, at every pause I made, she repeated the same question—

"What time will you go in the morning, dear?"

At last I touched her feelings, and she recovered her intellect, when I suddenly asked, if she would accompany me to England the next morning.

"Ay, that I will," cried she, "go with you through the wide world."

She burst into tears, and wept bitterly for some time.

"Ah! now I feel right again," said she; "this is what I wanted; but could not cry this many a day—never since the word came to me that you was going, and all was lost."

I assured her that I now expected to be happier than I had ever been.

"Oh!" cried she: "and have you never been happy all this time? What a folly it was for me, then, to do so wicked a thing! and all my comfort was, the thinking you was happy, dear. And what will become of you now? And is it on foot you'll go?"

Her thoughts rambled again.

"Whatever way I go, you shall go with me," said I. "You are my mother; and now that your son has done what he knows to be honest and just, he will prosper in the world, and will be truly happy; and so may you be happy, now that you have nothing more to conceal."

She shook her head.

"It's too late," said she, "quite too late. I often told Christy I would die before you left this place, dear; and so I will, you will see. God bless you! God bless you! and pray to him to forgive me! None that could know what I've gone through would ever do the like; no, not for their own child, was he even such as you, and that would be hard to find. God bless you, dear; I shall never see you more! The hand of death is upon me—God for ever bless you, dear!"

She died that night; and I lost in her the only human being who had ever shown me warm, disinterested affection. Her death delayed for a few days my departure from Glenthorn Castle. I stayed to see her laid in the grave. Her funeral was followed by crowds of people: by many, from the general habit of attending funerals; by many, who wished to pay their court to me, in showing respect to the memory of my nurse.

When the prayers over the dead were ended, and the grave closed, just as the crowd were about to disperse, I stood up on a monument belonging to the Glenthorn family; and the moment it was observed that I wished to address the multitude, the moving waves were stilled, and there was a dead silence. Every eye was fixed upon me with eager expectation. It was the first time in my life that I had ever spoken before numbers; but as I was certain that I had something to say, and quite indifferent about the manner, words came without difficulty. Amazement appeared in every face when I declared myself to be the son of the poor woman whom we had just interred. And when I pointed to the real Earl of Glenthorn, and when I declared that I relinquished to him his hereditary title and lawful property, my auditors looked alternately at me and at my foster-brother, seeming to think it impossible that a man, with face and hands so black as Christy's usually were known to be, could become an earl.

When I concluded my narrative, and paused, the silence still continued; all seemed held in mute astonishment.

"And now, my good friends," continued I, "let me bid you farewell; probably you will never see or hear of me more; but, whether he be rich or poor, or high or low-born, every honest man must wish to leave behind him a fair character. Therefore, when I am gone, and, as it were, dead to you, speak of me, not as of an impostor, who long assumed a name and enjoyed a fortune that was not his own; but remember that I was bred to believe myself heir to a great estate, and that, after having lived till the age of seven-and-twenty, in every kind of luxury, I voluntarily gave up the fortune I enjoyed, the moment I discovered that it was not justly mine."

"That you did, indeed," interrupted Christy; "and of that I am ready to bear witness for you in this world and in the next. God bless and prosper you wherever you go! and sure enough he will, for he cannot do other than prosper one that deserves it so well. I never should have known a sentence of the secret," continued he, addressing his neighbours, "if it had not been for his generosity to tell it me; and even had I found it out by any maracle, where would have been the gain of that to me? for you know he could, had he been so inclined, have kept me out of all by the law—ay, baffled me on till my heart was sick, and till my little substance was wasted, and my bones rotten in the ground; but, God's blessing be upon him! he's an honest man, and done that which many a lord in his place would not have done; but a good conscience is a kingdom in itself, and that he cannot but have, wherever he goes—and all which grieves me is that he is going away from us. If he'd be prevailed with by me, he'd stay where he is, and we'd share and share alike; but he's too proud for that—and no wonder—he has a right to be proud; for no matter who was his mother, he'll live and die a gentleman, every inch of him. Any man, you see, may be made a lord; but a gentleman, a man must make himself. And yourselves can witness, has not he reigned over us like a gentleman, and a raal gentleman; and shown mercy to the poor, and done justice to all, as well as to me? and did not he take me by the hand when I was persecuted, and none else in the wide world to befrind me; and did not he stand up for me against the tyrants that had the sway then; ay, and did not he put himself to trouble, day and night, go riding here and there, and spaking and writing for me? Well, as they say, he loves his ease, and that's the worse can be said of him; he took all this pains for a poor man, and had like to have lost his life by it. And now, wherever he is and whatever, can I help loving and praying for him? or could you? And since you will go," added he, turning to me with tears in his eyes, "take with you the blessings of the poor, which, they say, carry a man straight to heaven, if any thing can."

The surrounding crowd joined with one voice in applauding this speech: "It is he that has said what we all think," cried they, following me with acclamations to the castle. When they saw the chaise at the door which was to carry me away, their acclamations suddenly ceased—"But is he going?—But can't he stay?—And is he going this minute? troth it's a pity, and a great pity!"

Again and again these honest people insisted upon taking leave of me, and I could not force myself away without difficulty. They walked on beside my carriage, Christy at their head; and in this species of triumph, melancholy indeed, but grateful to my heart, I quitted Glenthorn Castle, passed through that park which was no longer mine, and at the verge of the county shook hands for the last time with these affectionate and generous people. I then bid my postilion drive on fast; and I never looked back, never once cast a lingering look at all I left behind. I felt proud of having executed my purpose, and conscious I had not the insignificant, inefficient character that had formerly disgraced me. As to the future, I had not distinctly arranged my plans, nor was my mind during the remainder of the day sufficiently tranquil for reflection. I felt like one in a dream, and could scarcely persuade myself of the reality of the events, that had succeeded each other with such astonishing rapidity. At night I stopped at an inn where I was not known; and having no attendants or equipage to command respect from hostlers, waiters, and inn-keepers, I was made immediately sensible of the reality, at least of the change in my fortune; but I was not mortified—I felt only as if I were travelling incognito. And I contrived to go to bed without a valet-de-chambre, and slept soundly, for I had earned a sound sleep by exertion both of body and mind.

CHAPTER XIX

In the morning I awoke with a confused notion that something extraordinary had happened; but it was a good while before I recollected myself sufficiently to be perfectly sensible of the absolute and irrevocable change in my circumstances. An inn may not appear the best possible place for meditation, especially if the moralizer's bedchamber be next the yard where carriages roll, and hostlers swear perpetually; yet so situated, I, this morning as I lay awake in my bed, thought so abstractedly and attentively, that I heard neither wheels nor hostlers. I reviewed the whole of my past life; I regretted bitterly my extravagance, my dissipation, my waste of time; I considered how small a share of enjoyment my wealth had procured, either for myself or others; how little advantage I had derived from my education, and from all my opportunities of acquiring knowledge. It had been in my power to associate with persons of the highest talents, and of the best information, in the British dominions; yet I had devoted my youth to loungers, and gamesters, and epicures, and knew that scarcely a trace of my existence remained in the minds of those selfish beings, who once called themselves my friends. I wished that I could live my life over again; and I felt that, were it in my power, I should live in a manner very different from that in which I had fooled away existence. In the midst of my self-reproaches, however, I had some consolation in the idea that I had never been guilty of any base or dishonourable action. I recollected, with satisfaction, my behaviour to Lady Glenthorn, when I discovered her misconduct; I recollected that I had always shown gratitude to poor Ellinor for her kindness; I recollected with pleasure, that when trusted with power I had not used it tyrannically. My exertions in favour of my foster-brother, when he was oppressed, I remembered with much satisfaction; and the steadiness with which I behaved, when a conspiracy was formed against my life, gave me confidence in my own courage; and, after having sacrificed my vast possessions to a sense of justice, no mortal could doubt my integrity: so that upon the whole, notwithstanding my past follies, I had a tolerably good opinion of myself, or rather good hopes for the future. I was certain, that there was more in me than the world had seen; and I was ambitious of proving that I had some personal merit, independently of the adventitious circumstances of rank and fortune. But how was I to distinguish myself?

Just as I came to this difficult question, the chambermaid interrupted my reverie, by warning me in a shrill voice, that it was very late, and that she had called me above two hours before.

"Where's my man! send up my man. Oh! I beg your pardon—nothing at all: only, my good girl, I should be obliged to you if you could let me have a little warm water, that I may shave myself."

It was new and rather strange to me to be without attendants; but I found that, when I was forced to it, I could do things admirably well for myself, that I had never suspected I could perform without assistance. After I had travelled two days without servants, how I had travelled with them was the wonder. I once caught myself saying of myself, "that careless blockhead has forgotten my nightcap." For some time I was liable to make odd blunders about my own identity; I was apt to mistake between my old and my new habits, so that when I spoke in the tone and imperative mood in which Lord Glenthorn had been accustomed to speak, people stared at me as if I were mad, and I in my turn was frequently astonished by their astonishment, and perplexed by their ease of behaviour in my presence.

Upon my arrival in Dublin, I went to a small lodging which Mr. M'Leod had recommended to me; it was such as suited my reduced finances; but, at first view, it was not much to my taste; however, I ate with a good appetite my very frugal supper, upon a little table, covered with a little table-cloth, on which I could not wipe my mouth without stooping low. The mistress of the house, a North-country woman, was so condescending as to blow my fire, remarking, at the same time, that coals were a very scarce article; she begged to know whether I would choose a fire in my bed-room, and what quantity of coals she should lay in; she added many questions about boarding, and small-beer, and tea, and sugar, and butter, and blankets, and sheets, and washerwomen, which almost overwhelmed my spirits.

"And must I think of all these things for myself?" said I, in a lamentable tone, and I suppose with a most deplorable length of face, for the woman could not refrain from laughing: as she left the room, I heard her exclaim, "Lord help him, he looks as much astray as if he was just new from the Isle of Skye."

The cares of life were coming fast upon me, and I was terrified by the idea of a host of petty evils; I sat ruminating, with my feet upon the bars of the grate, till past midnight, when my landlady, who seemed to think it incumbent upon her to supply me with common sense, came to inform me that there was a good fire burning to waste in the bed-room, and that I should find myself a great deal better there than sitting over the cinders. I suffered myself to be removed to the bedchamber, and again established my feet upon the upper bar of the grate.

"Lack! sir, you'll burn your boots," said my careful landlady; who, after bidding me good night, put her head back into the room, to beg I would be sure to rake the fire, and throw up the ashes safe, before I went to bed. Left to my own meditations, I confess I did feel rather forlorn. I reflected upon my helplessness in all the common business of life; and the more I considered that I was totally unfit for any employment or profession, by which I could either earn money, or distinguish myself, the deeper became my despondency. I passed a sleepless night, vainly regretting the time that never could be recalled.

In the morning, my landlady gave me some letters, which had been forwarded for me from Glenthorn Castle; the direction to the Earl of Glenthorn scratched out, and in its place inserted my new address, "C. O'Donoghoe, Esq., No. 6, Duke-street, Dublin." I remember, I held the letters in my hand, contemplating the direction for some minutes, and at length reading it aloud repeatedly, to my landlady's infinite amusement:—she knew nothing of my history, and seemed in doubt whether to think me extremely silly or mad. One of my letters was from Lord Y—, an Irish nobleman, with whom I was not personally acquainted, but for whose amiable character and literary reputation I had always, even during my days of dissipation, peculiar respect. He wrote to me to make inquiries respecting the character of a Mr. Lyddell, who had just proposed himself as tutor to the son of one of his friends. Mr. Lyddell had formerly been my favourite tutor, the man who had encouraged me in every species of ignorance and idleness. In my present state of mind I was not disposed to speak favourably of this gentleman, and I resolved that I would not be instrumental in placing another young nobleman under his guidance. I wrote an explicit, indignant, and I will say eloquent letter upon this occasion; but, when I came to the signature, I felt a repugnance to signing myself, C. O'Donoghoe; and I recollected, that as my history could not yet be public, Lord Y— would be puzzled by this strange name, and would be unable to comprehend this answer to his letter. I therefore determined to wait upon his lordship, and to make my explanations in person: besides my other reasons for determining on this visit, I had a strong desire to become personally acquainted with a nobleman of whom I had heard so much. His lordship's porter was not quite so insolent as some of his brethren; and though I did not come in a showy equipage, and though I had no laced footmen to enforce my rights, I gained admission. I passed through a gallery of fine statues, to a magnificent library, which I admired till the master of the house appeared, and from that moment he commanded, or rather captivated, my attention.

Lord Y— was at this time an elderly gentleman. In his address, there was a becoming mixture of ease and dignity; he was not what the French call maniéré; his politeness was not of any particular school, but founded on those general principles of good taste, good sense, and good-nature, which must succeed in all times, places, and seasons. His desire to please evidently arose not from vanity but benevolence. In his conversation, there was neither the pedantry of a recluse, nor the coxcombry of a man of the world: his knowledge was select; his wit without effort, the play of a cultivated imagination: the happiness of his expressions did not seem the result of care; and his allusions were at once so apposite and elegant, as to charm both the learned and the unlearned: all he said was sufficiently clear and just to strike every person of plain sense and natural feeling, while to the man of literature it had often a further power to please, by its less obvious meaning. Lord Y—'s superiority never depressed those with whom he conversed; on the contrary, they felt themselves raised by the magic of politeness to his level; instead of being compelled to pay tribute, they seemed invited to share his intellectual dominion, and to enjoy with him the delightful pre-eminence of genius and virtue.

I shall be forgiven for pausing in my own insignificant story, to dwell on the noble character of a departed friend. That he permitted me to call him my friend, I think the greatest honour of my life. But let me, if I can, go on regularly with my narrative.

Lord Y— took it for granted, during our first half-hour's conversation, that he was speaking to the Earl of Glenthorn: he thanked me with much warmth for putting him on his guard against the character of Mr. Lyddell: and his lordship was also pleased to thank me for making him acquainted, as he said, with my own character; for convincing him how ill it had been appreciated by those who imagined that wealth and title were the only distinctions which the Earl of Glenthorn might claim. This compliment went nearer to my heart than Lord Y— could guess.

"My character," said I, "since your lordship encourages me to speak of myself with freedom, my character has, I hope, been much changed and improved by circumstances; and perhaps those which might at present be deemed the most unfortunate, may ultimately prove of the greatest advantage, by urging me to exertion.—Your lordship is not aware of what I allude to; a late event in my singular history," continued I, taking up the newspapers which lay on his library table—"my singular history has not yet, I fancy, got into the public newspapers. Perhaps you will hear it most favourably from myself."

Lord Y— was politely, benevolently attentive, whilst I related to him the sudden and singular change in my fortune: when I gave an account of the manner in which I had conducted myself after the discovery of my birth, tears of generous feeling filled his eyes; he laid his hand upon mine when I paused—

"Whatever you have lost," said he, "you have gained a friend. Do not be surprised," continued he, "by this sudden declaration. Before I saw you this morning, your real character was better known to me than you imagine. I learnt it from a particular friend of mine, of whose judgment and abilities I have the highest opinion, Mr. Cecil Devereux; I saw him just after his marriage; and the very evening before they sailed, I remember, when Lady Geraldine and he were talking of the regret they felt in leaving Ireland, among the friends whom they lamented that they should not see again, perhaps for years, you were mentioned with peculiar esteem and affection. They called you their generous benefactor, and fully explained to me the claim you had to this title—a title which never can be lost. But Mr. Devereux was anxious to convince me that he was not influenced by the partiality of gratitude in his opinion of his benefactor's talents. He repeated an assertion, that was supported with much energy by the charming Lady Geraldine, that Lord Glenthorn had abilities to be any thing Tie pleased; and the high terms in which they spoke of his talents, and the strong proofs they adduced of the generosity of his character, excited in my mind a warm desire to cultivate his acquaintance; a desire which has been considerably increased within this last hour. May I hope that the Irish rapidity with which I have passed from acquaintance to friendship may not shock English habits of reserve; and may not induce you to doubt the sincerity of the man, who has ventured with so little hesitation or ceremony to declare himself your friend?"

I was so much moved by this unexpected kindness, that, though I felt how much more was requisite, I could answer only with a bow; and I was glad to make my retreat as soon as possible. The very next day, his lordship returned my visit, to my landlady's irrecoverable astonishment; and I had increasing reason to regard him with admiration and affection. He convinced me, that I had interested him in my concerns, and told me, I must forgive him if he spoke to me with the freedom of a friend: thus I was encouraged to consult him respecting my future plans. Plans, indeed, I had none regularly formed; but Lord Y—, by his judicious suggestions, settled and directed my ideas without overpowering me by the formality of advice. My ambition was excited to deserve his friendship, and to accomplish his predictions. The profession of the law was that to which he advised me to turn my thoughts: he predicted, that, if for five years I would persevere in application to the necessary preparatory studies, I should afterwards distinguish myself at the bar, more than I had ever been distinguished by the title of Earl of Glenthorn. Five years of hard labour! the idea alarmed, but did not utterly appal my imagination; and to prevent my dwelling upon it too long at the first, Lord Y— suddenly changed the conversation; and, in a playful tone, said, "Before you immerse yourself in your studies, I must, however, claim some of your time. You must permit me to carry you home with me to-day, to introduce you to two ladies of my acquaintance: the one prudent and old—if a lady can ever be old; the other, young, and beautiful, and graceful, and witty, and wise, and reasonable. One of these ladies is much prepossessed in your favour, the other strongly prejudiced against you—for the best of all possible reasons, because she does not know you."

I accepted Lord Y—'s invitation; not a little curious to know whether it was the old and prudent, or the young, beautiful, graceful, witty, wise, and reasonable lady, who was much prepossessed in my favour. Notwithstanding my usual indifference to the whole race of very agreeable young ladies, I remember trying to form a picture in my imagination of this all-accomplished female.

## CHAPTER XX

Upon my arrival at Y— house, I found two ladies in the drawing-room, in earnest conversation with Lady Y—. In their external appearance they were nearly what my friend had described; except that the beauty of the youngest infinitely surpassed my expectations. The elegance of her form, and the charming expression of her countenance, struck me with a sort of delightful surprise, that was quickly succeeded by a most painful sensation.

"Lady Y—, give me leave to introduce to you Mr. O'Donoghoe."

Shocked by the sound of my own name, I was ready to recoil abashed. The elderly lady turned her eyes upon me for an instant, with that indifference with which we look at an uninteresting stranger. The young lady seemed to pity my confusion; for though so well and so long used to varieties of the highest company, when placed in a situation that was new to me, I was unaccountably disconcerted. Ah! thought I, how differently should I be received were I still Earl of Glenthorn!

I was rather angry with Lord Y—, for not introducing me, as he had promised, to this fair lady; and yet the repetition of my name would have increased my vexation. In short, I was unjust, and felt an impatience and irritability quite unusual to my temper. Lady Y—addressed some conversation to me, in an obliging manner, and I did my best to support my part till she left me: but my attention was soon distracted, by a conversation that commenced at another part of the room, between her and the elderly lady.

"My dear Lady Y—, have you heard the extraordinary news? the most incredible thing that ever was heard! For my part, I cannot believe it yet, though we have the intelligence from the best authority. Lord Glenthorn, that is to say, the person we always called Lord Glenthorn, turns out to be the son of the Lord knows who—they don't mention the name."

At this speech I was ready to sink into the earth. Lord Y— took my arm, and led me into another room. "I have some cameos," said he, "which are thought curious; would you like to look at them?"

"Can you conceive it?" continued the elderly lady, whose voice I still heard, as the folding-doors of the room were open: "Changed at nurse! One hears of such things in novels, but, in real life, I absolutely cannot believe it. Yet here, in this letter from Lady Ormsby, are all the particulars: and a blacksmith is found to be Earl of Glenthorn, and takes possession of Glenthorn castle, and all the estates. And the man is married, to some vulgarian of course: and he has a son, and may have half a hundred, you know; so there is an end of our hopes; and there is an end too of all my fine schemes for Cecilia."

I felt myself change colour again. "I believe," said I to Lord Y—, "I ought not to hear this. If your lordship will give me leave, I will shut the door."

"No, no," said he, smiling, and stopping me; "you ought to hear it, for it will do you a great deal of good. You know I have undertaken to be your guide, philosopher, and friend; so you must let me have my own way: and if it should so happen, hear yourself abused patiently.—Is not this a fine bust of Socrates?"

Some part of the conversation in the next room I missed, whilst his lordship spoke. The next words I heard were—

"But my dear Lady Y—, look at Cecilia.—Would not any other girl be cast down and miserable in Cecilia's place? yet see, see how provokingly happy and well she looks."

"Yes," replied Lady Y—, "I never saw her appear better: but we are not to judge of her by what any other young lady would be in her place, for I know of none at all comparable to Miss Delamere."

"Miss Delamere!" said I to Lord Y—. "Is this the Miss Delamere who is heiress at law to—"

"The Glenthorn estate. Yes—do not let the head of Socrates fall from your hands," said his lordship, smiling.

I again lost something that was said in the next room; but I heard the old lady going on with—

"I only say, my dear, that if the man had been really what he was said to be, you could not have done better."

"Dearest mother, you cannot be serious," replied the sweetest voice I ever heard. "I am sure that you never were in earnest upon this subject: you could not wish me to be united to such a man as Lord Glenthorn was said to be."

"Why? what was he said to be, my dear?—a little dissipated, a little extravagant only: and if he had a fortune to support it, child, what matter?" pursued the mother: "all young men are extravagant now-a-days—you must take the world as it goes."

"The lady who married Lord Glenthorn, I suppose, acted upon that principle; and you see what was the consequence."

"Oh, my dear, as to her ladyship, it ran in the blood: let her have married whom she would, she would have done the same: and I am told Lord Glenthorn made an incomparably good husband. A cousin of Lady Glenthorn's assured me that she was present one day, when her ladyship expressed a wish for a gold chain to wear round her neck, or braid her hair, I forget for what; but that very hour Lord Glenthorn bespoke for her a hundred yards of gold chain, at ten guineas a yard. Another time she longed for an Indian shawl, and his lordship presented her next day with three dozen real India shawls. There's a husband for you, Cecilia!"

"Not for me, mamma," said Cecilia, laughing.

"Ah, you are a strange romantic girl, and never will be married after all, I fear."

"Never to a fool, I hope," said Cecilia.

"Miss Delamere will, however, allow," said Lady Y—, "that a man may have his follies, without being a fool, or wholly unworthy of her esteem; otherwise, what a large portion of mankind she would deprive of hope!"

"As to Lord Glenthorn, he was no fool, I promise you," continued the mother: "has not he been living prudently enough these three years? We have not heard of late of any of his extraordinary landaus."

"But I have been told," said Cecilia, "that he is quite uninformed, without any taste for literature, and absolutely incapable of exertion—a victim to ennui. How miserable a woman must be with such a husband!"

"But," said Lady Y—, "what could be expected from a young nobleman bred up as Lord Glenthorn was?"

"Nothing," said Cecilia; "and that is the very reason I never wished to see him."

"Perhaps Miss Delamere's opinion might be changed if she had known him," said Lady Y—,

"Ay, for he is a very handsome man, I have heard," said the mother. "Lady Jocunda Lawler told me so, in one of her letters; and Lady Jocunda was very near being married to him herself, I can tell you, for he admired her prodigiously."

"A certain proof that he never would have admired me," said Cecilia; "for two women, so opposite in every respect, no man could have loved."

"Lord bless you, child! how little you know of the matter! After all, I dare say, if you had been acquainted with him, you might have been in love yourself with Lord Glenthorn."

"Possibly," said Cecilia, "if I had found him the reverse of what he is reported to be."

Company came in at this instant. Lord Y— was called to receive them, and I followed; glad, at this instant, that I was not Lord Glenthorn. At dinner the conversation turned upon general subjects; and Lord Y—, with polite and friendly attention, drew me out, without seeming to do so, in the kindest manner possible.

I had the pleasure to perceive that Cecilia Delamere did not find me a fool. I never, even in the presence of Lady Geraldine, exerted myself so much to avoid this disgrace.

After all the company, except Mrs. and Miss Delamere, were gone, Lord Y— called me aside.

"Will you pardon," said he, "the means I have taken to convince you how much superior you are to the opinion that has been commonly formed of Lord Glenthorn? Will you forgive me for convincing you that when a man has sufficient strength of mind to rely upon himself, and sufficient energy to exert his abilities, he becomes independent of common report and vulgar opinion? He secures the suffrages of the best judges; and they, in time, lead all the rest of the world. Will you permit me now to introduce you to your prudent friend and your fair enemy? Mrs. Delamere—Miss Delamere—give me leave to introduce to you the late Earl of Glenthorn."

Of the astonishment in the opening eyes of Mrs. Delamere I have some faint recollection. I can never forget the crimson blush that instantaneously spread over the celestial countenance of Cecilia. She was perfectly silent; but her mother went on talking with increased rapidity.

"Good Heavens! the late Lord Glenthorn! Why, I was talking—but he was not in the room." The ladies exchanged looks, which seemed to say, "I hope he did not hear all we said of him."

"My dear Lord Y—, why did not you tell us this before? Suppose we had spoken of his lordship, you would have been answerable for all the consequences."

"Certainly," said Lord Y—.

"But, seriously," said the old lady, "have I the pleasure to speak to Lord Glenthorn, or have I not? I believe I began, unluckily, to talk of a strange story I had heard; but perhaps all this is a mistake, and my country correspondent may have been amusing herself at the expense of my credulity. I assure you I was not imposed upon; I never believed half the story."

"You may believe the whole of it, madam," said I; "the story is perfectly true."

"Oh! my good sir, how sorry I am to hear you say it is all true! And the blacksmith is really Earl of Glenthorn, and has taken possession of the castle, and is married, and has a son! Lord bless me, how unfortunate! Well, I can only say, sir, I wish, with all my heart, you were Earl of Glenthorn still."

After hearing from Lord Y— the circumstances of what he was pleased to call my generous conduct, Mrs. Delamere observed, that I had acted very generously, to be sure, but that few in my place would have thought themselves bound to give up possession of an estate, which I had so long been taught to believe was my own. To have and to hold, she observed, always went together in law; and she could not help thinking I had done very injudiciously and imprudently not to let the law decide for me.

I was consoled for Mrs. Delamere's reprehensions by her daughter's approving countenance. After this visit, Lord Y— gave me a general invitation to his house, where I frequently saw Miss Delamere, and frequently compared her with my recollection of Lady Geraldine —. Cecilia Delamere was not so entertaining, but she was more interesting than Lady Geraldine: the flashes of her ladyship's wit, though always striking, were sometimes dangerous; Cecilia's wit, though equally brilliant, shone with a more pleasing and inoffensive light. With as much generosity as Lady Geraldine could show in great affairs, she had more forbearance and delicacy of attention on every-day occasions. Lady Geraldine had much pride, and it often gave offence; Cecilia, perhaps, had more pride, but it never appeared, except upon the defensive: without having less candour, she had less occasion for it than Lady Geraldine seemed to have; and Cecilia's temper had more softness and equability. Perhaps Cecilia was not so fascinating, but she was more attractive. One had the envied art of appearing to advantage in public—the other, the more desirable power of being happy in private. I admired Lady Geraldine long before I loved her; I loved Cecilia long before I admired her.

Whilst I possibly could, I called what I felt for Miss Delamere only esteem; but when I found it impossible to conceal from myself that I loved, I resolved to avoid this charming woman. How happy, thought I, would the fortune I once possessed now make me! but in my present circumstances what have I to hope? Surely my friend Lord Y— has not shown his usual prudence in exposing me to such a temptation; but it is to be supposed, he thinks that the impossibility of my obtaining Miss Delamere will prevent my thinking of her, or perhaps he depends on the inertness and apathy of my temper. Unfortunately for me, my sensibility has increased since I have become poor; for many years, when I was rich, and could have married easily, I never wished to marry, and now that I have not enough to support a wife, I immediately fall desperately in love.

Again and again I pondered upon my circumstances: three hundred a-year was the amount of all my worldly possessions; and Miss Delamere was not rich, and she had been bred expensively; for it had never been absent from her mother's mind, that Cecilia would be heiress to the immense Glenthorn estate. The present possessor was, however, an excellent life, and he had a son stout and healthy, so all these hopes of Mrs. Delamere's were at an end; and as there was little chance, as she said (laughing), of persuading her daughter to marry Johnny, the young lord and heir apparent, it was now necessary to turn her views elsewhere, and to form for Cecilia some suitable alliance. Rank and large fortune were, in Mrs. Delamere's opinion, indispensable to happiness. Cecilia's ideas were far more moderate; but, though perfectly disinterested and generous, she was not so romantic, or so silly, as to think of marrying any man without the probability of his being able to support her in the society of her equals: nor, even if I could have thought it possible to prevail upon Miss Delamere to make an unbecoming and imprudent choice, would I have taken advantage of the confidence reposed in me by Lord Y—, to destroy the happiness of a young friend, for whom he evidently had a great regard. I resolved to see her no more— and for some weeks I kept my resolution; I refrained from going to Y— house. I deem this the most virtuous action of my life; it certainly was the most painful sacrifice I ever made to a sense of duty. At last, Lord Y— came to me one morning, and after reproaching me, in a friendly manner, for having so long absented myself from his house, declared that he would not be satisfied with any of those common excuses, which might content a mere acquaintance; that his sincere anxiety for my welfare gave him a right to expect from me the frankness of a friend. It was a relief to my mind to be encouraged in this manner. I confessed with entire openness my real motive: Lord Y— heard me without surprise.

"It is gratifying to me," said his lordship, "to be convinced that I was not mistaken in my judgment, either of your taste, or your integrity; permit me to assure you, that I foresaw exactly how you would feel, and precisely how you would act. There are certain moral omens, which old experience never fails to interpret rightly, and from which unerring predictions of the future conduct, and consequently of the future fate of individuals, may be formed. I hold that we are the artificers of our own fortune. If there be any whom the gods wish to destroy, these are first deprived of understanding; whom the gods wish to favour, they first endow with integrity, inspire with understanding, and animate with activity. Have I not seen integrity in you, and shall I not see activity? Yes; that supineness of temper or habit with which you reproach yourself has arisen, believe me, only from want of motive; but you have now the most powerful of motives, and in proportion to your exertions will be your success. In our country, you know, the highest offices of the state are open to talents and perseverance; a man of abilities and application cannot fail to secure independence, and obtain distinction. Time and industry are necessary to prepare you for the profession, to which you will hereafter be an honour, and you will courageously submit.

—'Time and industry, the mighty two,
Which bring our wishes nearer to our view.'

As to the probability that your present wishes may be crowned with success, I can judge only from my general knowledge of the views and disposition of the lady whom you admire. I know that her views with respect to fortune are moderate; and that her disposition and excellent understanding will, in the choice of a husband, direct her preference to the essential good qualities, and not to the accidental advantages, of the candidates for her favour. As to the mother's influence, that will necessarily yield to the daughter's superior judgment. Cecilia possesses over her mother that witchcraft of gentle manners, which in the female sex is always irresistible, even over violent tempers. Prudential considerations have a just, though not exclusive, claim to Miss Delamere's attention. But her relations, I fancy, could find means of providing against any pecuniary embarrassments, if she should think proper to unite herself to a man who can be content, as she would be, with a competence, and who should have proved himself able, by his own exertions, to maintain his wife in independence. On this last condition I must dwell with emphasis, because it is indispensable; and I am convinced that without it Miss Delamere's consent, even after she is of age, and at liberty to judge for herself, could never be obtained. You perceive, then, how much depends upon your own exertions; and this is the best hope, and the best motive, that I can give to a strong and generous mind. Farewell—Persevere and prosper."

Such was the general purport of what Lord Y— said to me; indeed, I believe that I have repeated his very words, for they made a great and ineffaceable impression upon my mind. From this day I date the commencement of a new existence. Fired with ambition,—I hope generous ambition,—to distinguish myself among men, and to win the favour of the most amiable and the most lovely of women, all the faculties of my soul were awakened: I became active, permanently active. The enchantment of indolence was dissolved, and the demon of ennui was cast out for ever.


CHAPTER XXI

If, among those who maybe tempted to peruse my history, there should be any mere novel readers, let me advise them to throw the book aside at the commencement of this chapter; for I have no more wonderful incidents to relate, no more changes at nurse, no more sudden turns of fortune. I am now become a plodding man of business, poring over law-books from morning till night, and leading a most monotonous life: yet occupation, and hope, and the constant sense of approaching nearer to my object, rendered this mode of existence, dull as it may seem, infinitely more agreeable than many of my apparently prosperous days, when I had more money, and more time, than I knew how to enjoy. I resolutely persevered in my studies.

About a month after I came to town, the doors of my lodging were blockaded by half a dozen cars, loaded with huge packing-cases, on which I saw, in the hand-writing which I remembered often to have seen in my blacksmith's bills, a direction to Christopher O'Donoghoe, Esquire—this side upwards: to be kept dry.

One of the carmen fumbled in what he called his pocket, and at last produced a very dirty note.

"My dear and honourable foster-brother, larning from Mr. M'Leod that you are thinking of studdeing, I send you inclosed by the bearer, who is to get nothing for the carrige, all the bookes from the big booke-room at the castle, which I hope, being of not as much use as I could wish to me, your honour will not scorn to accept, with the true veneration of

"Your ever-loving foster-brother, and grateful humble servant, to command.

"P.S. No name needful, for you will not be astray about the hand."

This good-natured fellow's present was highly valuable and useful to me.

Among my pleasures at this studious period of my life, when I had few events to break the uniform tenor of my days, I must mention letters which I frequently received from Mr. Devereux and Lady Geraldine, who still continued in India. Mr. Devereux was acquainted with almost all the men of eminence at the Irish bar; men who are not mere lawyers, but persons of literature, of agreeable manners, and gentlemanlike habits. Mr. Desvereux wrote to his friends so warmly in my favour, that, instead of finding myself a stranger in Dublin, my only difficulty was how to avoid the numerous invitations which tempted me from my studies.

Those gentlemen of the bar who were intimate with Mr. Devereux honoured me with particular attention, and their society was peculiarly useful, as well as agreeable, to me: they directed my industry to the best and shortest means of preparing myself for their profession; they put into my hands the best books; told me all that experience had taught them of the art of distinguishing, in the mass of law-precedents, the useful from the useless: instructed me in the methods of indexing and common-placing; and gave me all those advantages, which solitary students so often want, and the want of which so often makes the study of the law appear an endless maze without a plan. When I found myself surrounded with books, and reading assiduously day and night, I could scarcely believe in my own identity; I could scarcely imagine that I was the same person, who, but a few months before this time, lolled upon a sofa half the day, and found it an intolerable labour to read or think for half an hour together. Such is the power of motive! During the whole time I pursued my studies, and kept my terms, in Ireland, the only relaxation I allowed myself was in the society at Lord Y—'s house in Dublin, and, during my vacations, in excursions which I made with his lordship to different parts of the country. Lord Y— had two country-seats in the most beautiful parts of Ireland. How differently the face of nature appeared to me now! with what different sensations I beheld the same objects!

"No brighter colours paint th' enamell'd fields,
No sweeter fragrance now the garden yields;
Whence then this strange increase of joy?
Is it to love these new delights I owe?"

It was not to love that I owed these new delights, for Cecilia was not there; but my powers of observation were awakened, and the confinement and labour to which I had lately submitted gave value to the pleasures of rest and liberty, and to the freshness of country air, and the beautiful scenes of nature. So true it is, that all our pleasures must be earned, before they can be enjoyed. When I saw on Lord Y—'s estates, and on those of several other gentlemen, which he occasionally took me to visit, the neat cottages, the well-cultivated farms, the air of comfort, industry, and prosperity, diffused through the lower classes of the people, I was convinced that much may be done by the judicious care and assistance of landlords for their tenantry. I saw this with mixed sensations of pleasure and of pain—of pain, for I reflected how little I had accomplished, and how ill I had done even that little, whilst the means of doing good to numbers had been in my power. For the very trifling services I did to some of my poor tenants, I am sure I had abundant gratitude; and I was astonished and touched by instances of this shown to me after I had lost my fortune, and when I scarcely had myself any remembrance of the people who came to thank me. Trivial as it is, I cannot forbear to record one of the many instances of gratitude I met with from a poor Irishman.

Whilst I was in Dublin, as I was paying a morning visit to Lord Y—, sitting with him in his library, we heard some disturbance in the inner court; and looking out of the window, we saw a countryman with a basket on his arm, struggling with the porter and two footmen.

"He is here; I know to a certainty he is here, and I shall see him, say what you plase now!"

"I tell you my lord is not at home," said the porter.

"What's the matter?" said Lord Y—, opening the window.

"See, there's my lord himself at the window: are not you ashamed of yourself now?" said the footman.

"And why would I be ashamed that am telling no lies, and hindering no one?" said the countryman, looking up to us with so sudden a motion that his hat fell of. I knew his face, but could not recollect his name.

"Oh! there he is, his own honour; I've found him, and axe pardon for my boldness; but it's because I've been all day yesterday, and this day, running through Dublin after yees; and when certified by the lady of the lodgings you was in it here, I could not lave town without my errand, which is no more than a cheese from my wife of her own making, to be given to your honour's own hands, and she would not see me if I did not do it."

"Let him come up," said Lord Y—. "This," continued his lordship, turning to me, "reminds me of Henry the Fourth, and the Gascon peasant with his fromages de boeuf."

"But our countryman brings his offering to an abdicated monarch," said I.

The poor fellow presented his wife's cheese to me with as good a grace as any courtier could have made his offering. Unembarrassed, his manners and his words gave the natural and easy expression of a grateful heart. He assured me that he and his wife were the happiest couple in all Ireland; and he hoped I would one day be as happy myself in a wife as I desarved, who had made others so; and there were many on the estate remembered as well as he did the good I did to the poor during my reign.

Then stepping up closer to me, he said, in a lower voice, "I'm Jimmy Riley, that married ould Noonan's daughter; and now that it is all over I may tell you a bit of a secret, which made me so eager to get to the speech of your honour, that I might tell it to your own ear alone—no offence to this gentleman, before whom I'd as soon say it as yourself, becaase I see he is all as one as another yourself. Then the thing is—does your honour remember the boy with the cord round his body, looking for the birds' eggs in the rock, and the 'nonymous bit of a letter that you got? 'Twas I wrote it, and the gossoon that threw it to your honour was a cousin of my own that I sent, that nobody, nor yourself even, might not know him: and the way I got the information I never can tell till I die, and then only to the priest, becaase I swore I would not never. But don't go for to think it was by being a rubble any way; no man can, I thank my God, charge me with indifferency. So rejoiced to see you the same, I wish you a good morrow, and long life, and a happy death—when it comes."

About this time I frequently used to receive presents to a considerable amount, and of things which were most useful to me, but always without any indication by which I could discover to whom I was indebted for them: at last, by means of my Scotch landlady, I traced them to Mr. M'Leod. His kindness was so earnest and peremptory, that it would admit neither thanks nor refusals; and I submitted to be obliged to a man for whom I felt such high esteem. I looked upon it as not the least of his proofs of regard, that he gave me what I knew he valued more than any thing else—his time. Whenever he came to Dublin, though he was always hurried by business, so that he had scarcely leisure to eat or sleep, he used constantly to come to see me in my obscure lodgings; and when in the country, though he hated all letter-writing, except letters of business, yet he regularly informed me of every thing that could be interesting to me. Glenthorn Castle he described as a scene of riotous living, and of the most wasteful vulgar extravagance. My poor foster-brother, the best-natured and most generous fellow in the world, had not sufficient prudence or strength of mind to conduct his own family; his wife filled the castle with tribes of her vagabond relations; she chose to be descended from one of the kings of Ireland; and whoever would acknowledge her high descent, and whoever would claim relationship with her, were sure to have their claims allowed, and were welcome to live in all the barbaric magnificence of Glenthorn Castle. Every instance that she could hear of the former Lady Glenthorn's extravagance or of mine—and, alas! there were many upon record, she determined to exceed. Her diamonds, and her pearls, and her finery, surpassed every thing but the extravagance of some of the Russian favourites of fortune. Decked out in the most absurd manner, this descendant of kings, as Mr. M'Leod assured me, often indulged in the pleasures of the banquet, till, no longer able to support the regal diadem, she was carried by some of the meanest of her subjects to her bed. The thefts committed during these interregnums were amazing in their amount, and the jewels of the crown were to be replaced as fast as they were stolen. Poor Christy all this time was considered as a mean-spirited cratur, who had no notion of living like a prince; and whilst his wife and her relations were revelling in this unheard-of manner, he was scarcely considered as the master of the house: he lived by the fireside disregarded in winter, and in summer he spent his time chiefly in walking up and down his garden, and picking fruit. He once made an attempt to amuse himself by mending the lock of his own room door; but he was detected in the fact, and exposed to such loud ridicule by his lady's favourites, that he desisted, and sighing said to Mr. M'Leod—"And isn't it now a great hardship upon a man like me to have nothing to do, or not to be let do any thing? If it had not been for my son Johnny's sake, I never would have quit the forge; and now all will be spent in coshering, and Johnny, at the last, will never be a penny the better, but the worse for my consinting to be lorded; and what grieves me more than all the rest, she is such a negre, that I haven't a guinea I can call my own to send, as I'd always laid out to do at odd times, such little tokens of my love and duty, as would be becoming to my dear foster-brother there in Dublin. And now, you tell me, he is going away too, beyond sea to England, to finish making a lawyer of himself in London; and what friends will he find there, without money in his pocket? and I had been thinking this while past, ever since you gave me notice of his being to quit Ireland, that I would go up to Dublin myself to see him, and wish him a good journey kindly before he would go; and I had a little compliment here, in a private drawer, that I had collected unknownst to my wife; but here last night she lit upon it, and now that her hand has closed upon it, not a guinea of it shall I ever see more, nor a farthing the better of it will my dear foster-brother ever be, for it or for me; and this is what grieves me more than all, and goes to the quick of my heart."

When Mr. M'Leod repeated to me these lamentations of poor Christy, I immediately wrote to set his heart at ease, as much as I could, by the assurance that I was in no distress for money; and that my three hundred a year would support me in perfect comfort and independence, while "I was making a lawyer of myself in London." I farther assured my good foster-brother, that I was so well convinced of his affectionate and generous disposition towards me, that it would be quite unnecessary ever to send me tokens of his regard. I added a few words of advice about his wife and his affairs, which, like most words of advice, were, as I afterwards found, absolutely thrown away.

Though I had taken care to live with so much economy, that I was not in any danger of being in pecuniary embarrassments, yet I felt much distress of another kind in leaving Ireland. I left Miss Delamere surrounded with admirers; her mother using her utmost art and parental influence to induce Cecilia to decide in favour of one of these gentlemen, who was a person of rank and of considerable fortune. I had seen all this going on, and was bound in honour the whole time to remain passive, not to express my own ardent feelings, not to make the slightest attempt to win the affections of the woman who was the object of all my labours, of all my exertions. The last evening that I saw her at Lord Y—'s, just before I sailed for England, I suffered more than I thought it was in my nature to feel, especially at the moment when I went up to make my bow, and take leave of her with all the cold ceremony of a common acquaintance. At parting, however, in the presence of her mother and of Lord Y—, Cecilia, with her sweet smile, and, I think, with a slight blush, said a few words, upon which I lived for months afterwards.

"I sincerely wish you, sir, the success your perseverance so well deserves."

The recollection of these words was often my solace in my lonely chambers in the Temple; and often, after a day's hard study, the repeating them to myself operated as a charm that dissipated all fatigue, and revived at once my exhausted spirits. To be sure, there were moments when my fire was out, and my candle sinking in the socket, and my mind over-wearied saw things in the most gloomy point of view; and at these times I used to give an unfavourable interpretation to Cecilia's words, and I fancied that they were designed to prevent my entertaining fallacious hopes, and to warn me that she must yield to her mother's authority, or perhaps to her own inclinations, in favour of some of her richer lovers. This idea would have sunk me into utter despondency, and I should have lost, with my motive, all power of exertion, had not I opposed to this apprehension the remembrance of Lord Y—'s countenance, at the moment Cecilia was speaking to me. I then felt assured, that his lordship, at least, understood the words in a favourable sense, else he would have suffered for me, and would not certainly have allowed me to go away with false hopes. Re-animated by this consideration, I persevered—for it was by perseverance alone that I could have any chance of success.

It was fortunate for me, that, stimulated by a great motive, I thus devoted my whole time and thoughts to my studies, otherwise I must, on returning to London, have felt the total neglect and desertion of all my former associates in the fashionable world; of all the vast number of acquaintance who used to lounge away their hours in my company, and partake of the luxuries of my table and the festivities of my house. Some, whom I accidentally met in the street, just at my re-appearance in town, thought proper, indeed, to know me again at first, that they might gratify their curiosity about the paragraphs which they had seen in the papers, and the reports which they had heard of my extraordinary change of fortune; but no sooner had they satisfied themselves that all they had heard was true, than their interest concerning me ceased. When they found, that, instead of being Earl of Glenthorn, and the possessor of a large estate, I was now reduced to three hundred a year, lodging in small chambers in the Temple, and studying the law, they never more thought me worthy of their notice. They affected, according to their different humours, either to pity me for my misfortunes, or to blame me for my folly in giving up my estate; but they unanimously expressed astonishment at the idea of my becoming a member of any active profession. They declared that it was impossible that I could ever endure the labour of the law, or succeed in such an arduous career. Their prophecies intimidated me not; I was conscious that these people did not in the least know me; and I hoped and believed that I had powers and a character which they were incapable of estimating: their contempt rather excited than depressed my mind, and their pity I returned with more sincerity than it was given. I had lived their life, knew thoroughly what were its pleasures and its pains; I could compare the ennui I felt when I was a Bond-street lounger with the self-complacency I enjoyed now that I was occupied in a laborious but interesting and honourable pursuit. I confess, I had sometimes, however, the weakness to think the worse of human nature, for what I called the desertion and ingratitude of these my former companions and flatterers; and I could not avoid comparing the neglect and solitude in which I lived in London, where I had lavished my fortune, with the kindness and hospitalities I had received in Dublin, where I lived only when I had no fortune to spend. After a little time, however, I became more reasonable and just; for I considered that it was my former dissipated mode of life, and imprudent choice of associates, which I should blame for the mortifications I now suffered from the desertion of companions, who were, in fact, incapable of being friends. In London I had lived with the most worthless, in Dublin with the best company; and in each place I had been treated as, in fact, I deserved. But, leaving the history of my feelings, I must proceed with my narrative.

One night, after I had dined with an Irish gentleman, a friend of Lord Y—'s, at the west end of the town, as I was returning late to my lodgings, I was stopped for some time by a crowd of carriages, in one of the fashionable streets. I found that there was a masquerade at the house of a lady, with whom I had been intimately acquainted. The clamours of the mob, eager to see the dresses of those who were alighting from their carriages, the gaudy and fantastic figures which I beheld by the light of the flambeaux, the noise and the bustle, put me in mind of various similar nights of my past life, and it seemed to me like a dream, or reminiscence of some former state of existence. I passed on as soon as the crowd would permit, and took my way down a narrow street, by which I hoped to get, by a shorter way than usual, to my quiet lodgings. The rattling of the carriages, the oaths of the footmen, and the shouts of the mob still sounded in my ears; and the masquerade figures had scarcely faded from my sight, when I saw, coming slowly out of a miserable entry, by the light of a few wretched candles and lanterns, a funeral. The contrast struck me: I stood still to make way for the coffin; and I heard one say to another, "What matter how she's buried! I tell you, be at as little expense as possible, for he'll never pay a farthing." I had a confused recollection of having heard the voice before: as one of the bearers lifted his lantern, I saw the face of the woman who spoke, and had a notion of having seen her before. I asked whose funeral it was; and I was answered, "It is one Mrs. Crawley's—Lady Glenthorn that was," added the woman. I heard no more: I was so much shocked, that I believe I should have fallen in the street, if I had not been immediately supported by somebody near me. When I recovered my recollection, I saw the funeral had moved on some paces, and the person who supported me, I now found, was a clergyman. In a mild voice, he told me that his duty called him away from me at present, but he added, that if I would tell him where I could be found, he would see me in the morning, and give me any information in his power, as he supposed that I was interested for this unfortunate woman. I put a card with my address into his hands, thanked him, and got home as well as I could. In the morning, the clergyman called upon me—a most benevolent man, unknown to fame; but known to all the wretched within the reach of his consolatory religion. He gave me a melancholy account of the last days of the unhappy woman, whose funeral I had just seen. I told him who I was, and what she had been to me. She had, almost in her last moments, as he assured me, expressed her sense of, what she called, my generosity to her, and had shown deep contrition for her infidelity. She died in extreme poverty and wretchedness, with no human being who was, or even seemed, interested for her, but a maid-servant (the woman whose voice I recollected), whose services were purchased to the last, by presents of whatever clothes or trinkets were left from the wreck of her mistress's fortune. Crawley, it seems, had behaved brutally to his victim. After having long delayed to perform his promise of marrying her, he declared that he could never think of a woman who had been divorced in any other way than a mistress: she, poor weak creature, consented to live with him on any terms; but, as his passions and his interest soon turned to new objects, he cast her off without scruple, refusing to pay any of the tradesmen, who had supplied her while she bore his name. He refused to pay the expenses even of her funeral, though she had shared with him her annuity, and every thing she possessed. I paid the funeral expenses, and some arrears of the maid's wages, together with such debts for necessaries as I had reason to believe were justly due: the strict economy with which I had lived for three years, and the parting with a watch and some other trinkets too fine for my circumstances, enabled me to pay this money without material inconvenience, and it was a satisfaction to my mind. The good clergyman who managed these little matters became interested for me, and our acquaintance with each other grew every day more intimate and agreeable. When he found that I was studying the law, he begged to introduce me to a brother of his, who had been one of the most eminent special pleaders in London, and who now, on a high salary, undertook to prepare students for the bar. I was rather unwilling to accept of this introduction, because I was not rich enough to become a pupil of this gentleman's; but my clergyman guessed the cause of my reluctance, and told me that his brother had charged him to overrule all such objections. "My brother and I," continued he, "though of different professions, have in reality but one mind between us: he has heard from me all the circumstances I know of you, and they have interested him so much, that he desires, in plain English, to be of any service he can to you."

This offer was made in earnest; and if I had given him the largest salary that could have been offered by the most opulent of his pupils, I could not have met with more attention, or have been instructed with more zeal than I was, by my new friend the special pleader. He was also so kind as to put me at ease by the assurance, that whenever I should begin to make money by my profession, he would accept of remuneration. He jestingly said, that he would make the same bargain with me that was made by the famous sophist Protagoras of old with his pupil, that he should have the profits of the first cause I should win—certain that I would not, like his treacherous pupil Evathlus, employ the rhetorician's arms against himself, to cheat him out of his promised reward. My special pleader was not a mere man of forms and law rigmaroles; he knew the reason for the forms he used: he had not only a technical, but a rational knowledge of his business; and, what is still more uncommon, he knew how to teach what he had learnt. He did not merely set me down at a desk, and leave me skins after skins of parchment to pore over in bewildered and hopeless stupidity; he did not use me like a mere copying machine, to copy sheet after sheet for him, every morning from nine till four, and again every evening from five till ten. Mine was a law tutor of a superior sort. Wherever he could, he gave me a clue to guide me through the labyrinth; and when no reason could be devised for what the law directs, he never puzzled me by attempting to explain what could not be explained; he did not insist upon the total surrender of my rational faculties, but with wonderful liberality would allow me to call nonsense, nonsense; and would, after two or three hours' hard scrivening, as the case might require—for this I thank him more than all the rest—permit me to yawn, and stretch, and pity myself, and curse the useless repetitions of lawyers, sinking under the weight of declarations, and replications, and double pleas, and dilatory, pleas;

"Of horse pleas, traverses, demurrers,
Jeofails, imparlances, and errors.
Averments, bars, and profestandoes.'"

O! Cecilia, what pains did I endure to win your applause! Yet, that I may state the whole truth, let me acknowledge, that even these, my dullest, hardest tasks, were light, compared with the burden I formerly bore of ennui. At length my period of probation in my pleader's office was over; I escaped from the dusky desk, and the smell of musty parchments, and the close smoky room; I finished eating my terms at the Temple, and returned, even, as the captain of the packet swore, "in the face and teeth of the wind," to Dublin.

But, in my haste to return, I must not omit to notice, for the sake of poetical equity, that just when I was leaving England, I heard that slow but sure-paced justice at last overtook that wretch Crawley. He was detected and convicted of embezzling considerable sums, the property of a gentleman in Cheshire, who had employed him as his agent. I saw him, as I passed through Chester, going to prison, amidst the execrations of the populace.

## CHAPTER XXII

As I was not, as formerly, asleep in my carriage on deck, when we came within sight of the Irish shore, I saw, and hailed with delight, the beautiful bay of Dublin. The moment we landed, instead of putting myself out of humour, as before, with every thing at the Marine Hotel, I went directly to my friend Lord Y—'s. I made my sortie from the hotel with so much extraordinary promptitude, that a slip-shod waiter was forced to pursue me, running or shuffling after me the whole length of the street, before he could overtake me with a letter, which had been "waiting for my honour, at the hotel, since yesterday's Holyhead packet." This was a mistake, as the letter had never come or gone by any Holyhead packet; it was only a letter from Mr. M'Leod, to welcome me to Ireland again; and to tell me, that he had taken care to secure good well-aired lodgings for me: he added an account of what was going on at Glenthorn Castle. The extravagance of my lady had by this time reduced the family to great difficulties for ready money, as they could neither sell nor mortgage any part of the Glenthorn estate, which was settled on the son. My poor foster-brother had, it seems, in vain attempted to restrain the wasteful folly of his wife, and to persuade Johnny, the young heir-apparent, to larn to be a jantleman: in vain Christy tried to prevail on his lordship to "refrain drinking whisky preferably to claret:" the youth pleaded both his father's and mother's examples; and said, that as he was an only son, and his father had but a life-interest in the estate, he expected to be indulged; he repeated continually "a short life and a merry one for me." Mr. M'Leod concluded this letter by observing, "that far from its being a merry life, he never saw any thing more sad than the life this foolish boy led; and that Glenthorn Castle was so melancholy and disgusting a scene of waste, riot, and intemperance, that he could not bear to go there." I was grieved by this account, for the sake of my poor foster-brother; but it would have made a deeper impression upon me at any other time. I must own that I forgot the letter, and all that it contained, as I knocked at Lord Y—'s door.

Lord Y— received me with open arms; and, with all the kindness of friendship, anticipated the questions I longed, yet feared, to ask.

"Cecilia Delamere is still unmarried—Let these words be enough to content you for the present; all the rest is, I hope, in your own power."

In my power!—delightful thought! yet how distant that hope! For I was now, after all my labours, but just called to the bar; not yet likely, for years, to make a guinea, much less a fortune, by my profession.

Many of the greatest of our lawyers have gone circuit for ten or twelve years, before they made a Fashionable Life. hundred a year; and I was at this time four-and-thirty. I confessed to my Lord Y—, that these reflections alarmed and depressed me exceedingly: but he encouraged me by this answer— "Persevere—deserve success; and trust the rest, not to fortune, but to your friends. It is not required of you to make ten thousand or one thousand a year at the bar, in any given time; but it is expected from you to give proofs that you are capable of conquering the indolence of your disposition or of your former habits. It is required from you to give proofs of intellectual energy and ability. When you have convinced me that you have the knowledge and assiduity that ought to succeed at the bar, I shall be certain that only time is wanting to your actual acquisition of a fortune equal to what I ought to require for my fair friend and relation. When it comes to that point, it will, my dear sir, be time enough for me to say more. Till it comes to that point, I have promised Mrs. Delamere that you will not even attempt to see her daughter. She blames me for having permitted Cecilia and you to see so much of each other, as you did in this house when you were last in Ireland. Perhaps I was imprudent, but your conduct has saved me from my own reproaches, and I fear no other. I end where I began, with 'Persevere—and may the success your perseverance deserves be your reward.' If I recollect right, these were nearly Miss Delamere's own words at parting with you."

In truth, I had not forgotten them; and I was so much excited by their repetition at this moment, and by my excellent friend's encouraging voice, that all difficulties, all dread of future labours or evils, vanished from my view. I went my first circuit, and made two guineas, and was content; for Lord Y— was not disappointed: he told me it would, it must be so. But though I made no money, I obtained gradually, amongst my associates at the bar, the reputation for judgment and knowledge. Of this they could judge by my conversation, and by the remarks on the trials brought on before us. The elder counsel had been prepared in my favour, first by Mr. Devereux, and afterwards by my diligence in following their advice, during my studies in Dublin: they perceived that I had not lost my time in London, and that my mind was in my possession. They prophesied, that from the moment I began to be employed, I should rise rapidly. Opportunity, they told me, was now all that I wanted, and for that I must wait with patience. I waited with as much patience as I could. I had many friends; some among the judges, some among a more powerful class of men, the attorneys: some of these friends made for me by Mr. Devereux and Lady Geraldine; some by Lord Y—; some, may I say it? by myself. Yet the utmost that even the highest patronage from the bench can do for a young barrister is, to give him an opportunity of distinguishing himself in preference to other competitors. This was all I hoped; and I was not deceived in this hope. It happened that a cause of considerable moment, which had come on in our circuit, and to the whole course of which I had attended with great care, was removed, by an appeal, to Dublin. I fortunately, I should say prudently, was in the habit of constant attendance at the courts: the counsel who was engaged to manage this cause was suddenly taken ill, and was disabled from proceeding. The judge called upon me; the attorneys, and the other counsel, were all agreed in wishing me to take up the business, for they knew I was prepared, and competent to the question. The next day the cause, which was then to be finally decided, came on. I sat up all night to look over my documents, and to make myself sure of my points. Ten years before this, if any one had prophesied this of me, how little could I have believed them!

The trial came on—I rose to speak. How fortunate it was for me, that I did not know my Lord Y— was in the court! I am persuaded that I could not have uttered three sentences, if he had caught my eye in the exordium of this my first harangue. Every man of sensibility—and no man without it can be an orator— every man of sensibility knows that it is more difficult to speak in the presence of one anxious friend, of whose judgment we have a high opinion, than before a thousand auditors who are indifferent, and are strangers to us. Not conscious who was listening to me, whose eyes were upon me, whose heart was beating for me, I spoke with confidence and fluency, for I spoke on a subject of which I had previously made myself completely master; and I was so full of the matter, that I thought not of the words. Perhaps this, and my having the right side of the question, were the causes of my success. I heard a buzz of thanks and applause round me. The decree was given in our favour. At this moment I recollected my bargain, and my debt to my good master the special pleader. But all bargains, all debts, all special pleaders, vanished the next instant from my mind; for the crowd opened, Lord Y— appeared before me, seized my hand, congratulated me actually with tears of joy, carried me away to his carriage, ordered the coachman to drive home—fast! fast!

"And now," said he to me, "I am satisfied. Your trial is over—successfully over—you have convinced me of your powers and your perseverance. All the hopes of friendship are fulfilled: may all the hopes of love be accomplished! You have now my free and full approbation to address my ward and relation, Cecilia Delamere. You will have difficulties with her mother, perhaps; but none beyond what we good and great lawyers shall, I trust, be able to overrule. Mrs. Delamere knows, that, as I have an unsettled estate, and but one son, I have it in my power to provide for her daughter as if she were my own. It has always been my intention to do so: but if you marry Miss Delamere, you will still find it necessary to pursue your profession diligently, to maintain her in her own rank and style of life; and now that you have felt the pleasures of successful exertion, you will consider this necessity as an additional blessing. From what I have heard this day, there can be no doubt, that, by pursuing your profession, you can secure, in a few years, not only ease and competence, but affluence and honours—honours of your own earning. How far superior to any hereditary title!"

The carriage stopped at Lord Y—'s door. My friend presented me to Cecilia, whom I saw this day for the first time since my return to Ireland. From this hour I date the commencement of my life of real happiness. How unlike that life of pleasure, to which so many give erroneously the name of happiness! Lord Y—, with his powerful influence, supported my cause with Mrs. Delamere, who was induced, though with an ill grace, to give up her opposition.

"Cecilia," she said, "was now three-and-twenty, an age to judge for herself; and Lord Y—'s judgment was a great point in favour of Mr. O'Donoghoe, to be sure. And no doubt Mr. O'Donoghoe might make a fortune, since he had made a figure already at the bar. In short, she could not oppose the wishes of Lord Y—, and the affections of her daughter, since they were so fixed. But, after all," said Mrs. Delamere, "what a horrid thing it will be to hear my girl called Mrs. O'Donoghoe! Only conceive the sound of—Mrs. O'Donoghoe's carriage there!—Mrs. O'Donoghoe's carriage stops the way!"

"Your objection, my dear madam," replied Lord Y—, "is fully as well founded as that of a young lady of my acquaintance, who could not prevail on her delicacy to become the wife of a merchant of the name of Sheepshanks. He very wisely, or very gallantly, paid five hundred pounds to change his name. I make no doubt that your future son-in-law will have no objection to take and bear the name and arms of Delamere; and I think I can answer for it, that a king's letter may be obtained, empowering him to do so. With this part of the business allow me to charge myself."

I spare the reader the protracted journal of a lover's hopes and fears. Cecilia, convinced, by the exertions in which I had so long persevered, that my affection for her was not only sincere and ardent, but likely to be permanent, did not torture me by the vain delays of female coquetry. She believed, she said, that a man capable of conquering habitual indolence could not be of a feeble character; and she therefore consented, without hesitation, to entrust her happiness to my care.

I hope my readers have, by this time, too favourable an opinion of me to suspect, that, in my joy, I forgot him who had been my steady friend in adversity. I wrote to M'Leod, as soon as I knew my own happiness, and assured him that it would be incomplete without his sympathy. I do not think there was at our wedding a face of more sincere, though sober joy, than M'Leod's. Cecilia and I have been now married above a twelvemonth, and she permits me to say, that she has never, for a moment, repented her choice. That I have not relapsed into my former habits, the judicious and benevolent reader will hence infer: and yet I have been in a situation to be spoiled; for I scarcely know a wish of my heart that remains ungratified, except the wish that my friend Mr. Devereux and Lady Geraldine should return from India, to see and partake of that happiness of which they first prepared the foundation. They first awakened my dormant intellects, made me know that I had a heart, and that I was capable of forming a character for myself. The loss of my estate continued the course of my education, forced me to exert my own powers, and to rely upon myself. My passion for the amiable and charming Cecilia was afterwards motive sufficient to urge me to persevering intellectual labour: fortunately my marriage has obliged me to continue my exertions, and the labours of my profession have made the pleasures of domestic life most delightful. The rich, says a philosophic moralist, are obliged to labour, if they would be healthy or happy; and they call this labour exercise.

Whether, if I were again a rich man, I should have sufficient voluntary exertion to take a due portion of mental and bodily exercise, I dare not pretend to determine, nor do I wish to be put to the trial. Desiring nothing in life but the continuance of the blessings I possess, I may here conclude my memoirs, by assuring my readers, that after a full experience of most of what are called the pleasures of life, I would not accept of all the Glenthorn and Sherwood estates, to pass another year of such misery as I endured whilst I was "stretched on the rack of a too easy chair."

The preceding memoirs were just ready for publication, when I received the following letter:

"HONOURED FOSTER-BROTHER,

"Since the day I parted yees, nothing in life but misfortins has happened me, owing to my being overruled by my wife, who would be a lady, all I could say again it. But that's over, and there's no help; for all and all that ever she can say will do no good. The castle's burnt down all to the ground, and my Johnny's dead, and I wish I was dead in his place. The occasion of his death was owing to drink, which he fell into from getting too much money, and nothing to do—and a snuff of a candle. When going to bed last night, a little in liquor, what does he do but takes the candle, and sticks it up against the head of his bed, as he used oftentimes to do, without detriment, in the cabin where he was reared, against the mud-wall. But this was close to an ould window curtain, and a deal of ould wood in the bed, which was all in a smother, and he lying asleep after drinking, when he was ever hard to wake, and before he waked at all, it appears the unfortunit cratur was smothered, and none heard a sentence of it, till the ceiling of my room, the blue bedchamber, with a piece of the big wood cornice, fell, and wakened me with terrible uproar, and all above and about me was flame and smoke, and I just took my wife on my back, and down the stairs with her, which did not give in till five minutes after, and she screeching, and all them relations she had screeching and running every one for themselves, and no thought in any to save any thing at all, but just what they could for themselves, and not a sarvant that was in his right rason. I got the ladder with a deal of difficulty, and up to Johnny's room, and there was a sight for me— he a corpse, and how even to get the corpse out of that, myself could not tell, for I was bewildered, and how they took me down, I don't well know. When I came to my sinses, I was lying on the ground in the court, and all confusion and screaming still, and the flames raging worse than ever. There's no use in describing all—the short of it is, there's nothing remaining of the castle but the stones; and it's little I'd think o' that, if I could have Johnny back—such as he used to be in my good days; since he's gone, I am no good. I write this to beg you, being married, of which I give you joy, to Miss Delamere, that is the hare at law, will take possession of all immediately, for I am as good as dead, and will give no hindrance. I will go back to my forge, and, by the help of God, forget at my work what has passed; and as to my wife, she may go to her own kith and kin, if she will not abide by me. I shall not trouble her long. Mr. M'Leod is a good man, and will follow any directions you send; and may the blessing of God attind, and come to reign over us again, when you will find me, as heretofore,

"Your loyal foster-brother,

"CHRISTY DONOGHOE."

Glenthorn Castle is now rebuilding; and when it is finished, and when I return thither, I will, if it should be desired by the public, give a faithful account of my feelings. I flatter myself that I shall not relapse into indolence; my understanding has been cultivated—I have acquired a taste for literature, and the example of Lord Y— convinces me that a man may at once be rich and noble, and active and happy.


## THE DUN

*"Horrible monster! hated by gods and men."—PHILLIPS.*

"In the higher and middle classes of society," says a celebrated writer, "it is a melancholy and distressing sight to observe, not unfrequently, a man of a noble and ingenuous disposition, once feelingly alive to a sense of honour and integrity, gradually sinking under the pressure of his circumstances, making his excuses at first with a blush of conscious shame, afraid to see the faces of his friends from whom he may have borrowed money, reduced to the meanest tricks and subterfuges to delay or avoid the payment of his just debts, till, ultimately grown familiar with falsehood, and at enmity with the world, he loses all the grace and dignity of man."

Colonel Pembroke, the subject of the following story, had not, at the time his biographer first became acquainted with him, "grown familiar with falsehood;" his conscience was not entirely callous to reproach, nor was his heart insensible to compassion; but he was in a fair way to get rid of all troublesome feelings and principles. He was connected with a set of selfish young men of fashion, whose opinions stood him in stead of law, equity, and morality; to them he appealed in all doubtful cases, and his self-complacency being daily and hourly dependent upon their decisions, he had seldom either leisure or inclination to consult his own judgment. His amusements and his expenses were consequently regulated by the example of his companions, not by his own choice. To follow them in every absurd variety of the mode, either in dress or, equipage, was his first ambition; and all their factitious wants appeared to him objects of the first necessity. No matter how good the boots, the hat, the coat, the furniture, or the equipage might be, if they had outlived the fashion of the day, or even of the hour, they were absolutely worthless in his eyes. Nobody could be seen in such things—then of what use could they be to any body? Colonel Pembroke's finances were not exactly equal to the support of such liberal principles; but this was a misfortune which he had in common with several of his companions. It was no check to their spirit—they could live upon credit—credit, "that talisman, which realizes every thing it imagines, and which can imagine every thing." [See Des Casaux sur le Méchanisme de la Société.] Without staying to reflect upon the immediate or remote consequences of this system,

Pembroke, in his first attempts, found it easy to reduce it to practice: but, as he proceeded, he experienced some difficulties. Tradesmen's bills accumulated, and applications for payment became every day more frequent and pressing. He defended himself with much address and ingenuity, and practice perfected him in all the Fabian arts of delay. "No faith with duns" became, as he frankly declared, a maxim of his morality. He could now, with a most plausible face, protest to a poor devil, upon the honour of a gentleman, that he should be paid to-morrow; when nothing was farther from his intentions or his power than to keep his word: and when to-morrow came, he could, with the most easy assurance, damn the rascal for putting a gentleman in mind of his promises. But there were persons more difficult to manage than poor devils. Colonel Pembroke's tailor, who had begun by being the most accommodating fellow in the world, and who had in three years run him up a bill of thirteen hundred pounds, at length began to fail in complaisance, and had the impertinence to talk of his large family, and his urgent calls for money, etc. And next, the colonel's shoe and boot-maker, a man from whom he had been in the habit of taking two hundred pounds' worth of shoes and boots every year, for himself and his servants, now pretended to be in distress for ready money, and refused to furnish more goods upon credit. "Ungrateful dog!" Pembroke called him; and he actually believed his creditors to be ungrateful and insolent, when they asked for their money; for men frequently learn to believe what they are in the daily habit of asserting [Rochefoucault], especially if their assertions be not contradicted by their audience. He knew that his tradesmen overcharged him in every article he bought, and therefore he thought it but just to delay payment whilst it suited his convenience. "Confound them, they can very well afford to wait!" As to their pleas of urgent demands for ready money, large families, &c., he considered these merely as words of course, tradesmen's cant, which should make no more impression upon a gentleman than the whining of a beggar.

One day when Pembroke was just going out to ride with some of his gay companions, he was stopped at his own door by a pale, thin, miserable-looking boy, eight or nine years old, who presented him with a paper, which he took for granted was a petition; he threw the child half-a-crown. "There, take that," said he, "and stand out of the way of my horse's heels, I advise you, my little fellow."

The boy, however, still pressed closer; and, without picking up the half-crown, held the paper to Colonel Pembroke, who had now vaulted into his saddle.

"O no! no! That's too much, my lad—I never read petitions—I'd sooner give half-a-crown at any time than read a petition."

"But, sir, this is not a petition—indeed, sir, I am not a beggar."

"What is it then?—Heyday! a bill!—Then you're worse than a beggar—a dun!—a dun! in the public streets, at your time of life! You little rascal, why what will you come to before you are your father's age?" The boy sighed. "If," pursued the colonel, "I were to serve you right, I should give you a good horse-whipping. Do you see this whip?"

"I do, sir," said the boy; "but—"

"But what? you insolent little dun!—But what?"

"My father is dying," said the child, bursting into tears, "and we have no money to buy him bread, or any thing."

Struck by these words, Pembroke snatched the paper from the boy, and looking hastily at the total and title of the bill, read—"Twelve pounds fourteen—John White, weaver."—"I know of no such person!—I have no dealings with weavers, child," said the colonel, laughing: "My name's Pembroke—Colonel Pembroke."

"Colonel Pembroke—yes, sir, the very person Mr. Close, the tailor, sent me to!"

"Close the tailor! D—n the rascal: was it he sent you to dun me? For this trick he shall not see a farthing of my money this twelvemonth. You may tell him so, you little whining hypocrite!—And, hark you! the next time you come to me, take care to come with a better story—let your father and mother, and six brothers and sisters, be all lying ill of the fever—do you understand?"

He tore the bill into bits as he spoke, and showered it over the boy's head. Pembroke's companions laughed at this operation, and he facetiously called it "powdering a dun." They rode off to the Park in high spirits; and the poor boy picked up the half-crown, and returned home. His home was in a lane in Moorfields, about three miles distant from this gay part of the town. As the child had not eaten any thing that morning, he was feeble, and grew faint as he was crossing Covent Garden. He sat down upon the corner of a stage of flowers.

"What are you doing there?" cried a surly man, pulling him up by the arm; "What business have you lounging and loitering here, breaking my best balsam?"

"I did not mean to do any harm—I am not loitering, indeed, sir,—I'm only weak," said the boy, "and hungry."

"Oranges! oranges! fine China oranges!" cried a woman, rolling her barrow full of fine fruit towards him. "If you've a two-pence in the world, you can't do better than take one of these fine ripe China oranges."

"I have not two-pence of my own in the world," said the boy.

"What's that I see through the hole in your waistcoat pocket?" said the woman; "is not that silver?"

"Yes, half-a-crown; which I am carrying home to my father, who is ill, and wants it more than I do."

"Pooh! take an orange out of it—it's only two-pence—and it will do you good—I'm sure you look as if you wanted it badly enough."

"That may be; but father wants it worse.—No, I won't change my half-crown," said the boy, turning away from the tempting oranges.

The gruff gardener caught him by the hand.

"Here, I've moved the balsam a bit, and it is not broke, I see; sit ye down, child, and rest yourself, and eat this," said he, putting into his hand half a ripe orange, which he just cut.

"Thank you!—God bless you, sir!—How good it is!—But," said the child, stopping after he had tasted the sweet juice, "I am sorry I have sucked so much; I might have carried it home to father, who is ill; and what a treat it would be to him!—I'll keep the rest."

"No—that you sha'n't," said the orange-woman. "But I'll tell you what you shall do—take this home to your father, which is a better one by half—I'm sure it will do him good—I never knew a ripe China orange do harm to man, woman, or child."

The boy thanked the good woman and the gardener, as only those can thank who have felt what it is to be in absolute want. When he was rested, and able to walk, he pursued his way home. His mother was watching for him at the street-door.

"Well, John, my dear, what news? Has he paid us?"

The boy shook his head.

"Then we must bear it as well as we can," said his mother, wiping the cold dew from her forehead.

"But look, mother, I have this half-crown, which the gentleman, thinking me a beggar, threw to me."

"Run with it, love, to the baker's. No—stay, you're tired—I'll go myself; and do you step up to your father, and tell him the bread is coming in a minute."

"Don't run, for you're not able, mother; don't hurry so," said the boy, calling after her, and holding up his orange: "see, I have this for father whilst you are away."

He clambered up three flights of dark, narrow, broken stairs, to the room in which his father lay. The door hung by a single hinge, and the child had scarcely strength enough to raise it out of the hollow in the decayed floor into which it had sunk. He pushed it open, with as little noise as possible, just far enough to creep in.

Let those forbear to follow him whose fine feelings can be moved only by romantic, elegant scenes of distress, whose delicate sensibility shrinks from the revolting sight of real misery. Here are no pictures for romance, no stage effect to be seen, no poetic language to be heard; nothing to charm the imagination,—every thing to disgust the senses.

This room was so dark, that upon first going into it, after having been in broad daylight, you could scarcely distinguish any one object it contained; and no one used to breathe a pure atmosphere could probably have endured to remain many minutes in this garret. There were three beds in it: one on which the sick man lay; divided from it by a tattered rug was another, for his wife and daughter; and a third for his little boy in the farthest corner. Underneath the window was fixed a loom, at which the poor weaver had worked hard many a day and year—too hard, indeed—even till the very hour he was taken ill. His shuttle now lay idle upon his frame. A girl of about sixteen—his daughter—was sitting at the foot of his bed, finishing some plain work.

"Oh, Anne! how your face is all flushed!" said her little brother, as she looked up when he came into the room.

"Have you brought us any money?" whispered she: "don't say No loud, for fear father should hear you." The boy told her in a low voice all that had passed.

"Speak out, my dear, I'm not asleep," said his father. "So you are come back as you went?"

"No, father, not quite—there's bread coming for you."

"Give me some more water, Anne, for my mouth is quite parched."

The little boy cut his orange in an instant, and gave a piece of it to his father, telling him, at the same time, how he came by it The sick man raised his hands to heaven, and blessed the poor woman who gave it to him.

"Oh, how I love her! and how I hate that cruel, unjust, rich man, who won't pay father for all the hard work he has done for him!" cried the child: "how I hate him!"

"God forgive him!" said the weaver. "I don't know what will become of you all, when I'm gone; and no one to befriend you, or even to work at the loom. Anne, I think if I was up," said he, raising himself, "I could still contrive to do a little good."

"Dear father, don't think of getting up; the best you can do for us is to lie still and take rest."

"Rest! I can take no rest, Anne. Rest! there's none for me in this world. And whilst I'm in it, is not it my duty to work for my wife and children? Reach me my clothes, and I'll get up."

It was in vain to contend with him, when this notion seized him that it was his duty to work till the last. All opposition fretted and made him worse; so that his daughter and his wife, even from affection, were forced to yield, and to let him go to the loom, when his trembling hands were scarcely able to throw the shuttle. He did not know how weak he was till he tried to walk. As he stepped out of bed, his wife came in with a loaf of bread in her hand: at the unexpected sight he made an exclamation of joy; sprang forward to meet her, but fell upon the floor in a swoon, before he could put one bit of the bread which she broke for him into his mouth. Want of sustenance, the having been overworked, and the constant anxiety which preyed upon his spirits, had reduced him to this deplorable state of weakness. When he recovered his senses, his wife showed him his little boy eating a large piece of bread; she also ate, and made Anne eat before him, to relieve his mind from that dread which had seized it—and not without some reason—that he should see his wife and children starve to death.

"You find, father, there's no danger for to-day," said Anne; "and to-morrow I shall be paid for my plain work, and then we shall do very well for a few days longer; and I dare say in that time Mr. Close the tailor will receive some money from some of the great many rich gentlemen who owe him so much; and you know he promised that as soon as ever he was able he would pay us."

With such hopes, and the remembrance of such promises, the poor man's spirits could not be much raised; he knew, alas! how little dependence was to be placed on them. As soon as he had eaten, and felt his strength revive, he insisted upon going to the loom; his mind was bent upon finishing a pattern, for which he was to receive five guineas in ready money: he worked and worked, then lay down and rested himself,—then worked again, and so on during the remainder of the day; and during several hours of the night he continued to throw the shuttle, whilst his little boy and his wife by turns wound spools for him.

He completed his work, and threw himself upon his bed quite exhausted, just as the neighbouring clock struck one.

At this hour Colonel Pembroke was in the midst of a gay and brilliant assembly at Mrs. York's, in a splendid saloon, illuminated with wax-lights in profusion, the floor crayoned with roses and myrtles, which the dancers' feet effaced, the walls hung with the most expensive hot-house flowers; in short, he was surrounded with luxury in all its extravagance. It is said that the peaches alone at this entertainment amounted to six hundred guineas. They cost a guinea a-piece: the price of one of them, which Colonel Pembroke threw away because it was not perfectly ripe, would have supported the weaver and his whole family for a week.

There are political advocates for luxury, who assert, perhaps justly, that the extravagance of individuals increases the wealth of nations. But even upon this system, those who by false hopes excite the industrious to exertion, without paying them their just wages, commit not only the most cruel private injustice, but the most important public injury. The permanence of industry in any state must be proportioned to the certainty of its reward.

Amongst the masks at Mrs. York's were three who amused the company particularly; the festive mob followed them as they moved, and their bon-mots were applauded and repeated by all the best, that is to say, the most fashionable male and female judges of wit. The three distinguished characters were a spendthrift, a bailiff, and a dun. The spendthrift was supported with great spirit and truth by Colonel Pembroke, and two of his companions were great and correct in the parts of the bailiff and the dun. The happy idea of appearing in these characters this night had been suggested by the circumstance that happened in the morning. Colonel Pembroke gave himself great credit, he said, for thus "striking novelty even from difficulty;" and he rejoiced that the rascal of a weaver had sent his boy to dun him, and had thus furnished him with diversion for the evening as well as the morning. We are much concerned that we cannot, for the advantage of posterity, record any of the innumerable good things which undoubtedly were uttered by this trio. Even the newspapers of the day could speak only in general panegyric. The probability, however, is, that the colonel deserved the praises that were lavished upon his manner of supporting his character. No man was better acquainted than himself with all those anecdotes of men of fashion, which could illustrate the spendthrift system. At least fifty times he had repeated, and always with the same glee, the reply of a great character to a creditor, who, upon being asked when his bond debts were likely to be paid, answered, "On the day of judgment."

Probably the admiration which this and similar sallies of wit have excited, must have produced a strong desire in the minds of many young men of spirit to perform similar feats; and though the ruin of innumerable poor creditors may be the consequence, that will not surely be deemed by a certain class of reasoners worthy of a moment's regret, or even a moment's thought. Persons of tender consciences may, perhaps, be shocked at the idea of committing injustice and cruelty by starving their creditors, but they may strengthen their minds by taking an enlarged political view of the subject.

It is obvious, that whether a hundred guineas be in the pocket of A or B, the total sum of the wealth of the nation remains the same; and whether the enjoyments of A be as 100, and those of B as 0,—or whether these enjoyments be equally divided between A and B,—is a matter of no importance to the political arithmetician, because in both cases it is obvious that the total sum of national happiness remains the same. The happiness of individuals is nothing compared with the general mass.

And if the individual B should fancy himself ill-used by our political arithmetician, and should take it into his head to observe, that though the happiness of B is nothing to the general mass, yet that it is every thing to him, the politician of course takes snuff, and replies, that his observation is foreign to the purpose—that the good of the whole society is the object in view. And if B immediately accede to this position, and only ask humbly whether the good of the whole be not made up of the good of the parts, and whether as a part he have not some right to his share of good, the dexterous logical arithmetician answers, that B is totally out of the question, because B is a negative quantity in the equation. And if obstinate B, still conceiving himself aggrieved, objects to this total annihilation of himself and his interests, and asks why the lot of extinction should not fall upon the debtor C, or even upon the calculator himself, by whatever letter of the alphabet he happens to be designated, the calculator must knit his brow, and answer—any thing he pleases—except, I don't know—for this is a phrase below the dignity of a philosopher. This argument is produced, not as a statement of what is really the case, but as a popular argument against political sophistry.

Colonel Pembroke, notwithstanding his success at Mrs. York's masquerade in his character of a spendthrift, could not by his utmost wit and address satisfy or silence his impertinent tailor. Mr. Close absolutely refused to give further credit without valuable consideration; and the colonel was compelled to pass his bond for the whole sum which was claimed, which was fifty pounds more than was strictly due, in order to compound with the tailor for the want of ready money. When the bond was fairly signed, sealed, and delivered, Mr. Close produced the poor weaver's bill.

"Colonel Pembroke," said he, "I have a trifling bill here—I am really ashamed to speak to you about such a trifle—but as we are settling all accounts—and as this White, the weaver, is so wretchedly poor, that he or some of his family are with me every day of my life dunning me to get me to speak about their little demand—"

"Who is this White?" said Mr. Pembroke.

"You recollect the elegant waistcoat pattern of which you afterwards bought up the whole piece, lest it should become common and vulgar?—this White was the weaver from whom we got it."

"Bless me! why that's two years ago: I thought that fellow was paid long ago!"

"No, indeed, I wish he had been; for he has been the torment of my life this many a month—I never saw people so eager about their money."

"But why do you employ such miserable, greedy creatures? What can you expect but to be dunned every hour of your life?"

"Very true, indeed, colonel; it is what I always, on that principle, avoid as far as possibly I can: but I can't blame myself in this particular instance; for this White, at the time I employed him first, was a very decent man, and in a very good way, for one of his sort: but I suppose he has taken to drink, for he is worth not a farthing now."

"What business has a fellow of his sort to drink? He should leave that for his betters," said Colonel Pembroke, laughing. "Drinking's too great a pleasure for a weaver. The drunken rascal's money is safer in my hands, tell him, than in his own."

The tailor's conscience twinged him a little at this instant, for he had spoken entirely at random, not having the slightest grounds for his insinuation that this poor weaver had ruined himself by drunkenness.

"Upon my word, sir," said Close, retracting, "the man may not be a drunken fellow for any thing I know positively—I purely surmised that might be the case, from his having fallen into such distress, which is no otherwise accountable for, to my comprehension, except we believe his own story, that he has money due to him which he cannot get paid, and that this has been his ruin."

Colonel Pembroke cleared his throat two or three times upon hearing this last suggestion, and actually took up the weaver's bill with some intention of paying it; but he recollected that he should want the ready money he had in his pocket for another indispensable occasion; for he was obliged to go to Brookes's that night; so he contented his humanity by recommending it to Mr. Close to pay White and have done with him.

"If you let him have the money, you know, you can put it down to my account, or make a memorandum of it at the back of the bond. In short, settle it as you will, but let me hear no more about it. I have not leisure to think of such trifles—Good morning to you, Mr. Close."

Mr. Close was far from having any intention of complying with the colonel's request. When the weaver's wife called upon him after his return home, he assured her that he had not seen the colour of one guinea, or one farthing, of Colonel Pembroke's money; and that it was absolutely impossible that he could pay Mr. White till he was paid himself—that it could not be expected he should advance money for any body out of his own pocket—that he begged he might not be pestered and dunned any more, for that he really had not leisure to think of such trifles.

For want of this trifle, of which neither the fashionable colonel nor his fashionable tailor had leisure to think, the poor weaver and his whole family were reduced to the last degree of human misery—to absolute famine. The man had exerted himself to the utmost to finish a pattern, which had been bespoken for a tradesman who promised upon the delivery of it to pay him five guineas in hand. This money he received; but four guineas of it were due to his landlord for rent of his wretched garret, and the remaining guinea was divided between the baker, to whom an old bill was due, and the apothecary, to whom they were obliged to have recourse, as the weaver was extremely ill. They had literally nothing now to depend upon but what the wife and daughter could earn by needlework; and they were known to be so miserably poor, that the prudent neighbours did not like to trust them with plain work, lest it should not be returned safely. Besides, in such a dirty place as they lived in, how could it be expected that they should put any work out of their hands decently clean? The woman to whom the house belonged, however, at last procured them work from Mrs. Carver, a widow lady, who she said was extremely charitable. She advised Anne to carry home the work as soon as it was finished, and to wait to see the lady herself, who might perhaps be as charitable to her as she was to many others. Anne resolved to take this advice: but when she carried home her work to the place to which she was directed, her heart almost failed her; for she found Mrs. Carver lived in such a handsome house, that there was little chance of a poor girl being admitted by the servants farther than the hall-door or the kitchen. The lady, however, happened to be just coming out of her parlour at the moment the hall-door was opened for Anne; and she bid her come in and show her work—approved of it—commended her industry—asked her several questions about her family—seemed to be touched with compassion by Anne's account of their distress—and after paying what she had charged for the work, put half-a-guinea into her hand, and bid her call the next day, when she hoped that she should be able to do something more for her. This unexpected bounty, and the kindness of voice and look with which it was accompanied, had such an effect upon the poor girl, that if she had not caught hold of a chair to support herself she would have sunk to the ground. Mrs. Carver immediately made her sit down—"Oh, madam! I'm well, quite well now—it was nothing—only surprise," said she, bursting into tears. "I beg your pardon for this foolishness—but it is only because I'm weaker to-day than usual, for want of eating."

"For want of eating! my poor child! How she trembles! she is weak indeed, and must not leave my house in this condition."

Mrs. Carver rang the bell, and ordered a glass of wine; but Anne was afraid to drink it, as she was not used to wine, and as she knew that it would affect her head if she drank without eating. When the lady found that she refused the wine, she did not press it, but insisted upon her eating something.

"Oh, madam!" said the poor girl, "it is long, long indeed, since I have eaten so heartily; and it is almost a shame for me to stay eating such dainties, when my father and mother are all the while in the way they are. But I'll run home with the half-guinea, and tell them how good you have been, and they will be so joyful and so thankful to you! My mother will come herself, I'm sure, with me to-morrow morning—she can thank you so much better than I can!"

Those only who have known the extreme of want can imagine the joy and gratitude with which the half-guinea was received by this poor family. Half-a-guinea!—Colonel Pembroke spent six half-guineas this very day in a fruit-shop, and ten times that sum at a jeweller's on seals and baubles for which he had no manner of use.

When Anne and her mother called the next morning to thank their benefactress, she was not up; but her servant gave them a parcel from his mistress: it contained a fresh supply of needlework, a gown, and some other clothes, which were directed for Anne. The servant said, that if she would call again about eight in the evening, his lady would probably be able to see her, and that she begged to have the work finished by that time. The work was finished, though with some difficulty, by the appointed hour; and Anne, dressed in her new clothes, was at Mrs. Carver's door just as the clock struck eight. The old lady was alone at tea; she seemed to be well pleased by Anne's punctuality; said that she had made inquiries respecting Mr. and Mrs. White, and that she heard an excellent character of them; that therefore she was disposed to do every thing she could to serve them. She added, that she "should soon part with her own maid, and that perhaps Anne might supply her place." Nothing could be more agreeable to the poor girl than this proposal: her father and mother were rejoiced at the idea of seeing her so well placed; and they now looked forward impatiently for the day when Mrs. Carver's maid was to be dismissed. In the mean time the old lady continued to employ Anne, and to make her presents, sometimes of clothes, and sometimes of money. The money she always gave to her parents; and she loved her "good old lady," as she always called her, more for putting it in her power thus to help her father and mother than for all the rest. The weaver's disease had arisen from want of sufficient food, from fatigue of body, and anxiety of mind; and he grew rapidly better, now that he was relieved from want, and inspired with hope. Mrs. Carver bespoke from him two pieces of waistcoating, which she promised to dispose of for him most advantageously, by a raffle, for which she had raised subscriptions amongst her numerous acquaintance. She expressed great indignation, when Anne told her how Mr. White had been ruined by persons who would not pay their just debts; and when she knew that the weaver was overcharged for all his working materials, because he took them upon credit, she generously offered to lend them whatever ready money might be necessary, which she said Anne might repay, at her leisure, out of her wages.

"Oh, madam!" said Anne, "you are too good to us, indeed—too good! and if you could but see into our hearts, you would know that we are not ungrateful."

"I am sure that is what you never will be, my dear," said the old lady; "at least such is my opinion of you."

"Thank you, ma'am! thank you, from the bottom of my heart!—We should all have been starved, if it had not been for you. And it is owing to you that we are so happy now—quite different creatures from what we were."

"Quite a different creature indeed, you look, child, from what you did the first day I saw you. To-morrow my own maid goes, and you may come at ten o'clock; and I hope we shall agree very well together— you'll find me an easy mistress, and I make no doubt I shall always find you the good, grateful girl you seem to be."

Anne was impatient for the moment when she was to enter into the service of her benefactress; and she lay awake half the night, considering how she should ever be able to show sufficient gratitude. As Mrs. Carver had often expressed her desire to have Anne look neat and smart, she dressed herself as well as she possibly could; and when her poor father and mother took leave of her, they could not help observing, as Mrs. Carver had done the day before, that "Anne looked quite a different creature from what she was a few weeks ago." She was, indeed, an extremely pretty girl; but we need not stop to relate all the fond praises that were bestowed upon her beauty by her partial parents. Her little brother John was not at home when she was going away; he was at a carpenter's shop in the neighbourhood mending a wheelbarrow, which belonged to that good-natured orange-woman who gave him the orange for his father. Anne called at the carpenter's shop to take leave of her brother. The woman was there waiting for her barrow—she looked earnestly at Anne when she entered, and then whispered to the boy, "Is that your sister?"—"Yes," said the boy, "and as good a sister she is as ever was born."

"Maybe so," said the woman; "but she is not likely to be good for much long, in the way she is going on now."

"What way—what do you mean?" said Anne, colouring violently.

"Oh, you understand me well enough, though you look so innocent."

"I do not understand you in the least."

"No!—Why, is not it you that I see going almost every day to that house in Chiswell-street?"

"Mrs. Carver's?—Yes."

"Mrs. Carver's indeed!" cried the woman, throwing an orange-peel from her with an air of disdain—"a pretty come-off indeed! as if I did not know her name, and all about her, as well as you do."

"Do you?" said Anne; "then I am sure you know one of the best women in the world."

The woman looked still more earnestly than before in Anne's countenance; and then, taking hold of both her hands, exclaimed, "You poor young creature! what are you about? I do believe you don't know what you are about—if you do, you are the greatest cheat I ever looked in the face, long as I've lived in this cheating world."

"You frighten my sister," said the boy: "do pray tell her what you mean at once, for look how pale she turns!"

"So much the better, for now I have good hope of her. Then to tell you all at once—no matter how I frighten her, it's for her good—this Mrs. Carver, as you call her, is only Mrs. Carver when she wants to pass upon such as you for a good woman."

"To pass for a good woman!" repeated Anne, with indignation. "Oh, she is, she is a good woman—you do not know her as I do."

"I know her a great deal better, I tell you: if you choose not to believe me, go your ways—go to your ruin—go to your shame—go to your grave—as hundreds have gone, by the same road, before you. Your Mrs. Carver keeps two houses, and one of them is a bad house—and that's the house you'll soon go to, if you trust to her: now you know the whole truth."

The poor girl was shocked so much, that for several minutes she could neither speak nor think. As soon as she had recovered sufficient presence of mind to consider what she should do, she declared that she would that instant go home and put on her rags again, and return to the wicked Mrs. Carver all the clothes she had given her.

"But what will become of us all?—She has lent my father money—a great deal of money. How can he pay her?—Oh, I will pay her all—I will go into some honest service, now I am well and strong enough to do any sort of hard work, and God knows I am willing."

Full of these resolutions, Anne hurried home, intending to tell her father and mother all that had happened; but they were neither of them within. She flew to the mistress of the house, who had first recommended her to Mrs. Carver, and reproached her in the most moving terms which the agony of her mind could suggest. Her landlady listened to her with astonishment, either real or admirably well affected—declared that she knew nothing more of Mrs. Carver but that she lived in a large fine house, and that she had been very charitable to some poor people in Moorfields—that she bore the best of characters—and that if nothing could be said against her but by an orange-woman, there was no great reason to believe such scandal.

Anne now began to think that the whole of what she had heard might be a falsehood, or a mistake; one moment she blamed herself for so easily suspecting a person who had shown her so much kindness; but the next minute the emphatic words and warning looks of the woman recurred to her mind; and though they were but the words and looks of an orange-woman, she could not help dreading that there was some truth in them. The clock struck ten whilst she was in this uncertainty. The woman of the house urged her to go without farther delay to Mrs. Carver's, who would undoubtedly be displeased by any want of punctuality; but Anne wished to wait for the return of her father and mother.

"They will not be back, either of them, these three hours, for your mother is gone to the other end of the town about that old bill of Colonel Pembroke's, and your father is gone to buy some silk for weaving—he told me he should not be home before three o'clock."

Notwithstanding these remonstrances, Anne persisted in her resolution: she took off the clothes which she had received from Mrs. Carver, and put on those which she had been used to wear. Her mother was much surprised, when she came in, to see her in this condition; and no words can describe her grief, when she heard the cause of this change. She blamed herself severely for not having made inquiries concerning Mrs. Carver before she had suffered her daughter to accept of any presents from her; and she wept bitterly, when she recollected the money which this woman had lent her husband.

"She will throw him into jail, I am sure she will—we shall be worse off a thousand times than ever we were in our worst days. The work that is in the loom, by which he hoped to get so much, is all for her, and it will be left upon our hands now; and how are we to pay the woman of this house for the lodgings?—Oh! I see it all coming upon us at once," continued the poor woman, wringing her hands. "If that Colonel Pembroke would but let us have our own!—But there I've been all the morning hunting him out, and at last, when I did see him, he only swore, and said we were all a family of duns, or some such nonsense. And then he called after me from the top of his fine stairs, just to say, that he had ordered Close the tailor to pay us; and when I went to him there was no satisfaction to be got from him—his shop was full of customers, and he hustled me away, giving me for answer, that when Colonel Pembroke paid him, he would pay us, and no sooner. Ah! these purse-proud tradesfolk, and these sparks of fashion, what do they know of all we suffer? What do they care for us?—It is not for charity I ask any of them—only for what my own husband has justly earned, and hardly toiled for too; and this I cannot get out of their hands. If I could, we might defy this wicked woman—but now we are laid under her feet, and she will trample us to death."

In the midst of these lamentations, Anne's father came in: when he learned the cause of them, he stood for a moment in silence; then snatched from his daughter's hand the bundle of clothes, which she had prepared to return to Mrs. Carver.

"Give them to me; I will go to this woman myself," cried he with indignation: "Anne shall never more set her foot within those doors."

"Dear father," cried Anne, stopping him as he went out of the door, "perhaps it is all a mistake: do pray inquire from somebody else before you speak to Mrs. Carver—she looks so good, she has been so kind to me, I cannot believe that she is wicked. Do pray inquire of a great many people before you knock at the door."

He promised that he would do all his daughter desired.

With most impatient anxiety they waited for his return: the time of his absence appeared insupportably long, and they formed new fears and new conjectures every instant. Every time they heard a footstep upon the stairs, they ran out to see who it was: sometimes it was the landlady—sometimes the lodgers or their visitors—at last came the person they longed to see; but the moment they beheld him, all their fears were confirmed. He was pale as death, and his lips trembled with convulsive motion. He walked directly up to his loom, and without speaking one syllable, began to cut the unfinished work out of it.

"What are you about, my dear?" cried his wife. "Consider what you are about—this work of yours is the only dependence we have in the world."

"You have nothing in this world to depend upon, I tell you," cried he, continuing to cut out the web with a hurried hand—"you must not depend on me—you must not depend on my work—I shall never throw this shuttle more whilst I live—think of me as if I was dead—to-morrow I shall be dead to you—I shall be in a jail, and there must lie till carried out in my coffin. Here, take this work just as it is to our landlady—she met me on the stairs, and said she must have her rent directly—that will pay her—I'll pay all I can. As for the loom, that's only hired—the silk I bought to-day will pay the hire—I'll pay all my debts to the uttermost farthing, as far as I am able—but the ten guineas to that wicked woman I cannot pay—so I must rot in a jail. Don't cry, Anne, don't cry so, my good girl—you'll break my heart, wife, if you take on so. Why! have not we one comfort, that let us go out of this world when we may, or how we may, we shall go out of it honest, having no one's ruin to answer for, having done our duty to God and man, as far as we are able?—My child," continued he, catching Anne in his arms, "I have you safe, and I thank God for it!"

When this poor man had thus in an incoherent manner given vent to his first feelings, he became somewhat more composed, and was able to relate all that had passed between him and Mrs. Carver. The inquiries which he made before he saw her sufficiently confirmed the orange-woman's story; and when he returned the presents which Anne had unfortunately received, Mrs. Carver, with all the audacity of a woman hardened in guilt, avowed her purpose and her profession—declared that whatever ignorance and innocence Anne or her parents might now find it convenient to affect, she was "confident they had all the time perfectly understood what she was about, and that she would not be cheated at last by a parcel of swindling hypocrites." With horrid imprecations she then swore, that if Anne was kept from her she would have vengeance—and that her vengeance should know no bounds. The event showed that these were not empty threats—the very next day she sent two bailiffs to arrest Anne's father. They met him in the street, as he was going to pay the last farthing he had to the baker. The wretched man in vain endeavoured to move the ear of justice by relating the simple truth. Mrs. Carver was rich—her victim was poor. He was committed to jail; and he entered his prison with the firm belief, that there he must drag out the remainder of his days.

One faint hope remained in his wife's heart—she imagined that if she could but prevail upon Colonel Pembroke's servants, either to obtain for her a sight of their master, or if they would carry to him a letter containing an exact account of her distress, he would immediately pay the fourteen pounds which had been so long due. With this money she could obtain her husband's liberty, and she fancied all might yet be well. Her son, who could write a very legible hand, wrote the petition. "Ah, mother!" said he, "don't hope that Colonel Pembroke will read it—he will tear it to pieces, as he did one that I carried him before."

"I can but try," said she; "I cannot believe that any gentleman is so cruel, and so unjust—he must and will pay us when he knows the whole truth."

Colonel Pembroke was dressing in a hurry, to go to a great dinner at the Crown and Anchor tavern. One of Pembroke's gay companions had called, and was in the room waiting for him. It was at this inauspicious time that Mrs. White arrived. Her petition the servant at first absolutely refused to take from her hands; but at last a young lad, whom the colonel had lately brought from the country, and who had either more natural feeling, or less acquired power of equivocating, than his fellows, consented to carry up the petition, when he should, as he expected, be called by his master to report the state of a favourite horse that was sick. While his master's hair was dressing, the lad was summoned; and when the health of the horse had been anxiously inquired into, the lad with country awkwardness scratched his head, and laid the petition before his master, saying—"Sir, there's a poor woman below waiting for an answer; and if so be what she says is true, as I take it to be, 'tis enough to break one's heart."

"Your heart, my lad, is not seasoned to London yet, I perceive," said Colonel Pembroke, smiling; "why, your heart will be broke a thousand times over by every beggar you meet."

"No, no; I be too much of a man for that," replied the groom, wiping his eyes hastily with the back of his hand—"not such a noodle as that comes to, neither—beggars are beggars, and so to be treated—but this woman, sir, is no common beggar, not she; nor is she begging any ways—only to be paid her bill—so I brought it, as I was coming up."

"Then, sir, as you are going down, you may take it down again, if you please," cried Colonel Pembroke; "and in future, sir, I recommend it to you to look after your horses, and to trust me to look after my own affairs."

The groom retreated; and his master gave the poor woman's petition, without reading it, to the hair-dresser, who was looking for a piece of paper to try the heat of his irons.

"I should be pestered with bills and petitions from morning till night, if I did not frighten these fellows out of the trick of bringing them to me," continued Colonel Pembroke, turning to his companion. "That blockhead of a groom is but just come to town; he does not yet know how to drive away a dun—but he'll learn. They say that the American dogs did not know how to bark, till they learnt it from their civilized betters."

Colonel Pembroke habitually drove away reflection, and silenced the whispers of conscience, by noisy declamation, or sallies of wit.

At the bottom of the singed paper, which the hair-dresser left on the table, the name of White was sufficiently visible. "White!" exclaimed Colonel Pembroke, "as I hope to live and breathe, these Whites have been this half-year the torment of my life." He started up, rang the bell, and gave immediate orders to his servant, that these Whites should never more be let in, and that no more of their bills and petitions in any form whatever should be brought to him. "I'll punish them for their insolence—I won't pay them one farthing this twelvemonth: and if the woman is not gone, pray tell her so—I bid Close the tailor pay them: if he has not, it is no fault of mine. Let me not hear a syllable more about it—I'll part with the first of you who dares to disobey me."

"The woman is gone, I believe, sir," said the footman; "it was not I let her in, and I refused to bring up the letter."

"You did right. Let me hear no more about the matter. We shall be late at the Crown and Anchor. I beg your pardon, my dear friend, for detaining you so long."

Whilst the colonel went to his jovial meeting, where he was the life and spirit of the company, the poor woman returned in despair to the prison where her husband was confined.

We forbear to describe the horrible situation to which this family were soon reduced. Beyond a certain point, the human heart cannot feel compassion.

One day, as Anne was returning from the prison, where she had been with her father, she was met by a porter, who put a letter into her hands, then turned down a narrow lane, and was out of sight before she could inquire from whom he came. When she read the letter, however, she could not be in doubt—it came from Mrs. Carver, and contained these words:—

"You can gain nothing by your present obstinacy—you are the cause of your father's lying in jail, and of your mother's being as she is, nearly starved to death. You can relieve them from misery worse than death, and place them in ease and comfort for the remainder of their days. Be assured, they do not speak sincerley to you, when they pretend not to wish that your compliance should put an end to their present sufferings. It is you that are cruel to them—it is you that are cruel to yourself, and can blame nobody else. You might live all your days in a house as good as mine, and have a plentiful table served from one year's end to another, with all the dainties of the season, and you might be dressed as elegantly as the most elegant lady in London (which, by-the-bye, your beauty deserves), and you would have servants of your own, and a carriage of your own, and nothing to do all day long but take your pleasure. And after all, what is asked of you?—only to make a person happy, whom half the town would envy you, that would make it a study to gratify you in every wish of your heart. The person alluded to you have seen, and more than once, when you have been talking to me of work in my parlour. He is a very rich and generous gentleman. If you come to Chiswell-street about six this evening, you will find all I say true—if not, you and yours must take the consequences."

Coarse as the eloquence of this letter may appear, Anne could not read it without emotion: it raised in her heart a violent contest. Virtue, with poverty and famine, were on one side—and vice, with affluence, love, and every worldly pleasure, on the other.

Those who have been bred up in the lap of luxury; whom the breath of heaven has never visited too roughly; whose minds from their earliest infancy have been guarded even with more care than their persons; who in the dangerous season of youth are surrounded by all that the solicitude of experienced friends, and all that polished society, can devise for their security; are not perhaps competent to judge of the temptations by which beauty in the lower classes of life may be assailed. They who have never seen a father in prison, or a mother perishing for want of the absolute necessaries of life—they who have never themselves known the cravings of famine, cannot form an adequate idea of this poor girl's feelings, and of the temptation to which she was now exposed. She wept—she hesitated—and "the woman that deliberates is lost." Perhaps those who are the most truly virtuous of her sex will be the most disposed to feel for this poor creature, who was literally half famished before her good resolutions were conquered. At last she yielded to necessity. At the appointed hour she was in Mrs. Carver's house. This woman received her with triumph—she supplied Anne immediately with food, and then hastened to deck out her victim in the most attractive manner. The girl was quite passive in her hand. She promised, though scarcely knowing that she uttered the words, to obey the instructions that were given to her, and she suffered herself without struggle, or apparent emotion, to be led to destruction. She appeared quite insensible—but at last she was roused from this state of stupefaction, by the voice of a person with whom she found herself alone. The stranger, who was a young and gay gentleman, pleasing both in his person and manners, attempted by every possible means to render himself agreeable to her, to raise her spirits, and calm her apprehensions. By degrees his manner changed from levity to tenderness. He represented to her, that he was not a brutal wretch, who could be gratified by any triumph in which the affections of the heart have no share; and he assured her, that in any connexion which she might be prevailed upon to form with him, she should be treated with honour and delicacy.

Touched by his manner of speaking, and overpowered by the sense of her own situation, Anne could not reply one single word to all he said—but burst into an agony of tears, and sinking on her knees before him, exclaimed, "Save me! save me from myself!—Restore me to my parents, before they have reason to hate me."

The gentleman seemed to be somewhat in doubt whether this was acting or nature: but he raised Anne from the ground, and placed her upon a seat beside him. "Am I to understand, then, that I have been deceived, and that our present meeting is against your own consent?"

"No, I cannot say that—oh, how I wish that I could!—I did wrong, very wrong, to come here—but I repent—I was half-starved—I have a father in jail—I thought I could set him free with the money—but I will not pretend to be better than I am—I believe I thought that, beside relieving my father, I should live all my days without ever more knowing what distress is—and I thought I should be happy—but now I have changed my mind—I never could be happy with a bad conscience—I know—by what I have felt this last hour."

Her voice failed; and she sobbed for some moments without being able to speak. The gentleman, who now was convinced that she was quite artless and thoroughly in earnest, was struck with compassion; but his compassion was not unmixed with other feelings, and he had hopes that, by treating her with tenderness, he should in time make it her wish to live with him as his mistress. He was anxious to hear what her former way of life had been; and she related, at his request, the circumstances by which she and her parents had been reduced to such distress. His countenance presently showed how much he was interested in her story—he grew red and pale—he started from his seat, and walked up and down the room in great agitation, till at last, when she mentioned the name of Colonel Pembroke, he stopped short, and exclaimed, "I am the man—I am Colonel Pembroke—I am that unjust, unfeeling wretch! How often, in the bitterness of your hearts, you must have cursed me!"

"Oh, no—my father, when he was at the worst, never cursed you; and I am sure he will have reason to bless you now, if you send his daughter back again to him, such as she was when she left him."

"That shall be done," said Colonel Pembroke; "and in doing so, I make some sacrifice, and have some merit. It is time I should make some reparation for the evils I have occasioned," continued he, taking a handful of guineas from his pocket: "but first let me pay my just debts."

"My poor father!" exclaimed Anne; "to-morrow he will be out of prison."

"I will go with you to the prison, where your father is confined—I will force myself to behold all the evils I have occasioned."

Colonel Pembroke went to the prison; and he was so much struck by the scene, that he not only relieved the misery of this family, but in two months afterwards his debts were paid, his race-horses sold, and all his expenses regulated, so as to render him ever afterwards truly independent. He no longer spent his days, like many young men of fashion, either in DREADING or in DAMNING DUNS.

Edgeworthstown, 1802.

Maria Edgeworth – A Short Biography

Maria Edgeworth was born at Black Bourton, Oxfordshire on January 1st 1768, the second child of Richard Lovell Edgeworth and Anna Maria Edgeworth (née Elers).

Her early years were with her mother's family in England. Sadly, her mother died when Maria was only five. When her father married his second wife, Honora Sneyd, in 1773, the family went to live at his estate, Edgeworthstown, in County Longford, Ireland.

Maria was later sent to Mrs. Lattafière's school in Derby after Honora fell ill in 1775. There she studied dancing, French and other subjects. After Honora died in 1780 Maria's father married Honora's sister, Elizabeth, causing much social disapproved.

Maria transferred to Mrs. Devis's school in Upper Wimpole Street, London. Her father began to focus more attention on Maria in 1781 when she nearly lost her sight to an eye infection.

She returned home to Ireland at 14, and took charge of her younger siblings. She herself was home-tutored by her father in Irish economics and politics, science, literature and law. Despite her youth literature was in her blood.

She became her father's assistant in managing the Edgeworthstown estate, which had become run-down during the family's absence. Maria would now live and write there for the rest of her life.

With her father she began a lifelong academic collaboration. She meticulously detailed daily Irish life; a valuable lodestone of references for later use in her novels. Maria mixed with the Anglo-Irish gentry, and her aunt, Margaret Ruxton of Blackcastle, supplied her with the novels of Anne Radcliffe and William Godwin and encouraged her ambition to write.

Edgeworth's first published work in 1795 was 'Letters for Literary Ladies'. That same year 'An Essay on the Noble Science of Self-Justification', written for a female audience, states that the fair sex is endowed with an art of self-justification and women should use their gifts to continually challenge the force and power of men, especially their husbands, with wit and intelligence.

In 1796 her first children's book, 'The Parent's Assistant', which included the much loved short story 'The Purple Jar' was published.

In 1798 her father married for the fourth and last time, this time to Frances Beaufort. Frances was a year younger than Maria and they quickly became close.

'Practical Education' (1798) is a progressive work on education that combines the ideas of Locke and Rousseau with scientific inquiry. Edgeworth believed that "learning should be a positive experience and that the discipline of education is more important during the formative years than the acquisition of knowledge." The ultimate goal of Edgeworth's system was to create an independent thinker who understands the consequences of his or her actions.

Her first novel, 'Castle Rackrent' (1800) was published anonymously without her father's knowledge. It was an immediate success and firmly established Maria's appeal to the public.

'Belinda' (1801), was her first full-length novel. It dealt with love, courtship, and marriage, and she examined these as conflicts within her "own personality and environment; conflicts between reason and feeling, restraint and individual freedom, and society and free spirit." Startingly, 'Belinda' also included a depiction of interracial marriage between an African servant and an English farm-girl. Later editions of the novel, in line with unforgiving times, removed these sections.

Frances also pushed the family to travel more first London (1800), the Midlands (1802) and later the continent; first to Brussels and then to France. They met all the notables, with Maria even receiving a proposal of marriage from a Swedish courtier.

'Tales of Fashionable Life' (1809 and 1812) is a 2-series collection of short stories that often had its focus on the life of women. The second series was so successful that she was now the most commercially successful novelist of her age and ranked alongside her contemporaries Jane Austen and Sir Walter Scott.

On a visit to London in 1813, she met many notables including Lord Byron. She entered into a long correspondence with Sir Walter Scott after the publication of 'Waverley' in 1814, in which he acknowledged her influence, and they formed a lasting friendship. She visited him in Scotland at Abbotsford House in 1823 and the following year he visited Edgeworthstown.

After debating the issue with the economist David Ricardo, Maria came to believe that better management and the further use of science in agriculture would raise food production and help to lower prices. They were both in favour of Catholic Emancipation, enfranchisement for Catholics without property restrictions, agricultural reform and increased educational opportunities for women.

She worked particularly hard to improve the living standards of the poor in Edgeworthstown and to provide schools for the local children whatever their denomination.

After her father's death in 1817 she edited his memoirs, and extended them with her biographical addenda. Her father had married 4 times and sired 22 children. At the height of her creative endeavours, Maria had written, "Seriously it was to please my Father I first exerted myself to write, to please him I continued."

Maria worked for the relief of the famine-stricken Irish peasants during the Irish Potato Famine. She wrote 'Orlandino' and gave the proceeds to the Relieve Fund. However, during the famine her 'business head' insisted that only those tenants who had paid their full rent would receive any relief. She also punished any tenants who voted against her Tory preferences.

'Helen' (1834) is Maria Edgeworth's final novel, the only one she wrote after her father's death. Here the focus was on characters and situation and not moral lessons.

William Rowan Hamilton was elected president of the Royal Irish Academy and Maria's advice was constantly sought especially regarding literature in Ireland. She suggested that women should be allowed to participate in Academy events. Hamilton made Maria an honorary member in 1837.

After a visit to see her relations Maria was struck with severe chest pains and died suddenly of a heart attack in Edgeworthstown on 22nd May 1849. She was 81.

Maria Edgeworth is buried in the family tomb at St. John's Church, Edgeworthstown, Longford, Ireland.


Maria Edgeworth – A Concise Bibliography

Letters for Literary Ladies (1795) Second Edition (1798)
An Essay on the Noble Science of Self-Justification (1795)
The Parent's Assistant (1796)
Practical Education (1798) (2 Vols; collaborated with her father and step-mother)
Castle Rackrent (1800) Novel
Early Lessons (1801)
Moral Tales (1801)
Belinda (1801) Novel
The Mental Thermometer (1801)
Essay on Irish Bulls (1802)
Popular Tales (1804)
The Modern Griselda (1804)
Moral Tales for Young People (1805) (6 Vols)
Leonora (1806)
Essays in Professional Education (1809)
Tales of Fashionable Life (1809)
Ennui (1809) Novel
The Absentee (1812) Novel
Patronage (1814) Novel
Harrington (1817) Novel
Ormond (1817) Novel
Comic Dramas (1817)
Memoirs of Richard Lovell Edgeworth (1820) Editor
Rosamond: A Sequel to Early Lessons (1821)
Frank: A Sequel to Frank in Early Lessons (1822)
Tomorrow (1823) Novel
Helen (1834) novel
Orlandino (1848) Temperance novel

www.ingramcontent.com/pod-product-compliance
Lightning Source LLC
Chambersburg PA
CBHW021922170626
46807CB00007B/2944